CW01372704

YORKSHIRE'S PRIDE

Lord Hawke, who exerted the greatest influence over the development of Yorkshire cricket. (*Yorkshire Post*)

YORKSHIRE'S PRIDE

150 Years of County Cricket

JOHN CALLAGHAN

GUILD PUBLISHING
LONDON

This edition published 1984 by
Book Club Associates
By arrangement with Michael Joseph Ltd

© John Callaghan 1984

All Rights Reserved. No part of this publication may be reproduced, stored in a retrieval system, or transmitted, in any form or by any means, electronic, mechanical, photocopying, recording or otherwise, without the prior permission of the copyright owner.

British Library Cataloguing in Publication Data

Callaghan, John, *1938–*
   Yorkshire's pride: 150 years of county cricket.
   1. Yorkshire County Cricket Club – History
   I. Title
   796.35′863′094281   GV921.Y/

ISBN 0-7207-1505-9

Typeset, printed and bound in Great Britain
by Butler & Tanner Ltd Frome and London

CONTENTS

	Acknowledgments	6
	Preface	7
1	More Than a Game	11
2	In the Beginning (*c*1700–1863)	20
3	The Foundations are Laid (1863–1882)	28
4	The Golden Age (1883–1902)	35
5	Mixed Fortunes (1903–1914)	46
6	Picking Up the Pieces (1919–1925)	55
7	A Confusion of Captains (1926–1930)	64
8	Great Days (1931–1946)	71
9	After the Feast (1947–1958)	85
10	Back on the Mountain Top (1959–1970)	99
11	In the Wilderness (1971–1983)	111
12	Tackling the Tourists	129
13	The Run-makers	142
14	The All-rounders	160
15	The Destroyers	173
16	The Men Behind the Stumps	186
17	Record Stands	193
18	All in a Day's Work	213
19	The One-day Game	218
20	The Outsiders	227
	Appendix – County Records	231
	Index	237

ACKNOWLEDGMENTS

This book could not have been written without the generous help of several people. I am grateful to the editors of the *Yorkshire Post* and *Yorkshire Evening Post* for permission to use their files. I must also mention Roy Wilkinson, Yorkshire's leading cricket statistician, and Tony Woodhouse, whose vast knowledge of the county's past has been put at my disposal so willingly. Finally the trails laid by the Rev. R. S. Holmes, A. W. Pullin and J. M. Kilburn made the journey through Yorkshire's history both easier and more entertaining than might have been the case.

PREFACE

Cricket has been the Yorkshireman's abiding passion for more than 200 years and his in-born expertise at this most complicated of English games has earned a world-wide reputation for a handful of tiny villages tucked away in the shadow of the Pennine Hills. From Lascelles Hall and Kirkheaton in the Huddersfield area and from the Leeds suburb of Pudsey and similar centres of limited population, players have emerged to earn fame and, in some cases, fortune that would have been far beyond their reach in virtually any other walk of life.

They were the products of a club and league system which developed naturally throughout the county sustaining and strengthening the game's roots to ensure a rich growth.

Cricket itself was encouraged initially as an alternative to the unpleasant business of cock-fighting, and the earliest newspaper references underline its accepted moral virtue, for in 1751 'the Sheffield authorities engaged professional cricketers to amuse the populace and so draw them away from cock-fighting exhibitions'. Thus the pattern became established at the outset, with above-average performers employing their skills for a clear purpose and drawing due reward. In comparison, cricket in the South followed a gentler, less-demanding course.

The first generally recognised county match was staged on the Hyde Park Ground in Sheffield on September 2, 3, 4 and 5 1833, and the ensuing 150 years have contained a fascinating mixture of triumph and disaster, intermingling with outbreaks of administrative argument similar to that which focussed such an unwelcome spotlight on Yorkshire in the late 1970s.

It is an interesting point which students of environmental influence might profitably study that by far the majority of Yorkshire's great players have been born in a relatively tiny part of the vast county. So many spent their formative years and sharpened their skills in an area that could comfortably be encompassed by a circle with a twenty-mile radius based on the centre of Bradford. In Contrast, it is surprising that Sheffield, the birthplace of the county club in 1863, should inspire comparatively few capped players, despite figuring prominently in other ways.

One fascinating theory concerns the type of employment available for, while Sheffield grew as a steel centre, the old West Riding prospered through the woollen industry. This, in the days of hand looms, required a combination of quick hands and keen eyesight in the operation of the shuttle and pick by a workforce who subconsciously trained their reflexes for the cricket field as a matter of daily necessity.

These, though, are matters for speculation and debate. What cannot be doubted is Yorkshire's unchallenged superiority in terms of English cricket, for they have won the county championship thirty-one times outright and shared the honour on two other occasions. Surrey, with eighteen successes and two joint titles, stand next in line, but at a respectful distance which previous generations would understand.

The influx of overseas talent into our domestic competitions and a steady but marked decline in the standards of leagues have dramatically altered the balance of power, but on being appointed chairman of the Test selectors in 1982, Peter May, a man of experience and extensive first-hand knowledge, still felt able to repeat the well-worn theme that a strong Yorkshire side invariably means a strong England side.

This is largely the consequence of Yorkshire's loyalty to a tradition which insists on their players being born within the county. As we shall see, there have been significant exceptions to this rule, but generally the club have stuck to a policy which stems from a stubborn pride. To their credit, the committee ignored the easy option of buying success when a long sequence of poor results in the 1970s caused noisy disquiet, sparking internal conflict, and a referendum among their long-suffering members confirmed the wisdom of this decision.

The facts and figures of Yorkshire's glorious past are well documented in *Wisden* and other publications, but the background to these statistics is less well known. In some cases it has been forgotten altogether. The men are just as important as their deeds, however, for their legacy amounts to more than runs and wickets. They created an institution, sometimes painfully, sometimes gloriously, and they made it the best of its kind, leading the way and leaving others to follow at their own pace.

This account spread over 150 years is a tribute to the club and its

Preface

players. It takes some fascinating turns along its course and involves some marvellous personalities. It also sticks to the truth and avoids embellishment.

Emmott Robinson, one of the outstanding characters, once said to Neville Cardus, who tended to be generous with the colours in the word-pictures he painted to such good effect: 'Ah reckon, Mr Cardus, th'as invented me.' There is no need to exaggerate, however – Yorkshire cricket stands firmly on its own feet.

Chapter 1

MORE THAN A GAME

Bramall Lane, lost to cricket under the builder's hammer in 1973, was among the ugliest grounds in the world, yet the empty spaces of the football terraces, which in winter housed the followers of Sheffield United, echoed throughout the summer with a noisy character peculiar to Yorkshire. The relationship between players and spectators was a two-edged affair, an endless interplay of words and actions, and everyone adhered to the well understood and readily accepted high standards.

In the August of 1967, Geoff Pullar was steadily engaged in the task of rescuing Lancashire from a perilous position on an unreliable pitch, advancing at the same time with due caution towards his fifth Roses century, which was a record for his county in this most seriously of contested series.

Yorkshire, in the persons of Tony Nicholson and Richard Hutton, had apparently broken the back of the resistance by making full use of some early assistance in the conditions to capture five wickets for 26 runs. An expectant audience, substantially of one persuasion, enjoyed this procession hugely, but found the refusal of Pullar and David Lloyd to surrender rather more difficult to accept.

They suffered for a while in silence, admitting without much enthusiasm that Lancashire were entitled to at least a measure of respectability, although as the day wore on and runs came slowly, their collective patience began to run out.

At last Pullar edged Peter Stringer, a strongly-built Colt of around medium pace, and the ball flew high to the right of Phil Sharpe at first slip. Sharpe, the most nimble and sticky-fingered man in this position within living memory, accomplished a feat of spring-heeled agility to get a touch to the deflection, but he could not turn this fleeting chance into a catch. Eight thousand throats swallowed the roar of approval and Pullar plodded on.

His concentration must have been disturbed, however, for soon he aimed across the line at Ray Illingworth's offspin and captain Brian Close, dangerously near to the bat, palmed the ball upwards with a half-protective, half-controlled sweep of his arm that sent it lobbing gently to safety. It was a miracle that no permanent damage resulted.

Hardly had the crowd regathered its composure than a lofted drive against Nicholson skimmed ankle high and wide to the left of cover, where Ken Taylor made something out of nothing and saved four runs with a tremendous dive. In the circumstances, the catch he almost made would have been a conjuring trick.

High in the top tier of the pavilion balcony, a more senior member of the county club lunged to his feet and hurled a small attaché case to the floor releasing a cascade of sandwiches and a flood of tea, which spilled from a violently broken flask. 'You're throwing the damned game away,' he shouted in the general direction of the field before lapsing into a trance-like state which remained unbroken by a further burst of Yorkshire success during which the last five Lancashire wickets fell for 63 runs.

Those around him knew quite well how he felt. They shared his emotions because they expected Yorkshire cricketers to snap up every trifle with professional ease. An unwavering expertise was regarded as the norm. Excuses were for other teams. That has been the basic philosophy with the Broad Acres from the earliest days, long before the arrival of leagues brought the stimulation of competition.

It is, significantly, almost impossible to find people in Yorkshire taking part in any sport or pastime unless there is something tangible at the end of the road. Down the years, time snatched from the back-breaking routine of the coal mine or the mill has been too precious to waste on mere enjoyment, so even a handful of children playing tiddlywinks in the street are likely to organise rules and a method of settling the order of merit.

In much the same way, the youngest of those who fancied their chances at cricket have been ready to risk whatever money could be raised to 'make the contest worthwhile'. Tom Emmett, who came out of Crib Lane in Halifax carrying his kit in a copy of the *Evening Courier* to make his way as a five-shillings-a-match professional, enjoyed the thrill of playing for sums he could ill afford to lose.

'There was,' he said, 'a lot of rivalry among the boys who played on the Walk Top in the 1860s. It got to the length of arranging a single-wicket match and we played for twopence a man. It was such a terrible stake, but our side won.'

It was just as well they did, for the type of accident with which small boys are all too familiar marred the encounter.

'I sent the ball through the window of a nearby combing shed,' Emmett related. 'It hit a man named Harrowby, who was well known in the village. He came out covered with blood and swore he would have us before the magistrates. He looked so gory that I really thought it would be a case of manslaughter. Finally we clubbed up sufficient to pay for the broken glass and he agreed to get some plaster and forget about the magistrates.' Perhaps, thought the bowler who was to take 1,269 wickets for Yorkshire, which he captained between 1878 and 1882, the victim of his big-hitting was well pleased with the outcome of the match.

The difference between the competent and the very good quickly became defined once the pressure was on and those who demonstrated they could master their local contemporaries felt well able to hold their own with anyone. Hard-working, God-fearing people, they respected ability but bowed the knee to nobody. Their education might be limited, yet the men who founded Yorkshire cricket were sturdy, blessed with a native cunning and keenly aware of their place in the order of things.

Few travelled beyond the outskirts of the neighbourhood in which they were born in the 1880s, so it might be imagined that the opportunity to see some of the further-flung corners of the world would have been eagerly grasped. Yorkshiremen, however, had a healthy regard for what they knew best.

Ephraim Lockwood, one of the Lascelles Hall 'giants', rated around the 1870s as the finest cutter of the ball in the world, did not blink an eye at the majesty of Niagara Falls. He was taken to see this spectacle of nature while in America with a touring party. 'This is a sight worth seeing, isn't it? It's grand,' ventured his wicket-keeping colleague George Pinder. 'Nay, I make nowt of it. I'd sooner be at Lascelles Hall,' came the reply from the batsman referred to affectionately as 'Old Mary' by his team-mates.

Lockwood also had the chance to visit Australia with W.G. Grace in 1873, but said simply: 'Somehow I didn't fancy the outing at the time, so I stayed at home.' This down-to-earth realism, linked to an unflappable temperament, has continued to mark out Yorkshiremen. There was, for example, the Test debut of Arthur 'Ticker' Mitchell, a thoroughly organised batsman who epitomised his county's solid virtues and became the most feared and exacting of coaches.

This occurred in unusual circumstances against South Africa in 1935. Mitchell was enjoying an unexpected break, earned by an

Ephraim Lockwood, from Lascelles Hall, near Huddersfield. He earned a reputation as the finest cutter of the ball in the 1870s and 1880s.

early victory over Kent, as England got to grips with the tourists at Headingley. He turned his attentions to his neglected garden at nearby Baildon after allowing himself the luxury of an extra hour in bed. He had settled down to the weeding and was engrossed as a car screeched to a halt outside his gate.

He was more than a little surprised to see his county captain, Brian Sellers, striding down the path, a little breathless and obviously in a hurry. 'Come on, Arthur,' he gasped, 'Morris has a back strain and you are wanted for England.' The Morris in question was Leyland, the most loved of Yorkshire's left-handed batsmen, whose bad luck provided Mitchell with his chance.

The story might easily have been taken straight from the pages of schoolboy fiction. Mitchell had obviously nursed ambitions of playing for his country, but, although he appreciated the need for haste with the start of the Test only an hour away, he remained calm and collected. 'I shall,' he replied soberly, 'have to wash my hands first.'

He also had to change from his gardening clothes and put his shaving kit into his pocket for use at the ground, but nothing disturbed the professionalism that had served his county so well. England, batting first, soon fell into trouble, three wickets tumbling for 78, at which point Mitchell marched to the wicket and made 58, mostly on the leg side, with exactly the right mixture of caution and enterprise. By adding another 72 in the second innings in a much more adventurous style to answer his captain's call, he underlined both his own quality and the Yorkshireman's reliability in a crisis.

This has been proved time and again, with Len Hutton and later Geoff Boycott carrying almost singlehanded responsibility for their country's batting, and others, such as Willie Watson, highlighting consistency on a slightly lower plane with brilliant displays, usually when the going was most difficult.

Watson scored one of the most celebrated centuries in Test history – 109 on his first appearance against Australia at Lord's in 1953 – sharing in a partnership of 163 with Trevor Bailey that saved one match and made possible the winning of the Ashes for the first time in twenty years. The pressures, of course, were real enough, but Watson's nerve had been tested as a boy in short trousers playing for Paddock in the Huddersfield League, where he made runs against 'the paid men' who had no time for the dictates of chivalry towards a junior. If you were part of the action, you had to look after yourself, with no quarter given.

It is possible, incidentally, that the unrelenting nature of league competition has prevented any of the Yorkshire-born West Indians, Pakistanis or Indians from making their numerical presence in towns such as Bradford and Huddersfield apparent in county cricket terms. The failure of black youngsters to reach the nets has reflected their absence from the senior league sides, although the more mature overseas professionals often fill principal roles.

The tendency is for boys of immigrant stock to stick together in the minor organisations, arguably to Yorkshire's cost. If those from completely different ethnic backgrounds find difficulty in settling into the present set-up, they would have been much further out of their depth thirty or more years ago, when league games were fiercely contested.

Professionals had reputations to guard, particularly as their record would be closely scrutinised when the question of further engagements and payments arose, and each man had a shrewd idea of his worth. Emmett, for instance, was upset when he had to turn down an invitation to join the well-set-up Todmorden club, but his asking price 'seven shillings and sixpence and my railway fare' proved too high for the officials. He refused, though, to undervalue himself, preferring to live with the hope that Keighley, who he then assisted, would arrange a match with the Lancastrians. A couple of years later they did, Emmett scoring 119 not out and taking six wickets so that Todmorden immediately came to the conclusion that, after all, three halfcrowns represented a fair figure for his services.

Emmett also stuck out for a £5 fee when Yorkshire approached him for the first time and asked him to turn out against Notts County at Nottingham. He won the day, striking a note that found a sympathetic echo many years later in Illingworth, who left the county in 1968 because they would not guarantee him the security he thought he had earned. Illingworth may have left for Leicestershire with a heavy heart, but, like Emmett, he could not bring himself to compromise over such an important issue.

To do so would have been to betray his birthright and this aspect of the matter was at least as important as the hard cash, although few Yorkshiremen have been less than careful with the latter. The trend might almost have been set by Luke Greenwood, yet another of the Lascelles Hall run-makers of the nineteenth century. In his day it was the custom in certain parts of the country to give one shilling to anyone returning a lost ball. Grace once hammered him high over square leg and out of the ground for six. 'An old lady found this one,' said Greenwood, 'and toddled up with it to the wicket. She brought it to me and I said, "Nay, yon's him that hit it, yo mun go to him for t'brass."' W.G. paid up with a smile.

Not surprisingly collections for half-centuries or six wickets were carefully calculated in the leagues. Some batsmen were known to delay their fifties when well set until the late-comers were in a position to toss their coppers into the cap, while others rushed along near the end of a match to avoid losing out as the crowd hurried home for a belated tea. One such deserving soul, having struck the winning boundary and reached his half-century at the same instance, duly turned up outside the Methodist church next morning, fully attired in pads and batting gloves with his cap at the ready, working on the reasonable assumption that most of the congregation would have attended the 'other service' on the previous day and escaped without paying their dues. It is pleasing to discover that enterprise did not go unheeded.

Against such a stern background, children grew up quickly, learning in a matter of weeks what their contemporaries in other areas may have taken years to discover, if, indeed, they ever came to such knowledge, which brings us back to Watson and the way in which he rose to the occasion in such a critical moment at Lord's.

In his formative years, he had endured trial by physical ordeal too often to be worried by Ray Lindwall or Keith Miller. The reputation of this formidable Australian pair had been based on solid performance, but in this direction as well Yorkshiremen are always sceptical. They want to see for themselves, so they treat other mortals, however famous, as less than equal until convinced otherwise.

This has seldom helped them either to make friends or influence people, which might have been a disadvantage set against the aspirations of some, but it has persuaded most of their opponents to tread very carefully in their presence. Even the legendary W.G. Grace, who kept umpires in a constant state of fear and trembling by disputing almost every decision which went against him, could make nothing of the defiant, independent Yorkshireman.

While batting at Nottingham, Grace was given out, caught at the wicket by Joe Rowbotham, who donned the white coat of officialdom after a distinguished career as a batsman up to 1876. 'Joe, what have you done?' complained the champion, rubbing his forearm to indicate where he, at least, wanted to believe it had struck. 'Given you out,' came the unhesitating reply, 'and I shall do it again if it happens. All your rubbing won't alter that.'

It is, of course, easy to mistake this straightforward approach as conceit or arrogance, but invariably a Yorkshireman's opinion is based on logic and false modesty never brought success on or off the field. To this extent, those players who made the grade and settled regularly in the county side never grew away from the cradle that nurtured them. The links with the league clubs and the very able amateurs remained strong, with many a Saturday afternoon man believing quite sincerely that he was just as good as the more fortunate first-class cricketer, although he would seldom seek to prove the point by joining another county. For all those who changed their allegiance, there were many more who turned up their nose at the idea. Ex-county men also quite often went back to their roots to fill out their active days usefully by helping to set the standards. They watched over the youngsters of real potential and in this way Edgar Oldroyd, although disgruntled when Yorkshire released him in the 1930s, kept a watchful eye on the progress of the young Len Hutton.

There was, therefore, a steady supply of talent ready to step forward. When the Yorkshire team met one of the more prominent league sides shortly after the Second World War in an allegedly friendly fixture which contained an inevitable element of keen rivalry, they had to work very hard to complete the expected victory. To a large extent their task was made more difficult by the defiance of the amateur number seven, who fell narrowly short of fifty in a low scoring encounter.

Sellers, who had figured in the same position on the Yorkshire batting order, felt obliged to comment on the splendid innings. 'You must be one of the best number sevens in the county,' he said, offering what to many would have been high praise indeed. The recipient was neither flattered nor amused. Banging his glass down on the bar, he replied with conviction, 'See here, Mr Sellers, I am the best number seven in the county and that includes you.'

A rather more famous story has been handed down to illustrate the same point, although the truth has been distorted. England lost a Test match against Australia on home soil for the first time in 1882 by 7 runs, a result which brought into being the Ashes, and the villain of the piece was Edmund Peate, the prototype for the handful of world-class left-arm spinners who have raised the level of Yorkshire's challenge over so long a period.

Peate's crime, as number eleven, was to throw away his wicket, hitting out when the man at the other end was Charlie Studd, a darling of the crowd who had been the most successful batsman against the tourists. 'I could not trust Mr Studd,' explained Peate when criticised for an admittedly bad stroke – a remark which was quickly dismissed as foolishness. It is, though, worth adding that the expert opinion in the dressing room supported Peate's view.

Studd, who fell without scoring in the first innings and failed to get off the mark in the second, spent most of the time walking around with a blanket round his shoulders and with his teeth chattering while waiting his turn to bat. The great amateur appeared much the more agitated of the two.

A refusal to acknowledge nerves has enabled the White Rose representatives to serve England so well under the shadow of Sydney's infamous hill and out in the middle on so many grounds.

The present crop of Yorkshire players are the descendants of a distinguished line that stretches back to the beginnings of the game and demands special consideration for the county, even in troubled and controversial times. Throughout 150 years, Yorkshire has been the backbone of English cricket, because its inhabitants enjoy a special affinity with bat and ball – a relationship which has stood the test of time – and the summer sport will always have first claim on the county's affections.

Chapter 2

IN THE BEGINNING
(*c*1700–1863)

There is a school of thought, predictably with a great following throughout Yorkshire, that cricket had its beginnings in the North. This line of reasoning starts with the old game of stool ball, which was very popular, especially in the East Riding, as long ago as the early 1700s. Few rules existed, but a stool was laid on its side and an object stuffed with sawdust bowled at it while the 'batsman' defended the target with anything that happened to be available. These wooden stools, which could be found in most cottages, were, according to folklore, called crickets, which gives some substance to the claim.

From these humble origins, the sport grew slowly in the shadow of cock-fighting and boxing, which were both far more popular, and by 1751 accounts were set down of a match near Richmond between the Duke of Cleveland's eleven and a similar number representing the Earl of Northumberland. The patronage of the wealthy and influential nobility was vital, and the church also lent welcome support.

The burgesses in Leeds provided fourteen shillings and sixpence to pay cricketers in 1757 and the city became one of the first centres.

According to newspaper reports of May 1776, 'Yesterday a cricket match was played on Chapeltown Moor by the gentlemen of the town for five guineas and a dinner – married men against bachelors – which was won by the latter as there were six to come when the game was out.'

The spread of interest is confirmed in the fact that a club existed in York in 1784 and two years later the gentlemen of that city won a hundred guineas by defeating the gentlemen of Doncaster in a two-innings match. Not all the clubs which sprang up out of sudden enthusiasm survived though.

These pioneers were not above gilding the lily to attract the public and contests were often advertised as being for £500 or £1,000 when, in fact, very little money was at stake. The need to create a highly charged atmosphere was, therefore, quickly recognised and the actual money sometimes came from the players, who guaranteed so much each and took their dividends according to their share if they won. Of course, in some instances, the wealthy patrons accepted all the risks and took whatever profits might have accrued.

Businessmen also pondered the merits of the game, and the practice of supporting a sports club is, in one form or another, at least 150 years old, for there is evidence of a very rare three-innings match between the employees of two Sheffield factories. The reason for three innings is not clear, but the occasional match in the early 1800s followed this arrangement.

Details are scarce, largely because the scorers had neither pen nor paper, keeping a tally of the totals on sticks, with notches cut to count the runs. Individual batsmen's scores were not considered important, an attitude that would cause many modern run-makers to wince.

The most important progress in Yorkshire followed the building of a ground at Darnall, in Sheffield, which put the region firmly on the map around the turn of the century. There is reference to Ripon, which appears to have been one of the stronger clubs, meeting Nottingham in 1816, but the worthy citizens who made the Darnall project possible deserve the greatest credit for extending the scope of the county's activities.

The Marylebone Cricket Club visited Sheffield in 1825, beating All England in an eight-a-side contest, and subsequently All England thrashed the twenty-two of Yorkshire, but the lessons of this defeat were duly noted.

Even greater impetus stemmed from a fixture at Darnall between Sussex and All England, who met three times in various parts of the country to test a new style of bowling – round arm! This had been introduced in Sussex and was not immediately considered better than the under-arm method.

The Darnall event made a tremendous impact and cricket organisations prospered all over. Soon Huddersfield, Manchester, Halifax, Woodhouse, Armley, Bedale, Thirsk, Beverley, Bradford, Otley, Rotherham, Mexborough, Harrogate, Keighley, Scarborough, Redcar and Barnsley were engaged in keen rivalry. In the midst of all this activity, the series between Sheffield and Nottingham unquestionably assumed most importance as a constant thread in a random, ever-changing pattern. It could be demonstrated that the twenty-six fixtures in which these two cities took part from 1771 to 1860 were the forerunners of county competition, for they involved the leading players in those areas.

Sheffield had rather the worst of the argument, winning nine engagements to Nottingham's fourteen, but the continuity proved far more important than the results.

Inevitably differences arose on the way, and those who believe that the throwing controversy is an invention of our own generation can take comfort from the knowledge that this thorny issue caused trouble back in 1827. The Sheffield bowlers were 'called' several times in that year by the Nottingham umpires for 'jerking and throwing the ball' and, since the combatants could not reach agreement, play was suspended for a considerable time.

Finally, the whole business ended in uproar, with the two teams departing to find new and, presumably, more reliable officials. More straightforward decisions provoked heated debate, with one side or the other threatening to walk off, attitudes no doubt being shaped by the extent of the gambling on the outcome.

A leading hero was Tom Marsden, of Sheffield, whose candle burned brightly at both ends as he crowded a full life into thirty-eight eventful years. Marsden's best performance came in 1826, when a combined Sheffield and Leicestershire team beat Nottingham by an innings and 203 runs. He captured six wickets, but earned his place in the record books for an innings of 227 made in eight hours on his debut. Before this, probably as a consequence of the uneven and badly prepared pitches, only one first-class innings of 200 had been registered – by William Ward, who amassed 278 at Lord's in 1820.

Marsden's standing grew to such an extent that when he offered to meet any man in England at single wicket for £50 and to provide £10 towards his opponent's expenses in travelling to Darnall, there was no reply. Sadly, however, his powers declined rapidly and he endured utter humiliation at the hands of the celebrated Fuller Pilch, of Norfolk.

Pilch could be discussed in almost the same breath as any of the top batsmen of later years. He stood out as a leading figure in his own times and it was natural that he should be matched with Marsden for the championship of England, with £100 a side just to add to the interest. Pilch won the first encounter by an innings and 70 runs, scoring 77 against seven, and the second by 127 runs. These must have been lively affairs, for the rules allowed no fielders.

One other single-wicket match which merits a mention concerned Tom Hunt, who, although born in Chesterfield, came to prominence in Yorkshire and pitted his skills against a full Knaresborough team,

In the Beginning

winning by 8 runs over three days in 1845. The spectacle was marred by an unfortunate incident on the second day, when the appointed umpire got drunk and play had to be abandoned because no suitable replacement could be found.

Although these single-wicket games owed their success as much as anything to betting, they sowed the seeds from which the veritable forest of competition sprouted and without them it is unlikely that cricket would have taken such a grip on the imagination.

It is impossible to say exactly how or why it was decided to make up teams of eleven, for there are many instances of twelve a side or of eleven accomplished cricketers taking on twenty-two less able enthusiasts, but the game between Yorkshire and Norfolk in 1833 which marked the start of county cricket in the county involved the now familiar twenty-two.

Undoubtedly, Yorkshiremen took it as a good omen when their champions emerged triumphant by 120 runs and the full scorecard

Is this how it was? The gentlemen of York recreate the spirit of cricket from a bygone age.

for that fixture on the Hyde Park Ground at Sheffield on September 2, 3, 4 and 5 is worth studying. It was:

YORKSHIRE v NORFOLK
at Hyde Park Ground, Sheffield
2-5 September 1833

Yorkshire	first innings		second innings	
Woodhouse	run out	31	b N. Pilch	13
Vincent	b Daplyn	19	c Wilkinson	32
Smith	c F. Pilch	19	c Wilkinson	0
Marsden	b Daplyn	0	b F. Pilch	53
Dawson	c Pile	7	c Pile	6
Rawlins	c Pile	7	N. Pilch	12
Lupton	b F. Pilch	1	c Pile	0
Johnston	b F. Pilch	7	b N. Pilch	6
Barker	b F. Pilch	0	not out	4
Dearman	not out	14	c Wilkinson	40
Deakin	c Hogg	8	c W. Pilch	11
extras		25	extras	19
		138		196

Norfolk	first innings		second innings	
Simmence	b Marsden	3	b Marsden	0
N. Pilch	run out	10	b Dearman	22
Daplyn	lbw	5	c Vincent	0
Wilkinson	b Marsden	5	c Dearman	25
F. Pilch	c Vincent	10	c Vincent	23
Spinks	b Marsden	1	not out	14
Roberts	c Deakin	0	run out	21
Hogg	c Rawlins	1	run out	3
W. Pilch	run out	5	b Rawlins	8
Pile	b Dearman	20	b Marsden	11
Groom	not out	1	c Smith	0
extras		6	extras	20
		67		147

Bowlers clearly had to work hard to make their mark on posterity, for wickets then were given to the catchers, who took full credit for the dismissal and no bowling analyses were set down.

At this distance, Norfolk may seem strange opposition, but Sussex were the only other county club operating. Additionally, with the railway system in its infancy, Norfolk was much more accessible to Yorkshire than the southern clubs. Fuller Pilch, too, may have had a hand in the arrangements for the venture as he had an attachment to Sheffield Wednesday.

Yorkshire played that one game in 1833 and they met Norfolk twice in 1834 and 1836, but the public support generally remained lukewarm and the solitary fixture in 1835 was with Sussex. The first steps along the road that eventually led to such glory were, then, hesitant, and the county took part in a mere handful of matches between 1833 and 1861.

The All England eleven, founded in 1845 by William Clarke, an accomplished lob bowler, helped to keep first-class cricket alive in Yorkshire. The latter, however, had odds allowed to them to compensate for the vast difference in ability. They had fourteen, sixteen, eighteen or twenty-two players against the eleven of All England in twelve games, winning five, losing five, while they won seven and lost five of their engagements with Sussex, Manchester, Lancashire, Kent and Surrey.

Throughout this period Sheffield continued at the centre of things, even going so far as to challenge Yorkshire in 1849. Their confidence was justified in the sense that the city had provided the bulk of the county side since its inception and they went on to win three of the four matches. Yorkshire scored 816 runs for the loss of seventy-six wickets overall, while Sheffield made 850 runs for seventy-four wickets, Yorkshire's batsmen averaging 10.7 runs against Sheffield's 11.4.

All the important games were staged in Sheffield at the Darnall Ground, Hyde Park or Bramall Lane, where, it was claimed, 60,000 spectators could see every ball bowled. The Sheffield public soon earned respect for their knowledge and understanding, so when Tom Richardson, the Surrey and England pace bowler, heard of doubts being expressed about the legitimacy of his action he anxiously put the matter to the test in the city. 'I am sure that the folk there will spot if there is anything unfair about it,' he said, and when his bowling passed without comment he promptly assumed all was well.

Apart from Sheffield, places such as York, Harewood, Knaresborough, Dalton, near Huddersfield, and Bedale sent out their men to represent the county and the growth of the game forced another surge forward.

This came with the formation of a Public Match Fund Committee at a meeting in the Adelphi Hotel, Sheffield, on March 7, 1861. The approved resolution stated that the committee should be made up of the Bramall Lane management and one representative of any club prepared to put forward twenty shillings for the fund. M.J.

Ellison, destined to become the first Yorkshire County Cricket Club president, was elected treasurer of the fund and the Pitsmoor, Sheffield Wednesday and Hallam clubs soon subscribed, followed by Scarborough. The Yorkshire Year Book, incidentally, accords Mr T. R. Barker the honour of being president in 1863, and his name appears in the minute book, but diligent research by recognised county historians has unearthed no indication that he ever attended a meeting.

At this juncture, however, the Yorkshireman's basic suspicions formed a stumbling block. The widely-held view considered that this self-appointed body had no weight of authority and represented little more that the Sheffield interest, so no rush to put money into the fund materialised. As a consequence, the committee had to turn down an invitation from Lancashire in 1862, although they managed to finance home and away fixtures with Surrey, who won at the Oval by six wickets and were beaten at Bramall Lane by two wickets.

The sticking point for many was the fact that the Public Match Fund Committee did not represent the area as a whole and the local considerations which inspired this line of reasoning have lasted right up to the present day, when moves to centralise Yorkshire's activities on Headingley have been vigorously resisted.

The next scheme had to appeal to every corner of the county and it was unveiled on January 8, 1863, when the resolution stated: 'That a county club be formed, which shall consist of an unlimited number of members, the lowest subscription to such club being 10s. 6d., its object being to provide funds for playing first-class matches either in Sheffield or in other towns of the county according as arrangements may be made.'

Thus the enterprise became sufficiently extended, although the original committee consisted of twelve Sheffield men. The rules passed in 1863 included the promise that 'a central or any fixed ground shall not be considered requisite' and that 'matches shall be played at various localities'. Officials were at pains to emphasise that 'the county entirely disclaims the right or desire of interference with the particular concerns of any local clubs, their only object being to develop the cricketing powers of the county.'

This far-sighted administrative initiative drew a poor response, with only York showing a willingness to co-operate. Bradford even went so far as to threaten opposition, so it is Sheffield, the city which in the 1980s clung desperately to a slender link with a county club

In the Beginning

based in Leeds through the good graces of the Sheffield Amateur Sports Club at Abbeydale Park, that deserves recognition for organising Yorkshire into a fighting force.

Chapter 3

THE FOUNDATIONS ARE LAID (1863–1882)

The much feared Sheffield bias did not materialise in the choice of the eleven for the newly-formed club's first venture, which brought a draw with Surrey at the Oval on June 4, 5 and 6, 1863. Those on duty represented a fair enough mix of the leading players, the line-up being: John Thewliss (Lascelles Hall), John Berry and Edwin Dawson (Dalton), Roger Iddison and George Anderson (Bedale), George Atkinson (Ripon), Ikey Hodgson (Bradford), Joe Rowbotham, Edwin Stephenson and William Slinn (Sheffield) and Brian Waud (Leeds).

Surrey scored 315 to which Yorkshire replied with 257 before taking a grip on the proceedings by dismissing the home side for 60, with Slinn and Hodgson bowling unchanged to take five for 30 and five for 27 respectively. For some reason, although Iddison is accorded the distinction of being Yorkshire's first captain in the year-book, some references to this match state that Anderson led the team.

Even the democratic gesture with regard to selection did not put an end to the arguments and, while the Surrey game was the only one arranged by the Sheffield authorities, Bradford pressed their claims for equal consideration by meeting Nottinghamshire. For a long time queries arose as to who held the real responsibility for county cricket in Yorkshire.

The issue was further complicated in 1865, when Anderson, Atkinson, Iddison, Rowbotham and Stephenson refused to play against Surrey. Their action advertised ill-feeling which existed between North and South and politics entered into the calculations when Anderson sternly declined the offer of the Yorkshire captaincy in 1865. As the disputes raged, G. Wootton, playing for All England at Sheffield, took all ten Yorkshire wickets for 54 runs, becoming the first person to complete this feat against them.

Around this time the future of the club hung in the balance, so the committee did not arrange any matches in 1866, although three actually took place and in one of them Tom Emmett made his debut. The Halifax bowler and George Freeman took over from

The Foundations are Laid

Hodgson and Slinn to startle the cricketing world with their complementary skills. Freeman took fifty-one wickets at a cost of 7.4 runs each in 1867 and Emmett had thirty wickets for 5.2 runs, this pair's contribution enabling Yorkshire to win all their seven matches.

Despite the increasing prominence of the county club, unauthorised groups continued to take an uninvited hand and between 1863 and 1874, as the official body struggled for survival, some twenty-six 'pirate' fixtures were played.

The haphazard nature of the arrangements is best illustrated by the arrival on the scene of Ephraim Lockwood, destined to make an important mark, but, at the time of his debut, apparently ill-equipped for the role of leading batsman. Freeman and Luke Greenwood were injured in a bus accident in Derby and when Yorkshire reached London on the Saturday night of August 22, 1868, they found themselves short-handed. Lockwood's uncle, John Thewliss, put forward his nephew and, on the further recommendation of Emmett, the youngster was called up by a message which pursued him across the county as he had gone with Lascelles Hall to play at Yeadon.

Lockwood made a spectacular start, despite being in his own words, 'a raw lad, looking more like a collier than a cricketer'. He opened the Yorkshire innings with his uncle after Surrey had been dismissed for 195 and they put on 176 for the first wicket. Lockwood outscored his senior partner for quite a while, being not out 57 to Thewliss's 51 at the close of play on the first day. The crowd, rushing to get a close look at the newcomer as he left the field, were not unduly impressed by his appearance, one voice raising itself above the others to suggest: 'Why, he's more fit to eat a pennycake than play cricket.'

Gradually the more gifted and forceful came into national prominence, so, when Yorkshire won six out of seven games in 1870, the other being drawn, Freeman, whom W.G. Grace regarded as the best fast bowler he had seen, compensated for some indifferent batting by his team-mates with fifty wickets for 327 runs. Freeman was held in the highest regard by all his contemporaries, but, although very much a gentleman, he possessed a pride in his trade which allowed no liberties to be taken.

One incident underlines the fact that there was plenty of steel in his make-up. Knickerbockers became fashionable among the gentry towards the end of the nineteenth century and George Cayley, later to become Sir George Cayley Bart, went in to bat against Freeman without guards in order to display his legs in the new style. Freeman bristled instinctively at the implied slight. 'I'll have a go at those legs,' he said quietly. The first ball struck them, causing Cayley to flinch, and the second cracked into the shin bone with such force that the batsman thought it prudent to send for adequate protection. Honour satisfied, Freeman got down to the more serious business and bowled Cayley with the next delivery.

In 1870, Stephenson enjoyed a benefit and then retired, making way as wicket-keeper for George Pinder, from Sheffield, who soon became recognised as the best in the world in handling real pace. It was, in those days, the custom for the wicket-keeper to stand up to the stumps, whatever the bowling, and in playing with Freeman, Emmett and later Alan Hill, another from the Lascelles Hall nursery, Pinder dealt with the most hostile fast bowlers in the country.

Teams employed a long-stop to retrieve anything that beat the wicket-keeper and Pinder proudly became the first man to dispense with this insurance. A.N. Hornby, the Lancashire batsman, captaining the North against the South at Lord's, asked Pinder to manage without any assistance and the Yorkshireman responded with a magnificent display in which he conceded only four byes.

The funds of the club had improved by 1871 and the accounts revealed a profit of £300. Things were advancing at a pace and in 1873 a new chapter opened up with the county championship being put on a proper footing. Surrey set the ball rolling, although in the first place, they hoped chiefly to tighten up the qualification laws which allowed players to turn out for more or less anyone who approached them. As with everything else, there were some hiccoughs along the way. The rules by which the championship was decided changed a great deal and some odd results occurred.

The competition, in fact, drew comparatively little attention in its formative years and *Wisden's Almanack*, for example, preferred to deal primarily with MCC matches and the universities. Between 1873 and 1886, the title went, so far as most people were concerned, to the county with fewest defeats, although this system encouraged negative tactics and thus had its critics who, when it suited them, ignored the placings.

Subsequently, a win received one point and a draw half a point, while in the early 1890s the losses were simply deducted from the wins. Then percentages were introduced, which added to the confusion, but stood the test of time better than the other schemes.

The Foundations are Laid

Tom Emmett, who emerged from Crib Lane, Halifax, with his cricket gear wrapped in a copy of the *Halifax Courier* and went on to captain Yorkshire.

Gloucestershire, prospering from the inspiration of the remarkable Grace brothers, placed themselves firmly among the front-runners, taking the championship in 1873, 1874, 1876 and 1877. Yorkshire, by contrast, experienced some fruitless seasons, although by common consent they had three placings in the top four, this figure being based on the calculations which gained most favour. The basic weakness fed on a lack of consistency. A number of spectacular triumphs had to be set against some dreadful displays in which a lack of overall discipline, especially with regard to fielding, caused concern. In turn Anderson, Iddison, Rowbotham, Lockwood and Emmett had assumed the mantle of leadership without exercising complete control and the committee increasingly accepted the need for an amateur captain.

The question of jealousy among the professionals did not really arise, for Emmett, above all, was the subject of universal goodwill. Social attitudes were more important altogether. The committee minutes for 1878 reported that: 'T. Emmett be made captain in the absence of a gentleman.' Leadership, it was felt, even within the ranks of the team, should come from someone whose station in life fitted him to make decisions for and about others and who automatically stood out as a man apart.

Emmett, for instance, proved unduly modest about his own bowling, being at times reluctant to keep himself on because he feared the strictures of his colleagues, so it was as well for Yorkshire that the man they required to mould the excellent material on hand into an effective unit happened to be waiting in the wings.

The Hon. Martin Bladen Hawke transformed the club at all levels, imposing his will totally, and while his autocratic bearing has not endeared him to all cricket historians, there can be no disputing that he introduced many improvements which more than outweighed any disadvantages to be found in his admittedly high opinion of himself. Not all the benefits were bestowed on the playing side, for, as with the proverbial policeman, the cricketer's lot was not by any means a happy one and wide areas of discontent existed.

A lot fell on hard times at the end of their careers, much to the embarrassment of many attached to the county club. Luke Greenwood found himself almost penniless at sixty-four, keeping body and soul together by working on sports grounds and accepting the charity of his friends. Much worse was the fate of John Thewliss. He disappeared almost without trace, Yorkshire not being sure of his whereabouts after he retired. An enquiry from a well-wisher brought the reply: 'Think dead. If not, try Manchester.' This fine player was, as it turned out, living at 782 Oldham Road, Failsworth, near Manchester, earning coppers by trudging four miles under the burden of a heavy basket of laundry and by shovelling in loads of coal for the better off. Some cricketers were blamed for wasting their money, but financial returns were hardly substantial and covered only a handful of years.

Players were expected to be in London one day and in the North the next, covering their own expenses on around £5 or £6 a time which did not leave a lot to spare, particularly as winter pay had not been considered. Joe Rowbotham rushed through one hectic spell in which he recalled: 'We had to travel about 900 miles. We played at Brighton on the Monday and had to go on to Sheffield. Then we journeyed back to London and on to Truro.'

George Pinder also commented ruefully on the question of money. 'We got only £5 wherever we went. The largest number of games I played in was twenty-four in one season. That would be £120. Out of that I had to pay my hotel bills, my railway travelling and maintain my home, my wife and four children. We started in May, gave up in September and then we had seven months to get over. So you see, there was not a deal to throw away or spend.' As Pinder also discovered, cricket prevented him from following his trade as a grinder, leaving him hostage to fortune once he had to call it a day. A single man with only himself to account for may have managed all right, but most of the Yorkshire players were married men and found it hard going.

The Foundations are Laid

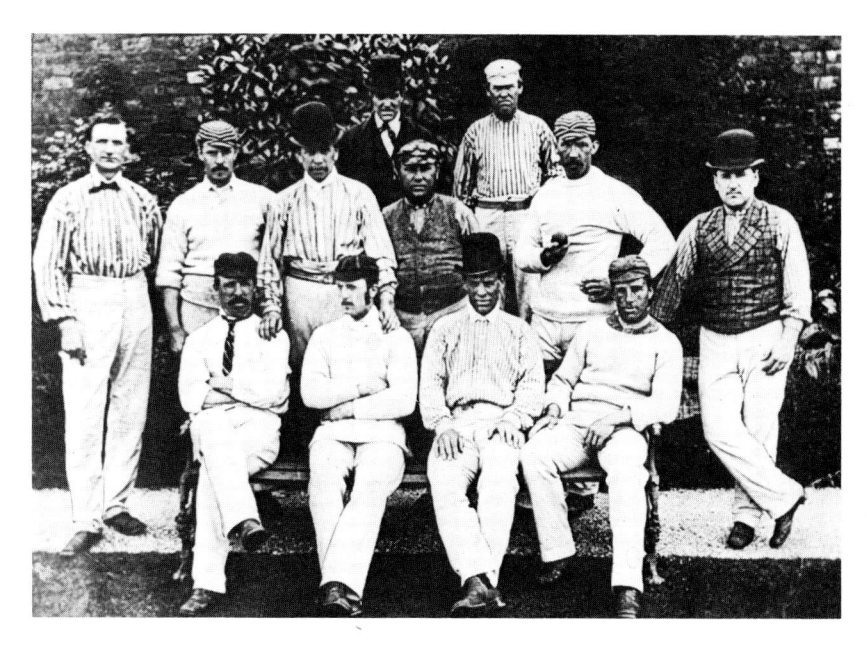

The days of brown boots and striped shirts. Yorkshire's line-up in 1875 looks distinctly odd, but the players were more than useful. They were (left to right): at back – G. Martin (umpire) and Thewliss; standing – Pinder, Ulyett, Armitage, Rowbotham, Hill, Greenwood; seated – Emmett, Hicks, Lockwood, Ullathorne.

Coupled with the expense was the sheer hardship of the long trips, which are wearying even with the motorway system to ease the strain and which must have been agonising a hundred years ago. George Anderson often protested at the trials and tribulations which became part and parcel of his life. 'Dublin to London, London to Glasgow and Edinburgh – those were the journeys we had to do,' he said, looking back to his association with the All England party. 'Often we went through the night and had to be ready for a prompt start the next day.

'I remember one difficulty we got into going from Wisbech to Sleaford. We had to do it one night by coach and the driver got lost, so we all wandered about Lincolnshire in the darkness until we stumbled across a signpost. We then struck a light and someone climbed up the post to find out the way we had to go. We landed at our destination at six in the morning and got onto the field by noon. On more than one occasion I have had to play in London on the Wednesday and in Glasgow the next morning – all for £5 a game.

After paying our expenses there was precious little left to get fat on, but most of our fellows were steady. I knew only one who could get drunk and still play the next day. You can take it from me that a man can't indulge and operate to the best of his game.'

Lord Hawke, to his credit, having put a lot right, admitted as late as 1904 that 'the remuneration of the professional is, in my opinion, even now none too good.' Yorkshire by then, however, were giving winter pay and had brought to fruition plans to look after their staff in their retirement. These included withholding small sums and investing them, which gives rise to other far-ranging debates on the rights of the working man to be in charge of his own financial affairs, but the committee's motives were honourable enough, while Lord Hawke also put up an incentive bonus.

'I award marks to each deserving professional, thus being able to recompense all departments,' he said. 'Each mark is worth five shillings and the cash equivalent is handed over to the individuals directly at the conclusion of the season.'

Lord Hawke made the welfare of the county player his hobby and the size of his achievement has to be measured in social as well as playing terms. He brought Yorkshire to the official and unquestioned championship for the first time in 1893 and altogether they took the title on eight occasions while he was captain. When not entirely successful, they had a formidable presence and his right to the highest ranking in the Yorkshire story cannot be challenged. It has been said that he inherited ten drunks and a parson, which exaggerates the eccentricities of his team, but it is true to say that without him some disorder would have persisted for a crippling period.

Chapter 4

THE GOLDEN AGE
(1883–1902)

Lord Hawke's value to Yorkshire cricket did not rest entirely with his qualities of leadership, for he acquitted himself usefully as a batsman with 13,429 runs for an average of 19.77. These figures were put together often from a place fairly low down the order with Lord Hawke batting when he found it necessary to press on quickly. He had no interest at all in averages, however, for in his mind nothing mattered except the team.

Admitting that their publication satisfied the public appetite, he often put forward the opinion that 'a man with his eye on statistics will try to keep up his wicket irrespective of his team's position'. Lord Hawke also thought that averages kept prominent cricketers too much in the public eye 'to the partial detriment of the sides they represent'. What he would have thought of the 1980s, dominated by the cult of hero-worship, is not difficult to imagine and it is hard to argue that cricket has gained anything from the exploitation of individual fame.

To gain an accurate indication of Lord Hawke's prowess, therefore, it has to be noted that he had an above-average reputation as an athlete at Eton and Cambridge University before coming almost by chance into the Yorkshire team. He was playing for the Yorkshire Gentlemen when the Reverend Edmund Carter invited him to turn out against I Zingari at Scarborough. Lord Hawke went on to play briefly under Emmett, declining an offer of the captaincy, before taking over in 1883.

Despite the splendid batsmen and bowlers at his command, Lord Hawke had to exhibit considerable patience, for the results continued to tantalise. The substance never quite matched the shadow. Promise was seldom fulfilled. Throughout this period Louis Hall, from Batley, 'the parson' Lord Hawke found in his ranks, built a record that has never been approached since.

Altogether this tall, solid batsman, who concentrated largely on his defence, carried his bat at his own pace through a completed innings fourteen times, which, to bring matters into perspective, compares with Geoff Boycott's seven and Herbert Sutcliffe's six.

'I cannot tell how I acquired a slow style,' said Hall, 'but I found it was of more value to my side than myself.' Remarkably, he compiled only nine centuries, but perhaps he never found the time to make more.

Surrounded by more spectacular strikers of the ball such as 'Happy Jack' Ulyett, his opening partner and a lively all-rounder, Hall found no reason for haste and Yorkshire were content to let him soldier on as he saw fit. Their real strength rested with the bowling, which is always the more effective arm of any really strong side, and Lord Hawke had at his disposal two legendary left-arm spinners in Edmund Peate and Bobby Peel.

Peate unbelievably began as one of Treloars' Clown Cricketers, a kind of variety act engaged in the south of England to entertain the public around 1875. They embarked on a tour of the country, finishing in Sheffield, where Peate sorrowfully reported: 'We were well mobbed and sodded. The grinders saw no fun in booby cricket.' After a brief attempt to become an acrobat, which came to a painful conclusion when he fell on his head, Peate turned to more serious matters, taking up appointments at Batley and Carlisle as a pace bowler until constant practice brought mastery of length and flight.

His career did not last long, failing eyesight forcing his premature retirement, but Peel picked up the torch in 1882, sustaining an art that was to flourish in Yorkshire through Wilfred Rhodes Hedley Verity and Johnny Wardle, who linked 1898 to 1958.

In the formative years of Lord Hawke's captaincy some of the young Colts failed to live up to expectation, so the progress followed an erratic course. In 1885 Yorkshire appeared for the first time in a match that yielded 1,000 runs, 1,039 being scored in the Sussex fixture at Brighton and 1,018 at Bradford, where Gloucestershire were the opposition. Ulyett and Hall set a new first-class record by scoring 123 and 108 for the first wicket in the two innings at Brighton, while the latter earned a somewhat less honourable mention in despatches at Canterbury, where he occupied the crease for seventy minutes without scoring.

On the bowling side, Peel confirmed his standing in the top flight with fourteen wickets for 33 runs as Nottinghamshire were shot out for 24 and 58 in 1888, only 165 runs being scored altogether – the lowest number in any completed Yorkshire match.

Between the years of 1883, when Lord Hawke took over, and 1892 Yorkshire rose to second place in the table three times and finished third on the same number of occasions, but they also had

Bobby Peel, from Churwell, near Leeds. One of Yorkshire's great line of slow left-arm bowlers. (*Overend Press*)

to live with the indignity of being seventh, eighth and sixth, with 1891 representing the low-water mark in their fortunes. Despite the presence of highly-rated university all-rounders in the Hon. F.S. Jackson and Ernest Smith, Yorkshire won only five of their seventeen matches, losing eleven, a sequence which brought a good deal of trouble.

Proposals aimed at revitalising the club flooded in. Some of them have been repeated by subsequent generations when Yorkshire's performances have not met requirements. They included searching more diligently for the talent that the critics were certain existed and had been overlooked only through a lack of interest on the committee's part. The idea of establishing the club in one centre with one ground also found favour. Not surprisingly, the officials came under heavy fire, with a clean sweep being noisily advocated.

The intention here was to create a new body with wider representation and gradually this came about, though not, happily, by means of a bloody revolution. The committee structure underwent major change in 1893 as the Sheffield seats were reduced from thirteen to seven. Bradford and Leeds acquired three each, while Barnsley, Craven, Dewsbury, Halifax, Huddersfield, Hull, Scarborough and

The Yorkshire team of 1890 were (left to right): back row – J.B. Wostinholme (secretary), Sherwin (umpire), Hunter, Wainwright, Haigh, Peel, the scorer (unknown); middle row – Tunnicliffe, F.S. Jackson, Lord Hawke (captain), Smith, Bairstow; front row – Hirst, Moorhouse, Denton, Brown.

Wakefield got one each. Events on the field, however, had a far greater significance, for in that same year Yorkshire won the championship.

A word of explanation here may help to clarify the position, for Yorkshire are credited in some cases with successes in 1867 and 1870 as well as a shared title with Nottinghamshire in 1869, but these can be regarded as unofficial. In one form or another county sides had been in competition for some time with a rough-and-ready method of compiling the table, the end product usually being the result of Press calculations.

Not until the meeting in London on December 11, 1872, inspired by Surrey's initiative, were rules formulated and it is from the following season that the championship is generally deemed to have

The Golden Age

started. Thus Yorkshire's 1893 triumph is the first to qualify for the seal of official approval.

This was entirely unexpected because Yorkshire went to the head of affairs with the same players who had managed to do no better than sixth the year before. The averages for that momentous summer were:

BATTING AVERAGES, 1893

	Innings	Not out	Runs	HS	Average
Brown	26	1	712	84	28.48
Tunnicliffe	26	3	653	77	28.39
Sellers	25	0	678	105	27.12
Hirst	23	9	287	43	20.50
Wainwright	24	1	453	78	19.69
Jackson	9	1	152	59	19.00
Moorhouse	22	5	302	39	17.76
Ulyett	22	2	342	73	17.10
Peel	23	1	343	69	15.59
Wardall	13	0	174	106	13.38
Lord Hawke	7	0	82	25	11.71
Hunter	23	10	116	32	8.92
Mounsey	8	1	62	27*	8.85
Smith	9	0	74	17	8.22

Also batted: Hayler 18* and 4; Whitehead 13 and 0; Frank 7; Waller 1.
* indicates not out

BOWLING AVERAGES, 1893

	O	M	R	W	Average
Jackson	77.1	28	160	13	12.30
Wainwright	600	209	1130	90	12.55
Peel	627.2	276	922	65	14.18
Wardall	165.1	84	209	14	14.92
Brown	71.4	21	159	10	15.90
Hirst	567.2	244	963	59	16.32
Smith	141	38	362	15	24.13
Moorhouse	98.4	56	150	4	37.50

Also bowled: Ulyett 2-0-12-0; Mounsey 9-2-16-0; Waller 10-6-10-2; Tunnicliffe 1-0-3-0; Hayley 5-0-18-0; Sellers 1-1-0-0.

The thing that stands out is the shortage of runs, with only Arthur Sellers, an amateur from Keighley, and Thomas Wardall scoring centuries. Sellers led the way with 105 and 103, but Yorkshire were dismissed for fewer than 150 on eight occasions. To balance this short-fall, the bowling operated with smooth efficiency and George Herbert Hirst, having made his debut in 1891, confirmed his worth as an all-rounder. His consistency is reflected in a batting average of 20 without a score higher than 43 and at Huddersfield, where Yorkshire won by ten wickets, his 35 swung the issue against Gloucestershire, prompting Grace to remark: 'I had no idea the beggar could bat so well.' If only he had known!

A few eyebrows must have been raised, too, at the absence of Lord Hawke, who took part in only six games, Ulyett being captain in the rest. Possibly it was a tribute to his lordship's authority that the machine ran so smoothly when he was away, but the championship triumph also brought great credit on the often under-rated professionals, who demonstrably knew how to behave in the heat of battle once they had been given the right lead.

Sadly, the authorities had to report that: 'The amount of subscriptions has increased, but is yet lamentably in arrears of what it should be to enable the committee to retain to the county the services of their most prominent young professionals and the committee hope that all members will do their utmost to induce their friends to join the club.'

From that point, Yorkshire's supremacy was never seriously dis-

The Hon. F.S. Jackson, the great amateur all-rounder who persuaded Lord Hawke to give Wilfred Rhodes his chance.

The Golden Age

puted in the long term until the 1950s, when Surrey took the title in seven successive years. Over fifty seasons, ignoring the savage disruptions caused by two world wars and the occasional slip, the White Rose bloomed to the envy and admiration of the cricketing world.

Yorkshire were champions twenty-three times, allowing the merest hint of fallibility now and again and all those doubts of the dark days of 1891 disappeared.

Indeed, the county made so much progress in the decade heralded by that first success that their ascendancy was conclusively underlined. Nottinghamshire and Surrey enjoyed moments of glory, but when Yorkshire swept them aside they had no answer. Early statisticians pounced on the opportunity to employ their expertise, sorting out the facts to put Yorkshire in a very favourable light. The comparison, based on returns when each of the three counties were at their best, gave Yorkshire a 66.85 percentage rating. Surrey's was 56.41 and Nottinghamshire's 53.84.

To clarify the position, Yorkshire won 146 of their 243 games, gaining 117 points out of a possible 175. Surrey had 122 victories from 174 outings, with 88 points from a maximum of 156, while Nottinghamshire's haul amounted to 42 points out of 78. The logic was clear enough.

The solitary cloud in an otherwise clear blue sky took the form of a Lancashire double and the clash at Old Trafford merits consideration among the most dramatic in the annals of Roses rivalry. Lancashire had won a low-scoring affair at Sheffield in 1872, but Yorkshire, bowled out for 55 and 68, then hit rock bottom in 1893 losing, by 5 runs, a match which yielded the lowest aggregate for a fixture in which forty wickets fell.

Lancashire, batting first, could muster no more than 64 and 50, Barker, at number seven, making the top score of 21 in their first innings. Yorkshire fared worse. Dismissed for 58 and 51, their sorry catalogue of batting failures in the two innings read: Sellers 13, Jackson 13, Smith 16, Brown 17, Tunnicliffe 13, Wainwright 7, Peel 13, Moorhouse 4, Ulyett 7, Hirst 1 and Hunter (not out twice) 2. Momentarily the champions had stumbled, but they quickly fell into step again, albeit looking over their shoulder and pondering the uncertainty of life.

New faces began to appear, including Frank Mitchell, an undergraduate at Cambridge University, and David Denton, from Wakefield, who blossomed into a dashing stroke-player. Although Surrey captured the major honours in 1894 and 1895, Yorkshire were building on a solid foundation. Their strength increasingly came from the collective spirit that characterised their work for many years, but the brilliance of Ted Wainwright from Sheffield, Hirst, David Hunter, the wicket-keeper, and J.T. Brown flourished as well. The fluent manner in which Wainwright could accelerate into a devastating spell was illustrated at Dewsbury in 1894, when he put apprehensive Sussex to the sword.

The bare details are that he collected a haul of thirteen wickets for 38 runs on a wicket made virtually impossible by heavy rain. He rushed the game to a timely conclusion with five wickets in seven balls, including the hat-trick, conveying the lasting impression that he had invented some system of remote control as the ball swerved, spun and cut through and round every stroke.

In 1896, Yorkshire put together their highest total – another mark on the history of the game that is never likely to be erased – by scoring 887 at the expense of a weary and increasingly dispirited Warwickshire attack at Birmingham. This massive affair occupied 650 minutes and included one 5 and 102 boundaries, sixes in those days having to be hit out of the ground.

In reply poor Warkshire limped to 203 in their first innings, Hirst taking eight for 59, but there was insufficient time to force victory. Opinion for once put Lord Hawke in the dock, where he stood accused of allowing the prospect of a record to over-rule his judgement. He had to plead guilty, but it represented a passing aberration and Yorkshire batted with tremendous authority all year, scoring 660 against Leicestershire and 543 off the Sussex attack in addition to fashioning five other totals in excess of 400. The details of the Warwickshire game are shown opposite.

Yorkshire's improved conditions gave their staff £2 per week throughout the winter 'on the express condition that they do not engage with any club or league during the summer'. Half the money was, however, retained at an interest rate of four per cent to be handed over to the player on his retirement.

The batting continued to impress, but, even with Schofield Haigh, another of the marvellous all-rounders from Huddersfield, creating a favourable impression, the bowling lacked the sting necessary to bring the championship back to the county. Injuries were a factor. So was the unfortunate incident which brought Peel's wonderful career to a sudden end in 1897. He had scored 11,131 runs for an average of 21.28 and taken 1,550 wickets at 15.09 runs each when

YORKSHIRE v WARWICKSHIRE
at Birmingham
7-9 May 1896

Yorkshire	first innings	
Jackson	c Law b Ward	117
Tunnicliffe	c Pallett b Glover	28
Brown	c Hill b Pallett	23
Denton	c W.G. Quaife b Santall	6
Moorhouse	b Ward	72
Wainwright	run out	126
Peel	not out	210
Milligan	b Pallett	34
Lord Hawke	b Pallett	166
Hirst	c Glover b Santall	85
Hunter	b Pallett	5
extras		15
		887

Fall of wickets: 1-63, 2-124, 3-141, 4-211, 5-339, 6-406, 7-448, 8-740, 9-876.
Bowling: Santall 65-9-223-2; Ward 62-11-175-2; Glover 30-1-154-1; Pallett 75.3-14-184-4; W.G. Quaife 8-1-33-0; Bainbridge 6-1-17-0; Hill 3-0-14-0; Lilley 6-1-13-0; W. Quaife 9-1-18-0; Diver 10-1-41-0.

Warwickshire	first innings		second innings	
Bainbridge	c Hunter b Hirst	5	b Wainwright	29
W. Quaife	b Hirst	0	not out	18
W.G. Quaife	not out	92		
Law	c Jackson b Hirst	7		
Lilley	b Hirst	0		
Hill	b Hirst	4		
Diver	b Peel	27		
Pallett	c Wainwright b Jackson	25		
Santall	b Hirst	29		
Glover	b Hirst	1		
Ward	b Hirst	3		
extras		10	extras	1
		203	(1 wkt)	48

Fall of wickets: 1-0, 2-7, 3-25, 4-25, 5-31, 6-78, 7-117, 8-170, 9-176.

Fall of wickets: 1-48.

Bowling: Hirst 40.1-16-59-8; Peel 31-21-27-1; Jackson 18-9-23-1; Wainwright 16-7-35-0; Milligan 13-5-14-0; Brown 4-0-24-0; Moorhouse 4-1-11-0.

Bowling: Milligan 5-1-15-0; Moorhouse 4-0-24-0; Peel 3-2-4-0; Wainwright 2.1-1-4-1.

he presented himself on the field against Middlesex at Sheffield on August 17 unfit for duty after enjoying good company too freely on the previous evening. His anxious team-mates did their best to shield him from the keen eye of Lord Hawke, but to no avail. Peel, who aggressively insisted on bowling in what he thought was the right

Headingley in the 1890s – a far cry from the ground today.

direction, making a sorry spectacle of himself in the process, had to go. His terrible misfortune, however, had a beneficial side-effect, opening the way for the most famous of all Yorkshire cricketers – Wilfred Rhodes.

Perhaps it was coincidence, but Rhodes's first year, 1898, brought Yorkshire another title and his association with them was supremely happy and successful for thirty-three years, during which everyone knew that the best all-rounder the world had known came from Kirkheaton, batted right-handed and bowled left. The single point of dispute concerned whether his name was Hirst or Rhodes.

Yorkshire's march along the path to glory contained a substantial landmark in the opening stand of 554 between J.T. Brown and 'Long John' Tunnicliffe at Chesterfield in 1898, the former surrendering his wicket after making exactly 300.

Surrey intruded to win the championship in 1899, but Yorkshire,

The Golden Age

'Long John' Tunnicliffe, who formed a famous opening partnership with John Brown.

in full, regal flow, completed a hat-trick in 1900, 1901 and 1902 and, in so doing, they won fifty-seven out of ninety-eight games, losing six. They simply destroyed all challengers, despite having to do without the services of the Hon. F. S. Jackson, an extremely able amateur all-rounder, good enough eventually to captain his county, who was away in South Africa. Hirst, Haigh and Rhodes, the great triumvirate, wreaked havoc, and in 1901 Nottinghamshire were despatched for 13 at Nottingham – the smallest score against Yorkshire and the second lowest total in first-class cricket. Rhodes took six wickets for 4 runs and Haigh four for 8.

The lengthening shadows of autumn which marked the end of the 1902 season, however, also stretched across Yorkshire's future. Middlesex and Lancashire in turn were destined to supplant them and success proved rather more elusive as Europe drifted towards the nightmare of 1914. The golden age was over.

Chapter 5

MIXED FORTUNES
(1903–1914)

Yorkshire were taking first-class cricket on a reasonably regular basis to Bradford, Leeds, Sheffield, Huddersfield, Hull, Dewsbury and Harrogate. Support for the club grew appreciably and 191,501 spectators paid at the turnstiles for the fifteen home fixtures in 1903. Receipts of £7,173 added to subscriptions of £3,276, which were welcome enough, but the contrast carried a warning note. The committee readily appreciated that attendance on the day could be seriously affected both by the weather and the form of the team, so the difference between takings and subscriptions caused mild concern, particularly as there were strong indications that changes would have to be made to the side.

The committee fought a long running battle to preserve the value of the members' ticket, regarding this guaranteed income as the 'cornerstone' of their finances, but in 1905 they found it necessary to reduce the privilege which permitted the free introduction of two ladies or two boys into the ground. This they reluctantly cut to one in the search for extra revenue and it is interesting to note that it was another seventy-eight years before a recommendation withdrawing this facility altogether briefly came up for consideration before being withdrawn in the face of noisy opposition.

Similarly, Yorkshire opposed a suggestion in 1908 by the Advisory County Cricket Committee that a proportion of members' subscriptions should go into a pool in each Test match year. Next the Board of Control objected to the free admission of local members to the Leeds Test, so Yorkshire spent £250 to defend the members' rights, although in this case subscribers to the Leeds club derived most benefit.

In many ways cricket has not changed all that much since then, for back in 1903 there were many proposals for improving the game. These included the widening of the wickets from eight to nine inches, to which the captains, the cricket sub-committee and the general committee of the MCC agreed. Yorkshire, while falling into line, added a cautionary note that 'the alteration should not become law until a good trial has been forthcoming'.

Mixed Fortunes 47

Another group advocated the introduction of a knockout competition, which Yorkshire immediately frowned upon, while others believed the imposition of a time limit on innings would bring a more positive approach. They gathered sufficient backing for an experiment to be conducted at Leeds, where Yorkshire and Nottinghamshire met with each innings restricted to four and a quarter hours. Provision was made for time saved on the first two innings to be added equally to the last two and boundaries could not exceed sixty yards.

Yorkshire won by 71 runs and, as everyone expected, both teams, anxious to keep up with the clock, were dismissed twice as they charged along in a frenzy of ill-considered haste. The result came at 12.45 on the third day, leaving plenty of time to spare and one theory in tatters.

So far as the more energetic aspects of the county's affairs were concerned, Yorkshire slipped to third place in the 1903 championship, losing five matches. Perhaps more significant was the accident to J.T. Brown junior, no relation to the better-known batsman of the same name. Brown, a pace bowler from Darfield, dislocated his shoulder in trying to find an extra yard of pace while bowling against Somerset. Despite immediate treatment, the mishap brought him down in full flight.

Two events overshadowed the general pattern of the 1904 season in which Yorkshire finished second to Lancashire. George Hirst took his benefit and the great affection and admiration he commanded ensured success. His total of £3,703 was surpassed only once up to 1945: in 1925, when Roy Kilner received £4,106.

The Harrogate wicket incident, however, gave considerably less cause for celebration. The fixture against Kent had to be abandoned on July 8 because of interference with the wicket on the previous night. Some spots were allegedly filled in, which must have been to the advantage of Kent, who had to bat last, and it was ruled that the game would not count as first-class.

In order to keep faith with the customers, the players went through the motions on the second day, Haigh taking a hat-trick with leg-breaks, but they gave up the ghost after that. The Harrogate groundsman steadfastly denied that he had been party to any doctoring of the wicket and the MCC declined to hold an inquiry, which left an unsolved mystery to exercise the minds of all concerned.

J.T. Brown – the batsman – retired through ill-health and Jackson approached the end of his active service, so the outcome of the campaign could be accepted with good grace. Indeed, subdued pleasure at the slight improvement gave way to general rejoicing as Yorkshire became champions again in 1905.

The title was gained the hard way, for Jackson led England in all five matches against Australia – his final fling bringing a 2-0 victory in the series – while Rhodes (four), Hirst (three), Denton and Haigh (one) all made Test appearances. Ignoring this handicap, Yorkshire headed the field and went on to beat the Rest of England by 65 runs in the annual end-of-season engagement. Hirst made another claim to immortality at Leicester, where he put together the biggest innings for Yorkshire – 341 with a six, fifty-three fours, seven threes and twenty twos.

David Denton, some thought him too rash for his own good.

Hirst, as it turned out, had been limbering up for bigger things. In the next season, 1906, he completed the unparalleled feat of the double double – 2,385 runs for an average of 45.86 and 208 wickets at 16.50 runs each. Rumour has it that when asked if he thought anyone else might repeat this almost impossible trick, Hirst replied: 'I don't know, but if they do they'll be tired,' and it is the magnitude of the physical requirement that captures the imagination. Hirst's concentration must also have been incredible.

He concluded on a superlatively high note at Bath, where he beat Somerset almost singlehanded, becoming the only man in any

Mixed Fortunes

first-class match to score two centuries and take more than five wickets in each of the opposition's innings. He made 111 out of 368 and then captured six for 70 as Somerset crumbled to 125. Acting captain Ernest Smith did not enforce the follow-on and Hirst went in at the fall of the first wicket to pass 2,000 runs in making 117 not out. This concession to individual needs did not affect the outcome, for Hirst then took another five for 45 as Somerset scraped their way to 134, Yorkshire winning by 389 runs.

He could not, though, keep Yorkshire at the top of the table, for Kent edged them out by a single run – the one by which Gloucestershire beat them in a low-scoring contest at Bristol.

Under the championship system, Yorkshire had simply to avoid defeat against Gloucestershire and Somerset in August to gain first place, but amidst scenes of wild West Country excitement the task proved unexpectedly beyond them.

The wet and wearisome summer of 1907, in which Yorkshire shared second place with Worcestershire and had two games with the champions, Nottinghamshire, abandoned, was quickly forgotten when the major honour came back to the county in 1908. The team did things in style after getting off to a sensational start by dismissing Northamptonshire twice at Northampton for an embarrassing 42 (27 and 15) – the smallest match total in any first-class English fixture. Yorkshire, batting first, made 333 for eight on the first day, but were then held up by heavy rain which threatened any further action. Finally, however, at 2.30 pm a resumption was possible and, in view of the wet outfield, they prolonged their innings, adding 23 runs in twenty-five minutes.

The home side, not in any event the strongest of opposition, were further weakened by injury and the absence of three leading amateurs, but, as one spectator observed: 'Their batting beggared description.' Hirst and Haigh bowled them out twice in two and a half hours, their returns being: Haigh 8–1–11–3 and 11–6–8–3; Hirst 8.5–4–12–6 and 11.2–8–7–6.

The one excuse Northamptonshire could offer was that Thompson, their best professional all-rounder, could not take part in either innings because of lumbago, but only one man, W.H. Kingston, reached double figures on aggregate. This is further evidence that life was comparatively easy in playing terms for the more accomplished cricketers when sides surrendered cheerfully simply because they lacked the ability to hold out. Eighteen of the nineteen completed innings totals of 19 or fewer in English cricket were registered before 1923, since when, we are often told, things have taken a turn for the worse.

Yorkshire actually got through the championship campaign unbeaten in twenty-eight matches – as they had been in 1900. They owed much to John Thomas Newstead, a bowler of above medium pace from Middlesbrough who discovered an aptitude for moving the ball into the bat rather like a fast offbreak. This, together with unrelenting accuracy, enabled him to take 131 first-class wickets for an average of 15.94. It was thought, reasonably enough, that another destructive force had been unearthed, but Newstead's decline was almost as rapid as his rise. Within a couple of years he had all but disappeared, having run out of steam.

Hirst, as ever, remained the perfect team man, able and willing. He scored 1,513 runs (39.81) and took 164 wickets (13.65). Rhodes just managed a hundred wickets in all matches, which could be regarded as someway below par for his course, but the bowling proved quite adequate as Yorkshire's batting struggled. The wonderful triumph was accomplished, despite the fact that only six batsmen averaged more than 20 with three of them topping the thirty mark.

The season also marked the twenty-fifth anniversary of Lord Hawke's appointment as captain, so during the Nottinghamshire game at Headingley he received a presentation. He chose six works of art that he proclaimed 'like Yorkshire cricket will last for ever and ever'.

Unhappily the next three years contained little to confirm that worthy prediction, for Yorkshire dropped to third in 1909 and eighth in 1910, equalling their worst season of 1891. Much greater distress stemmed from the sensational collapse at the Oval, where Yorkshire, seeking 113 to win, crashed to 26 all out in 1909 – their poorest effort until an even blacker day at Middlesbrough in 1965, when Hampshire put them out for 23. The sorry procession against Surrey is shown opposite.

The last five wickets fell with the total on 26 and only 16.1 overs were required for the innings. Admittedly the pitch was reported in *Wisden* as 'treacherous' and the glare of the sun from the pavilion windows troubled the batsmen, but Yorkshire lacked application.

Hawke, understandably, was less than pleased with the progress of the younger Colts, for what little success there was came Yorkshire's way thanks to Denton, Rhodes, Hirst and Haigh – 'The Old Brigade'.

Yorkshire	*Second innings*	
Rhodes	b Smith	0
Wilson	c Davis b Smith	2
Denton	b Smith	5
Rothery	c and b Rushby	4
Hirst	c Davis b Rushby	0
Drake	b Rushby	6
Bates	b Smith	4
Newstead	b Smith	0
Haigh	not out	0
Lord Hawke	b Rushby	0
Hunter	b Rushby	0
extras		5
		26

Fall of wickets: 1-2, 2-7, 3-12, 4-16, 5-16, 6-26, 7-26, 8-26, 9-26.
Bowling: Rushby 8.1-4-9-5; Smith 8-3-12-5.

Referring to defensive play in some quarters, Lord Hawke told the annual meeting: 'I would sooner we had lost matches by sporting cricket than that they should be drawn by unattractive play.' Occasional promise lifted the general depression and Yorkshire showed flashes of greatness, suddenly putting together their best fourth innings performance to beat Middlesex by two wickets in an amazing match at Lord's in 1910. They scored 331 for eight against all the odds, the concluding blow being struck with one delivery to spare.

During this period, David Hunter retired as wicket-keeper, giving way to Arthur Dolphin, who added something of his own to the illustrious chronicle of the men behind the stumps, and finally Lord Hawke announced his intention to retire after twenty-eight years in office.

Everard Radcliffe had already acted as captain for much of 1909 and 1910, so he hardly came new to the job when he took over in his own right in 1911. He had virtually no qualifications as a player, however, and gave way within a year to Sir Archibald White, whose appointment also rested entirely on the committee's desire to retain an amateur captain. Yorkshire, busily re-organising, gave opportunity to Major Booth – his christian name caused constant misunderstanding – and Alonzo Drake, while Roy Kilner began to show some form as a left-hand bat of genuine quality.

To assist in the coaching of youngsters, the committee built the winter shed at Headingley and put their faith in the future. The outcome was another championship in 1912 which gave Sir Archibald White the best possible start. None the less, he came in for more than his share of criticism, largely because the batting did not always live up to the livelier expectations. 'If you cannot win a match, why should you be beaten?' he asked, defending himself and his team, although he accepted that at times Benny Wilson and Edgar Oldroyd were 'inclined to be a little deliberate in their methods'.

Yorkshire's ninth title meant that in twenty years they had a record with which no one could compete. They had taken part in 515 championship matches, winning 280 and losing 65, their percentage of victories in the games that arrived at a positive conclusion being 80. Next in order of merit came Lancashire with 236 victories in 489 matches for a percentage of 71.

The weather was foul, however, in 1912, Yorkshire completing just one of their nineteen home fixtures without interruption. As a consequence a loss of almost £1,000 had to be faced on the year's workings. Lord Hawke felt justified in telling the annual meeting that Yorkshire would have 'a very excellent team for many years to come', but Kent and Surrey became champions in 1913 and 1914 and the war shattered so much before the world regained its normal rhythm.

Yorkshire actually won more games – sixteen to thirteen – in the 1913 championship, but Kent emerged as the better team. Injuries to Haigh, who was knocked down by a motor car, and Hirst proved serious blows, but the committee had every reason to be satisfied with the season's work, which involved an extra match against Lancashire at Liverpool to coincide with the King's visit to Merseyside.

The 1913 season also marked the return of Rockley Wilson, who did well enough as a slow bowler to earn a trip to Australia in 1921 after making his county debut in 1899. Wilson got his invitation to play for Yorkshire again after rumour reached the official ear that Hampshire, for whom he had a residential qualification as a master at Winchester, were showing interest. The Hampshire initiative reminded Yorkshire of Wilson's existence and he promptly made a century against Essex on his recall to the lists. Set against this good news came the retirement of Schofield Haigh, virtually irreplaceable as a right-arm seam bowler.

With war looming on the horizon, Yorkshire had a poor season in 1914, finishing fourth to Surrey. This placing, relatively low in Yorkshire's case, came about after eleven of the last twelve games had been won.

Mixed Fortunes

LEFT: Major Booth, a bowler who combined pace and skill, was killed on July 1, 1916, after enlisting in the Leeds 'Pals' in the First World War.

RIGHT: Alonzo Drake, the first Yorkshire bowler to take all ten wickets in an innings of a first-class match.

This also turned out to be the last season for both Booth and Drake. Booth, a second lieutenant, was killed on July 1, 1916, and Drake, medically unfit for military service, died suddenly three months after the end of hostilities. One of the sadder stories associated with Booth's tragic end concerned his sister, who, unable to accept the evidence of his death, kept a light burning in the window of the house in which they lived in the hope that one day he would return.

The loss to Yorkshire cricket was enormous. Drake had become the first Yorkshire bowler to take all ten wickets in an innings that fateful year. He had returns of five for 16 and ten for 35 on a badly prepared wicket at Weston-super-Mare. Booth, with five for 27 to his credit in the first innings, generously supported his colleague in the second, when Yorkshire had plenty of runs at their disposal. Booth bowled entirely to keep the batsmen playing him easily while Drake worked his way through the Somerset ranks at the other end. The details were:

Somerset	second innings	
Bisgood	c Dolphin b Drake	11
Braund	b Drake	9
Robson	c Birtles b Drake	3
Hylton-Stewart	st Dolphin b Drake	3
Hyman	st Dolphin b Drake	4
Poyntz	c Oldroyd b Drake	5
Hope	c and b Drake	19
Saunders	b Drake	0
Harcombe	b Drake	26
Bridges	not out	1
Chidgey	b Drake	4
extras		5
		90

Fall of wickets: 1–13, 2–20, 3–25, 4–28, 5–33, 6–38, 7–49, 8–52, 9–89.
Bowling: Booth 9-0-50-0; Drake 8.5-0-35-10.

Drake again forced his way into the modest headlines of the time when he became the only Yorkshire bowler to take four wickets in four balls, Derbyshire being the victims.

The popular idea that the war would be over in six months was exposed as a sorry illusion. Many thousands of lives were to be lost before cricket and the rest of the world could breathe easily once more.

Chapter 6

PICKING UP THE PIECES
(1919–1925)

The clearest sign in 1919 that all was well with the world after five years of madness came in the guise of another championship for Yorkshire, who played more matches than anyone else in romping clear of the field. They managed a percentage of 46.15, with twelve wins from twenty-six fixtures, but had to wait until the final matches to be sure of their reward. Rain prevented a finish to their match at Brighton, leaving them vulnerable, but Kent let their chance slip in failing to beat Middlesex and ended up on 42.85 per cent.

Yorkshire's public rightly took some of the credit for the healthy state of the club, for throughout the war many members forwarded their subscriptions and altogether £5,560 was received. A new start provided scope for experiment with two-day county cricket, an innovation which Yorkshire strongly opposed. The hours of play became 11.30 to 7.30, but by mid-season the venture had run out of support.

Apart from the difficulties of squeezing a meaningful contest into the abbreviated time span, there was the question of the public's eating habits, which were definitely out of step with the arrangements. This reduction to two days and the dismal weather were largely responsible for Yorkshire's eleven draws, which, of course, counted very much against them in the final analysis, for they adversely affected the percentages in the same way as defeats.

This was the first year of David Burton's captaincy. He had made one or two appearances before, getting an early taste in 1907 while a student at Cambridge University, and, like his predecessor, he had the good fortune to start at the top with his leadership. He had his own doubts as to the potential of the side, for Hirst was in his forty-eighth year and Rhodes in his forty-second, while, in addition to the loss of Booth and Drake, Kilner suffered severe wounds in the war.

Burton's fears, however, proved groundless, for three newcomers cast very much in the Yorkshire mould, forced their way into the reckoning – Herbert Sutcliffe, Abe Waddington and Emmott Robinson. Few years have thrown up such a rich crop. Sutcliffe had to serve his apprenticeship like anyone else, so arguably the best opening batsman of all time found himself in the middle order, Rhodes opening with Percy Holmes, the man who became linked with Sutcliffe in the best of all first-wicket partnerships. Predictably, Burton quickly promoted Sutcliffe, who responded to this expression of faith by heading the averages with 1,601 runs (48.51).

Waddington, the left-arm medium-pace bowler for whom Yorkshire were eagerly searching, also pushed his way immediately to the forefront, capturing one hundred wickets in all matches in his first season, despite not coming into the team until the beginning of July.

Robinson had reached the ripe old age of thirty-five when he finally found fame, one theory for the delay in using his obvious all-round skills being that Lord Hawke thought him too untidy in his dress to be a Yorkshire cricketer. He belied his years, however, in the field, where he acted as a spur to younger men as he soldiered on until forty-seven, a reliable batsman and a bowler of considerable subtlety.

Burton received one salutary lesson when he took a blow in the eye from Australian bowler Jack Gregory and missed several fixtures, during which Hirst led the side with great dignity and commonsense.

As Yorkshire wrestled with the task of co-ordinating their efforts, Middlesex assumed the mantle of champions in 1920 and 1921, but, the groundwork having been thoroughly done, a glorious burst brought four successive title triumphs.

The return to three-day cricket in 1920 drew approval from all quarters, but Yorkshire's bowling limitations prevented them from making the best use of the circumstances. Rhodes and Waddington took 296 wickets between them only to find that the other six bowlers could do no better than an aggregate of 181. The county's 'dynamic duo' also shared another distinction. each completing a hat-trick.

Amazingly Rhodes did it just the once in thirty-three glittering years – against Derbyshire at Derby – and, thus encouraged, Waddington followed suit at Northampton – in his first full season! Robinson had a splendid spell in the Roses match at Bradford. Lancashire got to within 52 runs of victory in the fourth innings with six wickets standing at lunch on the final day, but they lost by 22 as the Keighley bowler finished with nine for 36, dismissing all the last six batsmen.

Yorkshire could so easily have been back at the top in 1921, but

Picking up the Pieces 57

Emmott Robinson, one of the most popular cricketers in Yorkshire's history.

dreadful luck with the weather in four matches robbed them of their just deserts. These were against Lancashire at Headingley, Leicestershire at Leicester, Middlesex at Sheffield and Surrey at the Oval, where, in each instance, rain prevented what appeared to be the formality of victory.

The game at Leicester classically illustrated the weakness inherent in the championship regulations. Heavy rain on the first two days made it impossible to organise a businesslike finish. Leicestershire made 202 and Yorkshire finished on 201 for nine. The failure of the last pair, Arthur Dolphin and Rockley Wilson, to secure the lead, caused a good deal of comment since Yorkshire were better off with the contest being declared 'no result'.

They would have had two points for the lead, but failure to settle the first innings meant that the match simply did not count in the championship reckoning. These were still based on percentages, so Yorkshire must have been mathematically worse off with their two points. On the other hand, there were no signs of their holding back earlier in the day when Hirst and Robinson put on 116 for the sixth wicket. The pity was that the authorities were slow to see the point that had been accidentally but nevertheless well made.

The 1921 season also contained a spectacular debut by Cecil Tyson, who marked his first appearance by scoring 100 and 80 without being dismissed against Hampshire at Southampton. In doing so he convinced Yorkshire that they had found a left-hander of real worth, despite his advanced age of thirty-two, but he took part in only two more matches – against the Australians and Lancashire – before dropping out.

Tyson had an all-the-year engagement with Whitwood in the Yorkshire Council under which he acted as groundsman, adding an interest in the catering for good measure. Whitwood were distinctly anxious not to lose him as he had averaged around 50 after joining them from Tong Park in the Bradford League, so they approached the county committee to put forward their prior claim as soon as it became likely that he would be receiving regular invitations from Yorkshire.

Major Briggs, their captain, made it plain that they expected Tyson to be on call at weekends, and in doing so effectively settled the argument – Yorkshire looked elsewhere. The player himself understandably hoped to resolve the issue to everyone's satisfaction, but accepted his fate without rancour. 'I have no definite promise of an engagement with Yorkshire, so I am, in that sense, a casual player with no financial security,' he admitted. 'Whitwood have given me a regular income through an agreement with the colliery company and I shall honour that.'

He must have had his regrets deep down, for he had looked every bit the part in making that Southampton century as Hampshire had a few moments of their own in making Yorkshire struggle and Tyson still needed 11 runs with eight wickets down. George Macaulay gave him patient support for half an hour without scoring and he finally reached his target, a watchful, sure-footed defence and a stinging square-cut earning him general acclaim.

Form towards the end of the campaign indicated that Yorkshire were the strongest side in the championship, so their run of success, starting in 1922, came as no surprise, even without Hirst. He had taken up a coaching position at Eton the year before and bowed out at the end of the Scarborough Festival game against MCC, a fixture for which he returned to much appreciated action eight years further

Picking up the Pieces 59

on, enjoying one more outing 'for old times' sake'.

The eccentricities of the scoring system allowed Nottinghamshire to run them reasonably close in the first instance. Yorkshire won nineteen and lost two of their thirty games, while their nearest rivals claimed seventeen victories and suffered five defeats from twenty-eight fixtures. Turned into percentages based on points gained from points possible, though, the difference was a misleading 73.79 to 71.53.

A wide variety of bowling was Yorkshire's main strength, with Macaulay, improving rapidly as a spinner in his third season, Rhodes, Kilner and Waddington all topping the one-hundred wicket mark. Individually, nothing ranked alongside the feat of Waddington, who had the type of analysis that schoolboys invent in their wildest dreams – 7-4-6-7 at Hull, where Sussex were hustled out for 20 in their second innings as Yorkshire, improvising to make 125 serve their purpose, won by an innings and 10 runs.

The captaincy passed into the hands of Geoffrey Wilson, from Leeds, who impressed as a batsman at Harrow and went on to collect a Blue at Cambridge. He joined the county briefly in 1919, but lost touch with the first-class set-up until called up to lead the team and during his three years at the helm Yorkshire stayed firmly at the top of the tree. He coped well, too, in his first summer with the frustration of an appendix operation which kept him in hospital, Rockley Wilson deputising.

Their momentum nicely underway, Yorkshire were unstoppable in 1923 setting another record – this time for the number of victories. They won twenty-five out of thirty-two games, being beaten once – by three runs by Nottinghamshire at Leeds. Rhodes, Kilner and Macaulay all claimed over one hundred wickets, while Kilner added 1,126 runs to steady batting that endured moments of uncertainty. The ever-reliable Sutcliffe and Holmes were the standard-bearers without really excelling themselves as averages of 36.32 and 35.95 respectively indicate.

As they raced along, Yorkshire pushed aside the sturdy challenge of Harry Howell, who became the first Warwickshire bowler to take all ten wickets in a championship innings. They beat the Midlands county easily enough by 84 runs at Edgbaston, displaying a splendid resilience. Batting first on a pitch affected by rain which delayed the start until 4.30, they grafted their way typically to 67 for five, hanging on and looking for better things in time. Howell, at a pretty nasty pace, got the ball to rear from a variety of lengths, striking

Sutcliffe sickeningly on the jaw. The opener retired for treatment with blood gushing from the wound and, as they patched him up, his colleagues gritted their teeth and said very little. Actions speak louder than words, so Edgar Oldroyd got on with the job, his solid 44 defying the discomfort from several knocks on the fingers.

Howell continued to cut a swath through the Yorkshire ranks, despite an improvement in the pitch on the second day, and he finished with ten for 51 to qualify for a collection of £34 2s 6d. from an admiring audience of around 6,000, many drawn to the scene by the prospect of seeing the mighty tortured. Not to be outdone, however, Macaulay, with the air of a conjuror indulging in a sleight of hand, produced his first hat-trick to redress the balance and Yorkshire, scoring no more than 113 and 162 for six declared, got home with plenty in hand.

Crowds flocked to witness the deeds of valour and daring, with attendances climbing to 323,031 in 1921, when gross gate receipts amounted to £26,759. As a matter of fascinating and important comparison, Yorkshire took £20,111 at the turnstiles for championship games in 1982 and, even adding the Sunday League, had no more than £39,143 from a 'grand total' of 24,233 customers.

Edgar Oldroyd, although sometimes criticised for slow scoring, was a determined batsman very much in the Yorkshire tradition.

Subscriptions had risen to £6,061 in 1923, which meant that financially the club still depended on an attractive team basking in a fair amount of sunshine. They experienced no alarms on that score

Picking up the Pieces

in 1924, for the side continued as front-runners, although not by so great a distance. Support remained constant, but some of it had become too keen, leading up to a very unsavoury occurrence at Bramall Lane, where the Middlesex match ended in stalemate.

The umpires, H. Butt and W. Reeves, were subjected to so much abuse that they sent a written complaint to the MCC, stating that Waddington had made such a fuss about some decisions that he had incited the spectators. The Yorkshire committee invited the MCC to look into the affair while they concentrated on patching up the differences with Middlesex, who were threatening not to accept any fixtures with them in 1925. Waddington, shouldering the blame manfully, wrote an abject apology and the unpleasantness was smoothed over.

The biggest disaster on the field came in the Headingley Roses Match, Dick Tyldesley taking six for 18 as Yorkshire were hurried out for 33 in the second innings and to defeat by 24 runs. This apart, the batting improved on the previous season, but the bowling lost some of its edge, despite the application of Macaulay and Kilner.

Geoffrey Wilson retired, taking with him his one hundred per cent rating in the championship over three years, and in 1925 the captaincy passed to Major Arthur Lupton, most kindly described as 'a club cricketer of considerable experience and enthusiasm'. His inheritance was not quite so rich as might seem from a distance, for the troubles of 1924 left a sour taste in some mouths and Lord Hawke kept himself busy throughout the winter on diplomatic service.

The new captain experienced great difficulty in justifying his elevation to such high office, managing only 186 runs from twenty-three innings for an average of 9.78. Happily the other ten were nothing less than brilliant. *Wisden* summed up the summer succinctly. 'Once again the story of Yorkshire's success is a tale of all-round excellence.'

Holmes and Sutcliffe led the way, both averaging over 50, while the almost unplayable Macaulay's 176 wickets cost a miserly 15.21 runs each. Following a draw at Old Trafford, they won twelve successive matches – six by an innings and three by ten wickets, margins which permitted no argument about their superiority. Why, everyone wondered, had Holmes and Macaulay not been chosen to tour Australia in the previous winter? Macaulay must surely have been paying the price of upsetting the wrong people with his forth-

The style of Percy Holmes, who formed the greatest of the county's opening partnerships with Herbert Sutcliffe.

right approach, but there could be no disputing his right to stand shoulder to shoulder with the world's best bowlers.

One spectacular spell spotlighted both his ability and his determination. Sussex, chasing 263 for victory, wanted the last 40 runs with six wickets in hand, but Macaulay turned the contest upside down in the space of five overs and three balls, ripping out five wickets for 8 runs. Yorkshire won by 23. Holmes, for his part, savoured the honour of scoring 315 not out against Middlesex at Lord's, passing the 278 by Willie Ward which had stood for one hundred and five years as the highest innings at headquarters.

Throughout their years as champions, Yorkshire also held their own against the Rest of England in the match which annually brought down the curtain on the season and which was conducted in a thoroughly serious way with few, if any, concessions to frivolity.

Picking up the Pieces 63

They drew on three occasions and were overwhelmed only in 1924, when they lost by an innings and 124 runs. The match stretched over four days in 1925, drawing huge crowds to the Oval, where the receipts amounted to almost £2,000.

It is interesting to speculate at this stage whether there has ever been a stronger county side than the one which represented Yorkshire in that game. It read: Holmes, Sutcliffe, Oldroyd, Leyland, Rhodes, Kilner, Robinson, Macaulay, Waddington, Dolphin and Major Lupton. The first ten would surely have gained selection by virtually any side, including many at Test level, and the uncertainty that had hung in the air after the war had been displaced by a well-founded confidence. Yorkshire had been champions five times in seven years and their other placings were fourth and third.

Chapter 7

A CONFUSION OF CAPTAINS (1926–1930)

A favourite story in Yorkshire, while presumably apocryphal, undoubtedly contains a grain or two of truth. It concerns a day on which Major Lupton was seen to be fastening on his pads in readiness to take his place in the lower reaches of the batting order. One of the professionals respectfully stepped forward to advise: 'There is no need to hurry, Major, I think Wilfred's going to declare.' It must, of course, have been Rhodes, in partnership with Robinson who made most of the decisions, albeit by proxy, for Major Lupton had no worthwhile background knowledge to fit him for the role of captain. He got the job because of his station in life.

Major Lupton came to the first-class game as a forty-six-year-old, bringing with him from the circles of the Yorkshire Gentlemen's Club a reputation as an aggressive stroke-maker. That hardly helped him to take so big a step up the ladder and overall he has to be marked down as a passenger, scoring 668 runs to average 10.27. However admirable his leadership in the area of man management, he could hardly compensate for an obvious lack of ability, which makes it remarkable that in his three-year spell Yorkshire enjoyed an unbeaten sequence of sixty-nine matches in the championship.

It stretched back, actually, into Wilson's reign in 1924, for on August 26 Surrey beat them by 109 runs at the Oval. The next defeat came on May 29, 1927, at Hull, where Warwickshire got home by eight wickets.

The side, however, slipped to second place in 1926 and to third the following year. Shrewd judges found some consolation in the form of Morris Leyland, who was developing, after an uncertain start, into a player of world renown as a left-handed batsman in the classic style. Unfortunately, the flickering of individual genius did not promise to solve a major collective problem.

Obvious short-comings were magnified as Yorkshire wallowed slightly in the wake of the 'old enemy' Lancashire, who made the most of a brilliantly prosperous period in completing a hat-trick of championships in 1926, 1927 and 1928. The loss of Waddington in sorry circumstances hardly helped Yorkshire's cause. Possibly he

A Confusion of Captains

lost the keen edge of his enthusiasm in 1927, when his forty-five wickets cost 30.62 runs each, perhaps a shoulder injury upset him more than he cared to admit. Whatever the real reason, he refused terms offered by the county and stepped quietly out of the picture. Along with him went Dolphin, who made way for Arthur Wood.

The winter of 1927-28, however, was warmed by the flames of a far greater controversy than any that might centre on Waddington, for the committee admitted they were ready to abandon the principle of having an amateur captain. In doing so, they bowed to the logic of the situation. Lord Hawke transforming a disorganised army into an efficient fighting force was one thing, perpetuating a system for the sake of it was another altogether.

The shortage of suitable candidates focussed attention on the committee's dilemma. The men they thought suitable in one way were weak links in another. The highly successful Geoffrey Wilson scored an unnoticed 985 runs for an average of 12.31, while Major Lupton fell below this moderate level. There was, of course, no disgrace in this, for these gentlemen were serving the county as best they could, but the need to face up to reality had become so apparent that even Lord Hawke gave a measure of reluctant support to the dramatic change.

On Wednesday, November 2, Yorkshire announced that Herbert Sutcliffe, who was on his way to South Africa with the MCC, had been elected as captain. Not only this, he would remain a professional. Some idea of the heartsearching in high places can be gauged from the fact that serious consideration had been given to the idea of Sutcliffe becoming an amateur with Yorkshire guaranteeing a substantial testimonial to cover his losses. This was hypocrisy of the worst kind and sensibly the county backed down and abandoned any thought of subterfuge.

Twenty-eight of the thirty-two committee members attended the momentous meeting at the Queen's Hotel in Leeds to confirm that no other candidate had been discussed. Sutcliffe stood as the first and only choice. Lord Hawke, acknowledging his well-remembered prayer, 'Pray God no professional will ever captain England', put on a brave face.

'Possibly my old friend Jack Hobbs will laugh and say that I have gone back on my opinions. I was, however, talking about England and not Yorkshire, which is a different matter altogether,' he said. He went on to spoil that display of tact, for when asked for his personal opinion he is reported to have said: 'I am loyal to my committee and don't dare to pass comment.'

Alderman R. Ingham, from Bradford, a member of the cricket sub-committee, acted as official spokesman. 'The committee have discussed this very fully,' he said, 'and from all points of view they have come to the decision to offer Sutcliffe the captaincy as a professional. He already has knowledge of the possibility and I do not think there is any chance of his refusing.'

There was, as it turned out, every chance, for Sutcliffe did decline the heatedly debated promotion, but there is good reason to believe he did so under pressure.

He could not fail to be swept up in the whirlwind which followed Yorkshire's announcement. Some reaction remained thoughtfully guarded but nonetheless critical. Arthur Gilligan, the Sussex and England captain, for example, said: 'I have no objection to a professional captaining any side.' When pressed to say whether there was any strong body of opinion against such an appointment, however, he added: 'That is a delicate question I would rather not answer.'

The popular line had been best summed up by Lord Hawke, who firmly believed: 'There have always been disadvantages in having a professional captain of any county team. For instance, he can be nagged by his fellows in the dressing-room and is liable to be a butt for grumblers, while he can never exercise the same authority as an amateur.' It is hard to accept that this comment held good in Sutcliffe's case, yet opposition sprang up on all sides without his competence being queried in the slightest. The challenge was based on what rather than who he was and carried the day.

Were any representatives of that amateur lobby alive today they would no doubt point to the excessive caution of the professionals to support their argument and in many ways the wheel has turned full circle. Certainly there are quite a few influential voices being raised on behalf of the amateur spirit which might help to revive the ailing body of the game.

The Yorkshire authorities in 1927 faltered under a two-pronged assault which asserted that they were destroying the tradition of forty years and that, in any event, if they were to take this dreadful step they should have turned to Rhodes, the senior professional. Neither charge made much sense. Sutcliffe, with his immaculate dress and impeccable manners, had earned unquestioned respect inside and outside the dressing-room and, at thirty-four, he represented a much better choice than the fifty-year-old Rhodes, who was contemplating retirement.

A Confusion of Captains

Captains all. Sir William Worsley, who stepped into the breach to lead Yorkshire when Herbert Sutcliffe stood down, is pictured third from the left. With him (from left to right) are: Michael Crawford, Brian Sellers, Ted Lester, who was in charge of the second team, Ronnie Burnet and Billy Sutcliffe.

Reason disappeared, buried under a landslide of prejudice, and on December 9 Sutcliffe generously got the club out of their difficulty by sending a telegram which read: 'Official invitation received yesterday. Many thanks to you and your committee for great honour. Have carefully considered question and regret to decline. Am willing to play under any captain elected.' This last sentence, which seems superfluous, presumably had to be inserted to emphasise that the great batsman bore no grudge.

The 'great honour' went instead to Captain – later to become Sir – William Worsley, from Hoveringham Hall, Malton. The jubilant adherents to the amateur policy proudly forecast that he 'should be able to strengthen Yorkshire's batting by contributing the dash and enterprise which are needed in the middle part of the order'. These were the qualities normally associated with batsmen who played for the love of the game and thus paid no attention to averages or the need to earn the security of another season's engagement, but such extravagant claims actually made life much more difficult for a well liked and gallant gentleman. Worsley could hardly hope to live up to these expectations and the administrative about-turn condemned the team to further uncertainty. Yorkshire had eight captains in twenty-two years.

A terrible tragedy befell the county in the spring of 1928 when Roy Kilner died. He went with Morris Leyland to coach in India and on the way home fell desperately ill with paratyphoid. Rushed to Barnsley Fever Hospital as soon as he reached England, he passed away there on April 5 to the sorrow of the entire cricketing world. Few men have attracted so much genuine affection and, at thirty-seven, he was in the prime of life.

Without both Kilner and Waddington, Yorkshire's resources were stretched alarmingly, the more so as Rhodes and Robinson, two solid props in the foundation of their attack, had little left to offer.

The side went through their twenty-eight-match championship programme in 1928 unbeaten, but they could not find real penetration and suffered similar frustration in the following summer when Bill Bowes made his debut. Despite the Corinthian climate, some matters did not come through close investigation too well and the Nottinghamshire fixture at Trent Bridge was a disgrace. Yorkshire recovered from 130 for six to reach 498, with Percy Holmes, first in and last out, grinding away for a valuable 285. Nottinghamshire, the eventual champions, settled for a draw, using up seven and a quarter hours to make 190 for four, an exhibition which gives the lie to the assumption that the old days were always good.

Rhodes made 1930 his last season and, as he scored only 478 runs and took seventy-three wickets, it was clear that even his exceptional powers were on the wane. Under Alan Barber, who replaced Worsley as captain, Yorkshire finished third, which did not please either the players or their supporters, but the future loomed bright with promise, principally in the person of Hedley Verity. The natural successor to Rhodes as a left-arm spinner, Verity cut down sixty-four victims in 406 overs – a splendid striking rate – going straight to the top of the first-class averages. Verity and Rhodes, briefly operating in tandem, must have been a formidable combination and

A Confusion of Captains

A famous trio. Hedley Verity, Bill Bowes and Herbert Sutcliffe line-up with a very young Billy Sutcliffe, who went on to captain the county, getting into the picture. (*Yorkshire Post*)

they proved too much for Gloucestershire at Bristol, where the former had five for 18 in the first innings and the latter eight for 74 in the match, which brought Yorkshire victory by an innings and 187 runs.

The tortured reasoning behind some of the regulations actually hindered the smooth passage of play and Barber fell into an embarrassing trap at Hull, where heavy rain washed out the first day of the return fixture with Gloucestershire. Having put in the opposition, bowled them out cheaply and gained what he regarded as a useful lead, the Yorkshire captain declared at 6 pm in an attempt to make progress.

After some debate, which resulted in a lengthy delay, he found that he had infringed Law 54. This stated: 'The in-side may declare their innings at an end in a match of three days or more at any time on the second day; in a two-day match the captain of the batting side has power to declare his innings at close at any time, but such a declaration may not be made on the first day later than one hour and forty minutes before the time agreed upon for drawing stumps.' The thinking behind that complicated piece of legislation is baffling, but future generations will presumably express equal wonderment at some of the decisions reached by the modern guardians of cricket's best interests.

Chapter 8

GREAT DAYS
(1931–1946)

The bright summer of Yorkshire's cricketing experience, brought to full fruition by Brian Sellers, was ushered in under the skilful control of Frank Greenwood, and the county were more than a little fortunate to find in these two captains men who measured up to every requirement. In the years 1931 to 1946 the county were champions eight times, failing only in 1934, when fifth behind Lancashire, and 1936, when Derbyshire captured their solitary title and Yorkshire dropped to third.

What they might have done but for the horrors of the Second World War is guesswork, but all the evidence indicates that they would have reigned supreme.

Barber actually contributed satisfactorily in 1930 with 792 runs (average 19.32), but Greenwood, playing under him, as he had done under Worsley in 1929, did considerably better. Greenwood gained his early experience in the Huddersfield League, confirming his worth in the Colts before being singled out as the man to lead the side.

Yorkshire swept back to what they regarded as their rightful place in the grand manner, obtaining 287 from a maximum of 420 points. They conceded a single defeat, which came in pursuit of victory, and although the circumstances were frowned upon it is not unreasonable to suppose that Greenwood's enterprise encouraged the introduction of the law which today permits matches to be decided over one innings in the championship when play is severely curtailed by rain.

Tedious weather at the start of the summer forced Yorkshire to spend four long days in the pavilion. They idled away the hours at Bradford and were further frustrated at Sheffield, where no play was possible until the last day. A boring stalemate seemed inevitable until Greenwood and his Gloucestershire counterpart Beverley Lyon put their heads together to good purpose. The regulations gave fifteen points for an outright win, five for first innings lead and three to the losers on the first innings. Both sides were ready to gamble for high stakes.

Yorkshire won the toss and put in Gloucestershire. Emmott Robinson's first ball went unchallenged for four byes and the players marched off, much to the alarm of the hardy spectators, who peered into the skies for signs of yet more rain. These fears were quickly allayed, for the action soon resumed. Gloucestershire had declared and Yorkshire did likewise after Walter Hammond's first ball had also been allowed to pass for four byes.

The real business then got underway, Gloucestershire winning by forty-seven runs after reaching 171 in three hours. They left Yorkshire half an hour less to get the runs which was fair enough, taking the toss into account, and the need for haste forced elementary batting errors, although Yorkshire never wavered in their intention of hitting out to the end.

The contrived finish sparked off considerable debate in which Lord Hawke took a forceful part. 'It cannot possibly be to the advantage of our game if the laws, written and unwritten, are tampered with as they were by arrangements which necessitated that bowlers should not try to get the batsmen out and that batsmen should not try to score off the ball,' he thundered. 'Personally I am sorry Mr Greenwood got into the clutches of Mr Lyon and made himself party to the first freak declaration in the history of serious cricket. Ye Gods, is the game to be ruled by young men, some of whom are prepared to take the unwritten law into their own hands?'

Displeasure could not have been more vigorously expressed, and Lord Hawke hammered away at length on the theme of declining standards, but Greenwood said nothing and courageously repeated the manœuvre with Northamptonshire at Bradford, where the first two days were again washed out, and this time Yorkshire won by five wickets. On balance, Greenwood had the better of the argument with Lord Hawke and deserves recognition for his pioneering work, which helped to lift a deep depression.

Seven of the first twelve matches fell foul of the weather to some extent, but the foundations for the championship success were well and truly laid by an eleven-match run which included ten wins. The season also confirmed Verity's meteoric rise to the highest plane, for against Warwickshire at Headingley he became the second Yorkshire bowler to take all ten wickets in an innings – the cost being 36 runs.

He had not been awarded his county cap when he celebrated his twenty-sixth birthday in the most sensational way on May 18. Showing remarkable composure and maturity, he took the day's

Great Days

Hedley Verity (left) receives the congratulations of his own captain, Frank Greenwood (centre), and Warwickshire captain Bob Wyatt after taking 10 for 36 at Headingley on May 18, 1931. (*Yorkshire Post*)

play and shaped it to his own purpose by sheer brilliance, for the initial exchanges had been straightforward as Warwickshire made 201 and Yorkshire 298.

Verity suffered the indignity of being hit for six by Bob Wyatt but, far from being overawed, he remained accurate and demanding as he spun the ball viciously. Mitchell assisted with three neat catches, setting the pattern that was to continue for several years – and Verity's sixteenth over contained four wickets to the first and last two deliveries, yet each time he was denied the hat-trick. He almost denied himself the outstanding distinction of all ten wickets, too, for, diving unselfishly at short leg, he came very close indeed to claiming a catch for Macaulay. In jarring his right arm as he fell he lost the ball and had to have treatment for the injury which was bandaged. He did hold another catch, this time off his own bowling to remove the last man, and Yorkshire won by an innings and 25 runs. The scorecard of the Warwickshire second innings is shown overleaf.

Verity and Bill Bowes, the new boys really, took the bowling honours. Verity's 138 wickets cost 12.34, while Bowes was only

Warwickshire

	second innings	
Wyatt	c Holmes b Verity	23
Croom	c Greenwood b Verity	7
Bates	c Mitchell b Verity	19
Kilner	c Mitchell b Verity	0
Parsons	c Leyland b Verity	9
Hill	c Wood b Verity	8
Smart	c Mitchell b Verity	0
Foster	st Wood b Verity	0
Tate	lbw b Verity	0
Paine	c and b Verity	0
Mayer	not out	6
extras		0
		72

Fall of wickets: 1-16, 2-33, 3-33, 4-51, 5-59, 6-59, 7-59, 8-59, 9-59.
Bowling: Bowes 5-1-7-0; Robinson 4-1-9-0; Verity 18.4-6-36-10; Macaulay 18-11-20-0.

slightly less successful with 109 victims at 15.29 runs each in conditions that had been less suited to his faster bowling. Sutcliffe stood head and shoulders above his batting colleagues with an average of 97.57.

One note of sadness came with the retirement of Robinson, whose merits have to be assessed with regard to personality as well as performance. A fine all-rounder, he was a shrewd student of the game's tactics and a brilliant fielder close to the wicket.

Success in 1932 was predictable enough, although this time both Lancashire and Hampshire beat Yorkshire, but all else paled into insignificance in the shadow of the record first-wicket partnership between Holmes and Sutcliffe, who put on 555 against Essex at Leyton, and the most deadly spell of bowling in first-class cricket.

The opening pair stayed together until almost one o'clock on the second day in an impressive display of stamina, especially by Holmes, who had a nasty attack of lumbago. Essex, utterly demoralised, were shot out for 78 and 164 in reply, the match being concluded early on the Friday with Yorkshire having an innings and 313 runs to spare.

Verity's peak came at Headingley, where he destroyed Nottinghamshire, who, batting first, acquired a substantial advantage when a thunderstorm stopped play on the second day. Yorkshire, with the worst of the conditions, lost nine wickets for 163 and declared 71 behind in an attempt to derive some benefit from the drying conditions.

Great Days 75

There were no immediate fireworks as Nottinghamshire moved steadily to 38 without loss at lunch, but in the afternoon their last ten wickets fell for 29, all to Verity, who dominated to an extent unequalled before or since, collecting a hat-trick and twice taking two wickets in two balls. Holmes and Sutcliffe – who else? – completed the formality of winning the match by calmly knocking off the 139 runs required without alarm. The details of that Nottinghamshire innings were:

Nottinghamshire	*second innings*	
Keeton	c Macaulay b Verity	21
Shipstone	c Wood b Verity	21
Walker	c Macaulay b Verity	11
Carr	c Barber b Verity	0
A. Staples	c Macaulay b Verity	7
Harris	c Holmes b Verity	0
Gunn	lbw b Verity	0
Lilley	not out	3
Larwood	c Sutcliffe b Verity	0
Voce	c Holmes b Verity	0
S. Staples	st Wood b Verity	0
extras		4
		67

Fall of wickets: 1-44, 2-47, 3-51, 4-63, 5-63, 6-63, 7-64, 8-64, 9-67.
Bowling: Bowes 5-0-19-0; Macaulay 23-9-34-0; Verity 19.4-16-10-10.

Two other occasions stood out in the glittering progress. Against Essex, for whose bowling he had taken an obvious liking, Sutcliffe raced to his century in two hours and then accelerated, another 94 coming in forty breathless minutes. Together with Leyland, he delighted a Scarborough crowd by plundering 102 from six overs and the pair made 149 in fifty-five minutes – all this at the expense of an attack which included the exceptional pace of Ken Farnes.

Horace Fisher, a medium-paced left-arm bowler, was one of the unsung heroes, completing the first all lbw hat-trick against Somerset at Sheffield. He had taken six for 11 in the previous fixture with Leicestershire at Bradford, while Verity had none for 10. Fisher went on to claim five for 12 as Somerset crumbled to hopeless defeat, his lbw trio being N.S. Mitchell-Innes, W.H. Andrews and W.T. Luckes. Not content, Fisher added 76 not out, but although he headed the county's bowling averages in the championship with nineteen wickets at 12.52 each, he did not make the grade.

Less obvious at the time but of long-term importance was the work of Sellers, who gradually settled into the scheme of things. He

Bramall Lane in the 1930s. The ground has now been swallowed up by Sheffield United Football Club, but then it housed one of the most knowledgeable crowds in the world. The top balcony in the pavilion offered a marvellous view. (*Yorkshire Post*)

managed an aggregate of 672 in twenty-nine innings for an average of 26.88. A modest figure to the likes of Sutcliffe (87.46), Leyland (60.11) and Holmes (47.30), it secured him the captaincy in 1933.

This burly, forthright, sometimes rude but always fair man went on to earn a place second only to Lord Hawke in the club's annals. As a leader both on the field and in the committee room he commanded unswerving loyalty because he gave nothing less himself.

Sellers came to prominence as understudy to Greenwood, whose business commitments threatened and then limited his availability to the stage at which new arrangements had to be made. The son of Keighley's Arthur Sellers, he followed the same path as Greenwood in graduating through the league system – in his case in Bradford – and quickly attracted the nickname of 'Crackerjack'.

Although well aware that the players under him knew much more about the subtleties, he assumed unhesitating authority at once.

Great Days

While still finding his feet, he asked Sutcliffe's advice as Nottinghamshire's second innings got underway at Headingley. 'Don't waste time with the seamers,' came the reply. 'Rub the ball in the dirt and put on the spinners.' Instead, Sellers called up Bowes. 'Why bother asking my opinion if you ignore it?' complained a for once irate Sutcliffe. 'I know what you said, but if nothing happens we'll try it your way,' came the unabashed reply. 'Remember, we can rub the ball in the dirt later, but we can't get another new one.'

Thus the new captain indicated that, in addition to having a mind of his own, he thought things carefully through. Sellers also spent a lot of time studying the tactics of the game, so that within a few years he rarely needed to ask anyone anything and he was probably the best of all Yorkshire's captains. If we jump forward in time slightly, we get another example of the way in which Sellers paid close attention to detail. Ted Lester, the hard-hitting Scarborough batsman, became only the sixth man to score a century in each innings of a championship match for the county when he took 126 and 142 off Northamptonshire at Northampton in 1947. In a hurry to take his place on the coach which the team were using while on tour, he neglected to put on a tie. Sellers quickly drew his attention to this omission, so Lester had to open up his suitcase and dress himself properly before the coach set off. At least everyone knew where they stood.

It is, therefore, no disrespect to Greenwood to say that his departure at the end of 1932 allowed Yorkshire to strengthen their hand in gaining their third successive title. Beaten in three games, they still enjoyed a substantial superiority and by mid-August the rest of the field had been left far behind.

Verity, Bowes and Macaulay, with 391 wickets collectively, spearheaded the charge, but Bowes broke down and struggled towards the end, so Yorkshire owed a great debt to Macaulay, who relied mainly on spin delivered from around the wicket and benefited from superb close-catching support. Here Arthur Mitchell excelled, while Arthur Wood maintained the high standards associated with the county's wicket-keepers.

Mitchell also headed the batting averages in 1934 with 55.06, moving up the order to partner Sutcliffe in the absence of Holmes, who retired at the end of the previous summer. The year, though, turned into a poor one for Yorkshire, who were called upon to supply the backbone of England's unsuccessful Ashes challenge. Leyland and Verity appeared in all five Tests against Woodfull's

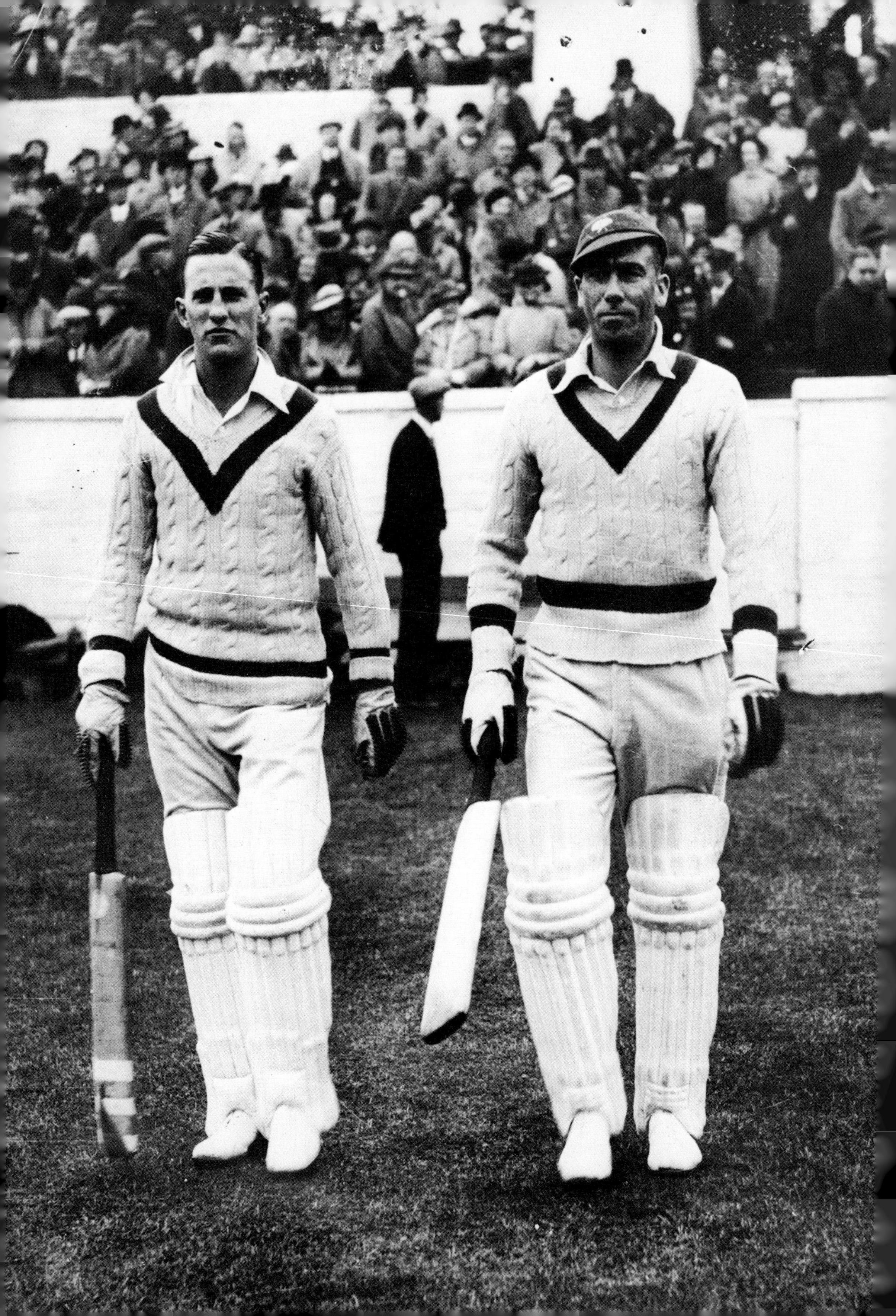

Great Days

Australians, Sutcliffe had four caps and Bowes three, so the fall to fifth place could be excused.

When they were available, these leading personalities filled their accustomed roles with sparkling efficiency, but Yorkshire lost to Sussex, Gloucestershire, Warwickshire and Essex during Test match time. Warwickshire actually won at Scarborough after being bowled out for 45 – the lowest score of the season – for they made 216 with a wicket in hand at the second attempt. Adding to Yorkshire's worries was a decline in the potency of Macaulay, who retired in 1935 partly as a consequence of rheumatism.

The end of Holmes coincided with the beginning of Len Hutton, for in 1934 the Pudsey prodigy, already acclaimed by Sutcliffe as the 'marvel of the age', got his first trials, starting with a duck but convincing powerful admirers with the perfection of his run-making methods. These, allied to a serene inner sense of purpose and effortless concentration, made him very special and by the end of July he had become the county's youngest century-maker at eighteen years and thirty-three days, putting together an innings of 196 against Worcestershire. He did not play in the next game, because Sutcliffe returned and his progress was steady as well as sure, so as Yorkshire reclaimed the title in 1935 Hutton did little more than gather experience.

Verity and Bowes were again magnificently lethal, while the stylish Wilf Barber matched Sutcliffe in averaging more than 50 with the bat. Yorkshire won nineteen matches and lost one, playing the sort of aggressive cricket which epitomised their captain's character, although poor Sellers had to survive the near catastrophe of four successive ducks at the start of the season.

Frank Smailes, a lively medium-paced right-arm bowler, settled in as a regular partner for Bowes, chipping in with welcome runs as a bonus. The one blemish came at Huddersfield, where Essex, in the course of inflicting a shock defeat, dismissed Yorkshire for 31. Morris Nichols took four for 17, hammered 146 runs and then added seven for 37 to complete the champions' misery.

Reputations were duly restored and the county finished on a high note by beating The Rest, who had gone thirty years since losing – also to Yorkshire, who thus completed a long-distance double

OPPOSITE: The young Len Hutton going out to open the Yorkshire innings with Arthur Mitchell.

before spending a month in Jamaica as guests of the local cricket association.

Anti-climax followed with third place behind Derbyshire in 1936. This was no disgrace with the weather turning one or two promising situations into dull draws, but it was disappointing. Smailes continued to fill a key role, bowling some tidy offbreaks to supplement his normal seam-up, but Yorkshire fell short of their own high hopes. They also had to labour long and hard in 1937, when the championship hung in the balance.

Middlesex were finally pipped at the post as Yorkshire gained brilliant victories over Sussex and Hampshire on the run-in. Hutton advanced smoothly into the England side – as everyone knew he would – supplying Yorkshire with eight centuries to make up for the Test calls which were the fore-runners of so many more. He topped the county averages with 55.74, confirming every prediction. Admittedly the attack still relied too heavily on Verity, Bowes and Smailes, but Yorkshire felt they could cope.

As the championship race aroused increasing interest all over the country, Middlesex put forward an imaginative proposition. Their captain, Walter Robins, sent a telegram to Sellers, suggesting that, whatever the final placings, the two teams should meet in a special challenge match over four days. Two considerations prompted Robins. 'The idea,' he explained, 'arose because so much has been said and written about Middlesex playing fewer matches than Yorkshire. We were also rather lucky to beat them at Lord's, where we were favoured by the weather. The return game was spoiled by rain at Sheffield when in an interesting state, so a challenge match would clear up matters.

'There is no champion county versus The Rest fixture this year and I think that after such an interesting season it would do cricket a tremendous amount of good were it to be played.'

Sellers replied: 'Challenge accepted at £10 a man. Choose your own ground.' The players, indeed, were very eager, but the project almost ran aground on the rocks of officialdom, with Lord Hawke yet again setting his face against any innovation. 'Personally, I would have nothing to do with it and I hope the committee turn the idea down,' he said. For some reason, they ignored this advice and, pausing only to ban any betting, agreed to let the game go ahead.

Unfortunately, it remained cold and damp for the match, which was over in three days, but the exercise raised £700 for charity as

Great Days 81

Yorkshire gained a crushing victory by an innings and 115 runs. Honour for them was more than satisfied. Hutton got 121 and Mitchell 86 in a total of 401 before Bowes, Smailes and Verity disposed of Middlesex for 185 and 101.

This supremacy extended throughout 1938, despite the arrival of another Australian touring party which meant the usual heavy interference from the Test selectors. Yorkshire had five representatives in the England ranks at the Oval, where Hutton put the final seal on this greatness with a monumental world record 364 in thirteen hours and twenty minutes.

The county won five of the nine fixtures which clashed with the international programme and lost one, being grateful all the while that the weather for a change came to their aid. Injuries proved a tedious burden, but Yorkshire soldiered cheerfully along the road which led to further glory in 1939.

As cricket jostled for space in newspapers littered with the rumours of war, Yorkshire unfolded some splendid cricket. The campaign was not quite completed when hostilities broke out, but no one could deny their right to pride of place again. Sellers had the machine running so smoothly that often the opposition feebly melted away.

Taking the field without Hutton, Wood, Verity and Bowes against Derbyshire at Sheffield, they were put out for 83. Lesser men might have given it up and waited for the return of reinforcements. Instead,

Derbyshire	*second innings*	
Smith	b Smailes	8
Alderman	c Smurthwaite b Smailes	0
Worthington	c Mitchell b Smailes	32
Townsend	b Smailes	0
G. Pope	lbw b Smailes	1
Rhodes	b Smailes	18
Hounsfield	not out	21
A. Pope	b Smailes	4
Gladwin	b Smailes	0
Elliott	b Smailes	6
Mitchell	st Fiddling b Smailes	6
extras		1
		97

Fall of wickets: 1-0, 2-19, 3-19, 4-21, 5-56, 6-61, 7-71, 8-71, 9-79.

Bowling: Smailes 17.1-5-47-10; Smurthwaite 14-5-43-0; Yardley 2-0-5-0; Robinson 1-0-1-0.

Yorkshire went to work with such a will that Derbyshire could muster no more than 20. They quickly collected 310, setting the stage for Smailes, who had four for 11 in the first Derbyshire innings. He responded to the weight of responsibility by taking all ten wickets for 47 as Yorkshire gathered in the points.

The conclusion to a wonderful period came at Brighton, where Yorkshire turned up without Sutcliffe, who had received orders from the War Office. No one knew exactly what to do next, but the players responded to Sellers's lead. 'We must carry on until told otherwise,' he said. The last game before the war resulted in victory by nine wickets. Sussex were routed for 33 and in his final spell Verity's figures were 6-1-9-7.

Yorkshire's party travelled sadly and silently on the way home. The future looked bleak. Very soon Sellers, Leyland and Smailes were serving with an artillery unit at Harrogate. Bowes became a gunner and Verity joined the Green Howards. He took part in the Sicily landings, was wounded showing great gallantry and taken prisoner. Verity died in Italy on July 31, 1943 – a true genius who, in happier times, must surely have set standards and records beyond the reach of others. As it is, he fulfilled a fraction of his potential. Aged thirty-four when war stopped play, he could have counted on at least another ten years in cricket.

Bowes, captured in North Africa in 1942, spent horrible years in German and Italian camps, losing over four stones in weight. Norman Yardley, another talented amateur, served in Northern Ireland, India, Iran and Egypt in addition to spending nine months in hospital after having his leg nearly blown off.

Hutton, as a member of the Army Physical Training Corps, badly fractured his left forearm. The damage appeared to be so serious that his career was in danger, but patient work by specialist surgeons ensured a full recovery. Full, that is, in medical terms, for batsman Hutton had to readjust to having one arm fractionally longer than the other.

Once peace had been declared, there was a rush to get things moving and the championship resumed in 1946 with Yorkshire taking the title. Sutcliffe, Wood and Mitchell were all too old to gather together the threads, but Sellers had the hard core of a useful eleven at his disposal. The committee sent for Arthur Booth, almost a newcomer to first-class cricket at forty-three.

The left-arm spinner had bowled twenty-seven overs to take one for 41 in 1931, but he could not compete with Verity and contented

Great Days

Yorkshire in 1946. The players (left to right) are: back row – B. Heyhirst (masseur), Robinson, Hutton, Coxon, Smailes, Watson, Beaumont, Booth, H. Walker (scorer); front row – Barber, Bowes, Sellers (captain), Gibb, Leyland.

himself with league cricket until the crisis and the opportunity came. He justified official faith with 111 wickets for an average of 11.61 which served to show how unlucky he had been not to have a county career, while Ellis Robinson emerged as the leading wicket-taker with his offspin.

Sellers led from the front, filling third place in the batting averages – 964 runs (33.24) as Yorkshire won sixteen and lost one of their twenty-six matches, but retirement for him lay just around the corner.

Leyland, Barber and Cyril Turner were also ready to make way for younger men. Turner had been on the staff from 1925, an all-rounder of tremendous worth who never allowed his personal ambitions to interfere with what he saw as his duty. He could not expect a regular place, but he played often as a deputy for others to

Norman Yardley, the most gifted of Yorkshire's amateur players and a knowledgeable captain.

emphasise that he would have been eagerly snapped up by most other counties. There are many quiet yet able men in cricket and Turner stands alongside the best of them.

The time had come for the committee to rebuild and they could not hope to discover overnight adequate replacements for the players who had carried Yorkshire to the highest pinnacles of achievement. Sutcliffe, Hutton, Mitchell, Leyland, Barber, Yardley, Sellers, Smailes, Wood, Verity, Bowes, Holmes and Macaulay, they were all giants of whom it could be honestly said 'we may never see their like again'.

Chapter 9

AFTER THE FEAST
(1947–1958)

Yorkshire hardly expected to reproduce the magnificent form of the 1930s, but the decline to eighth place in 1947 was not easy to stomach all the same. The year involved enforced experiment with unfamiliar personnel figuring in the twenty-six who crowded into the first-team averages. Among them was Ted Lester, who climbed to the top of the list with 73.00. Gerald Smithson, a left-hander, also raised a few eyebrows, so did Vic Wilson, a burly branch of farming stock, who, like Lester, gave the ball a powerful crack. Rather more elegant was Willie Watson, who would help to ensure the right balance in the batting line-up.

Bowes, geared down to a much reduced pace, was on borrowed time, but his sixty-one wickets cost fewer than anyone else's and a record benefit of £8,000 rewarded much hard toil and highly consistent bowling. Support came from Ron Aspinall and Alec Coxon, from Huddersfield, both serviceable seam bowlers, while Booth gave way to Johnny Wardle, who learned his trade in the south of the county. Ellis Robinson remained workmanlike, but overall the magic had disappeared and in their heart of hearts Yorkshiremen knew that demanding times lay ahead.

The difficulties were greater than the sternest critic could have imagined, however, for in twelve years Yorkshire managed one championship – and that had to be shared with Middlesex in 1949. For the rest, it was all Surrey, whose team under Stuart Surridge, a captain bearing a marked similarity to Sellers, claimed seven titles in a row in the 1950s.

No blame for these barren years attaches to Norman Yardley, who led the side from 1948 to 1955, for he never let Yorkshire down, scoring 11,632 runs (31.95) and taking 192 wickets (30.29). The Hon. F.S. Jackson alone did better than that among the amateurs and Yardley also was adept tactically. He got a firm grounding at St Peter's School, York, and Cambridge University, taking part with natural athletic ease in soccer, rugby, hockey and squash, going on to become North of England champion at the latter game for a record five times.

Arthur Booth and Arthur Mitchell put the Colts through their paces. Among those looking, listening and learning are Ken Taylor (extreme left), Dickie Bird (centre) and Mel Ryan (extreme right). (*Yorkshire Post*)

He got off to a troubled start in 1948 owing to illness, which forced him to rest from a number of games. Since Sellers stood in whenever possible and Frank Smailes took over when neither of the amateurs was available, the team must have been unsettled, too, but they battled their way into fourth place.

Hutton, dogged by illness and required regularly by England, missed several fixtures, but nevertheless his average of 92.05 was nearly double that of Watson, the second most successful run-maker. The gap in class between Hutton and his colleagues prompted some worried discussion, for while Yorkshiremen are proud of their heroes they are uneasy about total dependence.

Coxon made his Test debut and Wardle captured 148 wickets in all matches, but there was still a lot to do. Realistic assessment indicated that the shared honour with Middlesex in 1949 was something of an illusion, although Yorkshire finished with typical determination to recover lost ground.

To this extent at least the side were impressive, winning all the last six matches under pressure. Hutton stood out as the backbone, his matchless technique defying the handicap of his long-standing injury. He reached 1,000 runs by June 8, the earliest date for any Yorkshireman, and his 1,294 runs in June became the most by a batsman in any month, his scores being: 146 not out (*v* Scotland at Hull), 201 and 91 not out (*v* Lancashire at Old Trafford), 104 and 76 (*v* Northamptonshire at Bradford), 0 and 0 (*v* Worcestershire at Worcester), 113 and 28 (*v* Middlesex at Lord's), 165 and 100 (*v* Sussex at Hove), and 80 (*v* Sussex at Headingley).

These were, of course, for Yorkshire, and Hutton also made 101, 0, 23 and 66 opening for England against New Zealand. Almost as an elegant after-thought, Hutton collected another 1,050 in August to join Charles Fry, Ranjitsinhji and Sutcliffe in being credited with 1,000 runs in two separate months in a season.

A most bizarre day's play unfolded at Headingley on July 1, for Sussex, represented by James Langridge and George Cox, batted through it to achieve a draw. It remains Yorkshire's only wicketless full day's play. Sussex had been bowled out for 181 under overcast skies, to which Yorkshire replied with 520 for seven, Wilson and Lester thrashing the bowling to confirm the easing of the pitch.

As Sussex lost three relatively cheap second-innings wickets, the outcome seemed assured, but the fourth pair stayed together from eleven o'clock in the morning until tea, by which time Yorkshire had employed ten bowlers and Sussex had advanced their total by 326 runs. No one could – or wanted to – believe these gory statistics.

Yorkshire's enthusiasm for reshaping their side brought into service three brilliant youngsters, which makes it all the more surprising that that collective success proved elusive. Frank Lowson, Brian Close and Fred Trueman all entered first-class cricket in 1949 – an exceptional trio by any reckoning. A sign of the problem came in that year and the next when Yorkshire lost to Oxford University, who, although much stronger then than in later years, were generally reckoned to be sparring partners for the professionals.

In the first place, the Varsity boys were recording their first victory over Yorkshire since 1896 and when they repeated the dose they disposed of a strong challenge. The margin, too, was conclusive – eight wickets – and Yorkshire lost each of their first three matches in 1950 amidst gathering gloom.

Comfort was derived from a double over Surrey, joint champions with Lancashire, and Yorkshire picked up the pieces to take a respectable third place.

Keeping fit in the winter, these Yorkshire players combined into a useful soccer team. They are (left to right): back row – Close, Watson, Wilson, Lester, Trueman, Sutcliffe, Halliday; front row – Leadbeater, Yardley, Hutton, Brennan. (*Yorkshire Post*)

Watson missed a sizeable chunk of the summer because he was with England's World Cup soccer party in South America, while Close, who had already represented his country, fell into step with the demands of National Service. The bowling, with Trueman erratic, rested largely on the shoulders of Wardle, who got through a back-breaking 1,321 overs for 144 wickets, while Eddie Leadbeater, from Huddersfield, took pleasure from regular exposure as that most un-Yorkshirelike of attackers, the leg-spinner.

Within their limitations, Yorkshire continued to compete strongly, rising to second place in 1951, when they were definitely as good as the champions, Warwickshire, who did not have to cope with England calls. Yorkshire were represented in all five Tests against South Africa. Hutton had mainly deputised as captain, but Geoffrey Keighley, born by mischance in France, did duty when Yardley's responsibilities as chairman of the selectors kept him away from the county.

After the Feast 89

Bob Appleyard took his 150th wicket in the 1951 season against Essex at Bradford and then received his county cap from captain Norman Yardley. Fred Trueman had every reason to smile, too, for he also received the official seal of approval at the same time. (*Yorkshire Post*)

Hutton's brilliance illuminated the scene without dazzling Wilson and Lowson, who scored steadily, while the bowling improved considerably. Impetus here came from Bob Appleyard, who celebrated his first full season with 200 wickets, captured with a mixture of swing and spin. His haul, amazing for a man of twenty-seven, made it easier for Yorkshire to bear the loss of Coxon, who had returned to the leagues, and Close, still in the army.

It also kept the spotlight off Trueman, who grabbed 75 wickets with his much greater pace. This search for extra speed occasionally led to massive inaccuracies, but Trueman could be wickedly dangerous and at Sheffield he did the hat-trick at Nottinghamshire's expense, taking eight for 68 as the ball flew from not much short of a length. Five of his victims were bowled and he soon learned that the careful variation between a short and full length could be lethal in favourable conditions. The batsman expecting a bouncer could be deceived into error simply by pitching further up – a case of a physical game being played in the mind.

Yorkshire's search for a wicket-keeper to replace Wood, who stepped down in 1946, ended with Don Brennan, an amateur of unobtrusive skill which won him England caps in 1951.

They also discovered a batsman of exciting potential in Doug Padgett. He became Yorkshire's youngest player when he made his debut against Somerset at Taunton on June 6 – forty-four days short of his seventeenth birthday.

The term unique is often misused in the search for a sporting superlative, but nothing else adequately describes the events at Bramall Lane on May 29, 1951. Yorkshire began it needing nine to avoid the follow-on against Somerset after heavy rain had first delayed the start on the previous day and then complicated their life by making the pitch difficult. Their last wicket could not prevent the massive indignity at the hands of opposition regarded as their natural prey in normal circumstances, but this failure was a blessing in disguise.

Somerset's best course would probably have been to bat again, declare and set Yorkshire a formidable last-innings examination, but, no doubt excited at the prospect of an innings victory, they went into the field a second time and took a sound thrashing for their pains. With Hutton and Lowson setting off at an impressive pace, Yorkshire turned the tables. In three spectacular hours they translated a deficit of 157 into a lead of 112.

This represented a splendid feat in its own right, but Don Brennan, acting captain because Yardley was indisposed, had no intention of accepting the draw, however honourable. He declared, leaving Somerset to make 113 and giving his spinners 110 minutes in which to bowl them out. It was the sort of calculated gamble on which Yorkshire based so many of their triumphs, risking defeat because that was the only way in which they could come within touching distance of the extra points.

Almost at once Somerset were gripped by the familiar fingers of panic. Three men were out inside ten minutes and the scoreboard acknowledged only five runs. The drying pitch gave the bowlers more hope and Wardle and Appleyard made full use of every bit of assistance. Although Somerset needed merely to score at three an over, they threshed about violently and helped to destroy themselves.

Within eighty minutes Yorkshire had disposed of the Somerset second innings to win by 50 runs only some six hours after following on, and only in the distant erratically reported past could there be

After the Feast 91

YORKSHIRE v SOMERSET
at Bramall Lane
27–29 May 1951

Somerset	*first innings*		*second innings*	
Gimblett	b Appleyard	8	b Appleyard	0
Angell	b Appleyard	27	c Hutton b Appleyard	0
Hill	c Brennan b Trueman	3	c Hutton b Wardle	1
Tremlett	c Wardle b Leadbeater	81	st Brennan b Wardle	11
Buse	b Trueman	38	c Brennan b Wardle	8
Lawrence	not out	30	c Brennan b Wardle	0
Smith	b Appleyard	2	not out	0
Rogers	c Hutton b Leadbeater	24	b Appleyard	19
Stephenson	c Leadbeater b Trueman	3	c Brennan b Wardle	7
Robinson	lbw b Leadbeater	5	c Trueman b Wardle	4
Redman	b Leadbeater	10	b Leadbeater	8
extras		3	extras	4
		234		62

Fall of wickets: 1-11, 2-28, 3-55, 4-149, 5-168, 6-171, 7-212, 8-217, 9-222.

Fall of wickets: 1-0, 2-5, 3-5, 4-31, 5-39, 6-46, 7-46, 8-48, 9-62.

Bowling: Trueman 24-4-73-3; Appleyard 27-7-49-3; Halliday 9-4-16-0; Wardle 25-15-36-0; Leadbeater 17.5-2-57-4.

Bowling: Appleyard 13-3-35-3; Wardle 14-6-23-6; Leadbeater 1.5-1-0-1.

Yorkshire	*first innings*		*second innings*	
Hutton	b Buse	9	c Stephenson b Robinson	65
Lowson	c Redman b Buse	20	st Stephenson b Lawrence	43
Halliday	lbw b Redman	2	c Tremlett b Buse	55
Sutcliffe	b Buse	10	c Tremlett b Robinson	12
Wilson	c Lawrence b Redman	16	c Stephenson b Redman	56
Lester	lbw b Buse	0	not out	5
Wardle	b Buse	7	c Stephenson b Lawrence	26
Leadbeater	run out	0	c Rogers b Lawrence	7
Brennan	b Buse	3		
Appleyard	not out	5		
Trueman	st Stephenson b Redman	2		
extras		3	extras	0
		77	(for 7 wkts dec.)	269

Fall of wickets: 1-13, 2-15, 3-40, 4-45, 5-45, 6-67, 7-67, 8-67, 9-72.

Fall of wickets: 1-86, 2-132, 3-206, 4-226, 5-252, 6-257, 7-269.

Bowling: Redman 22.4-9-41-3; Buse 22-10-33-6.

Bowling: Redman 15-3-69-1; Buse 19-5-56-1; Robinson 29-6-74-2; Lawrence 24.5-4-70-3.

a matching performance. If there is one it lurks in surprising obscurity.

One other unusual statistic attaches itself to the occasion, for there were no extras in the Yorkshire second innings, which stretched over eighty-eight overs and that, too, in its way is unique, indicating among other things that the ball did not get past the bat very often and that no error of batting judgment brought about that nuisance of the game – the leg bye.

They could do no better than second again in 1952 as Surrey set off on their great run and the shattering blow to soundly based optimism turned out to be the crippling illness which struck down Appleyard. As he fought a lone battle with tuberculosis, Wardle waged war single-handed on Yorkshire's opponents. The left-arm spinner sent down 1,522 overs – six hundred more than the next man – and took 158 wickets. Close, doing the double of 1,000 runs and 100 wickets, lent promising support, but with Trueman having been called up by the Royal Air Force the bowling could not match the batting, which looked stronger than any in the country.

The feeling was that the title might well be within the county's grasp in 1953, particularly if Appleyard could be restored to good health, but he did not play and a catalogue of misfortune sent them tumbling down to twelfth, their worst position. Trueman, along with Hutton, as captain, Wardle and Watson featured in the Ashes triumph over Australia in which Yardley had a role as selector, but even at full strength Yorkshire did not have the sparkle normally associated with their endeavours.

Close added to their worries by injuring himself at soccer, the outcome being a cartilage operation that left him with time for only two games. On the brighter side, Ray Illingworth, who had come into the team in 1951, did well with both bat and ball mastering to an increasing degree the arts of offspin.

The mirage of a major success danced on the horizon, shimmering into view in 1954, when Yorkshire put the disappointment of the previous summer's disaster behind them and headed the title race for much of the time. In the final analysis, Surrey had a decisive advantage, but Yorkshire won thirteen of their twenty-eight engagements, the upturn in their fortunes stemming entirely from an improvement in the bowling.

Appleyard's recovery was so complete that he managed 881 overs and captured 127 wickets for an average of 14.55. Fractionally

After the Feast 93

behind came Trueman, with a smoother action that allowed for greater control. His tally of 114 wickets at 15.39 gave Yorkshire a cutting edge that broke through all but the best-organised resistance, so that a short-fall in the batting could be ignored. Six players compiled averages over 28, though, which meant that there was a reliability in depth.

Huddersfield became the scene of the county's first tie. Yorkshire's first innings yielded 351 for four, to which Leicestershire replied with 328. Deteriorating weather encouraged some swing, which Terry Spencer exploited to the full with nine for 63 as Yorkshire collapsed to 113 all out. Leicestershire experienced difficulties, too, and when Wardle delivered the last ball of extra time the scores were level. Spencer, yet again the centre of excited attention, pushed down the line and ran as hard as he knew how. He could not beat Wardle's reflexes and was run out.

This purposeful group obviously meant business, and the front row reads (left to right): Wardle, Hutton, Yardley, Lowson, Trueman, Appleyard, Halliday, Leadbeater, Lester. (*Yorkshire Post*)

YORKSHIRE v LEICESTERSHIRE
at Huddersfield
16–18 June 1954

Yorkshire

	first innings		second innings	
Hutton	c Firth b Munden	60	c Firth b Spencer	6
Lowson	b Walsh	38	b Spencer	8
Wilson	c Palmer b Walsh	138	b Spencer	18
Lester	c Boshier b Palmer	33	b Spencer	34
Watson	not out	80	b Spencer	0
Yardley			b Spencer	22
Close			c Firth b Palmer	1
Wardle			b Spencer	0
Booth			c Smithson b Spencer	8
Appleyard			not out	1
Trueman			b Spencer	8
extras		2	extras	7
	(4 wkts dec.)	351		113

Fall of wickets: 1–82, 2–123, 3–183, 4–351.

Fall of wickets: 1–13, 2–18, 3–43, 4–43, 5–82, 6–85, 7–87, 8–97, 9–108.

Bowling: Spencer 25-3-70-0; Boshier 17-3-51-0; Palmer 12-4-33-1; Walsh 20.5-0-77-2; Jackson 14-3-52-0; Munden 23-4-66-1.

Bowling: Spencer 23-6-63-9; Palmer 12-6-18-1; Jackson 10-2-25-0.

Leicestershire

	first innings		second innings	
Lester	b Close	74	b Trueman	4
Hallam	b Trueman	24	b Trueman	2
Tompkin	st Booth b Wardle	149	c and b Appleyard	6
Palmer	c Hutton b Wardle	15	b Wardle	31
Jackson	c Booth b Trueman	1	c Lester b Trueman	4
Smithson	c and b Close	25	c Lowson b Trueman	0
Munden	b Appleyard	19	run out	31
Walsh	b Wardle	0	c Hutton b Wardle	28
Firth	not out	8	st Booth b Wardle	3
Spencer	st Booth b Appleyard	0	run out	8
Boshier	c Watson b Wardle	1	not out	1
extras		12	extras	18
		328		136

Fall of wickets: 1–58, 2–183, 3–216, 4–223, 5–281, 6–315, 7–315, 8–327, 9–328.

Fall of wickets: 1–8, 2–15, 3–19, 4–21, 5–29, 6–72, 7–123, 8–123, 9–127.

Bowling: Trueman 22-1-83-2; Appleyard 31-11-62-2; Yardley 6-1-22-0; Wardle 44.4-18-82-4; Close 21-3-67-2.

Bowling: Trueman 18-2-44-4; Appleyard 20-8-38-1; Wardle 13-4-36-3.

After the Feast 95

Not all Yorkshire's failures were products of their own shortcomings and in 1955 they commanded widespread admiration by running Surrey close. Their 268 points broke the record under the scoring system introduced in 1938, but Surrey gained sixteen more, and they had to contend with injury to Appleyard, who took little part in the second half of the season. Had he been able to back up Trueman and Wardle all the time the tables might have been turned.

Hutton also had his moments of real concern, back trouble eventually bringing down the curtain on one of the truly great careers. 'Great' is an over-used word in sporting circles, but Hutton's exceptional talents make it appropriate in his case. It was also in this season that wicket-keeper Jimmy Binks began his long and amazingly reliable run in the senior side, holding his place until retiring at the end of the 1969 campaign.

Yardley gave early warning of his intention to resign, so in July Yorkshire unanimously elected Bill Sutcliffe as captain. The decision could scarcely have taxed the official mind, for Sutcliffe had shown that he was more than the son of a famous father. He had also taken over the leadership at odd times when Yardley could not be there. Weight of runs demanded the award of his cap in 1952 after a visit to India with the Commonwealth party in the winter of 1950–51 and in 1955 only Watson stood above him in the Yorkshire averages.

For some reason, though, he rarely received the acceptance to which he was entitled. He could never quite escape the shadow of Herbert, so speculation unkindly linked the appointment with his family connection. Perhaps left alone to make his own way he would have emerged as a fine batsman, for he possessed both character and technique, but people in too many quarters marked him down as a failure.

With Sutcliffe in charge Yorkshire finished seventh and third behind Surrey. Criticism rained down, but he was distinctly unlucky for Trueman had a miserable year in 1956 with only thirty-three wickets, while Mike Cowan, a left-arm seamer about whom enthusiastic forecasts were made, broke down with a back strain.

Things got marginally better in 1957, with Yorkshire climbing four places, but arguments confused selection policies, which used Appleyard as an opening bowler. The complaint here was that the bowling had been weakened to cover for suspect batting and the question of team discipline arose. Sutcliffe publicly stressed that the team spirit was good without being entirely convincing and it cannot be denied that some players had grown into the belief that they were special cases, meriting special treatment to the detriment of the senior squad as a whole.

By mid-August 1957, Sutcliffe wrote to the president, T.L. Taylor, relinquishing the captaincy 'very definitely for business reasons'. He had unselfishly operated with the interests of the county at heart and could never be accused of considering his own position as a batsman first, but it could be contended that a firmer hand would have served a worthwhile purpose.

The committee had to take this point into account when they met to consider the next step and they took their time over naming the new man. They did not decide to invite Ronnie Burnet to shoulder the burden until November and then the subject of their deliberations discovered the good news by buying a paper.

Driving through York, he spotted a billboard which proclaimed 'New Yorkshire Captain'. Stopping to buy a paper, he learned from the Stop Press that he had got the job. Approval did not immediately attach itself to the appointment, for Burnet, at thirty-nine, had no aspirations to anything higher than the Minor Counties competition, but his reputation in that field persuaded the committee that he was the disciplinarian they wanted.

He could not have tackled a more demanding job and in his first year he teetered on the brink of disaster. The county crashed to eleventh place in the table, Watson departed to Leicestershire before the season began and a fire broke out at Headingley, destroying the clock tower and the Press Box. The weather turned foul and caused twenty-four blank days - seventeen of them in Yorkshire - so receipts went down by almost £5,000 in 1957.

On top of all this came a furious row sparked by the sacking of Wardle. This broke only four days after the left-arm spinner had been selected to go to Australia with the MCC and Yorkshire had already publicised their intention to dispense with Appleyard and Lowson when secretary John Nash announced that they 'would not be calling upon Wardle next season'.

Brian Sellers, established as one of the MCC selectors, admitted: 'There was no indication of this happening when I sat down to help pick the England party for Australia. It was a lightning decision and had not been discussed until this afternoon.' Asked if he reconciled the move with Wardle's selection for the most important of all tours, he added: 'They are two different things. He may be good enough for England but not Yorkshire.' The superficially casual manner in

After the Feast

The men who sacked Johnny Wardle on August 11, 1958, are pictured at the historic meeting at Bradford Park Avenue. From left to right they are: seated – Michael Crawford, Sir William Worsley, Ronnie Burnet, Norman Yardley, John Nash (secretary) and Clifford Hesketh (chairman); standing – John Temple, Brian Sellers, Harold Dawson and Fred Popplewell. (*Yorkshire Post*)

which so worthy and hard-working a member of the team had been dispensed with came as an unpleasant shock to the public, for Wardle, with his ready wit and ability to communicate, was popular.

His team-mates saw another side to his nature, however, and he had been known to express his opinion forcefully both to colleagues and to his captain, who had clear terms of reference and demanded loyalty. Whatever the real reason, Wardle went amidst scenes of great anger.

Yorkshire had made an embarrassing about-turn, for in the first weeks of the campaign, when Burnet had been nursing a leg strain, Wardle was given the captaincy. Now he responded with some cutting comments in newspaper articles. Later he was to say: 'Yorkshire sacked me because I refused to accept the authority of the quite hopeless old man appointed captain,' but by then he had lost his tour place as well and dropped out of the first-class picture.

Yorkshire defended their action by issuing a statement which read: 'In past years Wardle has been warned on several occasions that his general behaviour on the field and in the dressing-room left much to be desired. As no improvement was shown this year the decision to dispense with his services was made as it was unanimously considered that it was essential to have discipline and a happy, loyal team before a lasting improvement could be expected.' The unpleasantness inevitably left a nasty taste, but the players were quick to make their position clear.

Vic Wilson, senior professional on the departure of Wardle, said: 'The players are not only one hundred per cent behind the skipper, but so much so that we are prepared, if necessary, to tell the county committee that and assure them we are ready to back Mr Burnet as loyally in the future as we have tried to do in the past.'

On the credit side, Bryan Stott, a dashing left-hander from Yeadon, and Ken Taylor, another Huddersfield product, formed a business-like opening partnership. Phil Sharpe also did well, Don Wilson stepped into Wardle's shoes and Trueman took sixty-two wickets for a cost of 11.91. With so much of the county in a turmoil the re-organisation did not hit many headlines, but Burnet had masterminded another step forward.

Chapter 10

BACK ON THE MOUNTAIN TOP (1959–1970)

Ronnie Burnet's brave stance, solidly supported by the committee, who stood their ground in the face of a withering cross-fire from a section of their membership, produced guidelines which passed the most exacting test over the next decade as Yorkshire justified the stern imposition of authority. The team climbed back to the top of the mountain. Their championship triumph in 1959 shocked the most optimistic among their admirers, including the down-to-earth Brian Sellers, who had not shrunk from the thought that it would take up to three years for the side to mature. Nor was the upsurge a flash in the pan.

Yorkshire went on to finish first seven times in ten years and while their standards may not have been quite so exacting as in previous periods of ascendancy, they maintained a constant level of competence.

Burnet fully deserved the praise which accompanied the amazing transformation in his second year of office. He had a comparatively young and inexperienced squad, who must have nursed some secret fears, and there were precious few signs of the behind-the-scenes labours bearing fruit as the county limped into the second half of the programme hovering uncertainly in mid-table. The demands on the leadership were enormous, but Burnet knew where he was going and, gradually gaining in confidence, the players began to pick up the tempo.

They beat Sussex by an innings and 40 runs at Bradford, Warwickshire by six wickets at Sheffield, despite losing the second day to rain, and Essex at Colchester with eleven minutes to spare. This spurt carried them to the top of the table and they were never thereafter out of the top three.

To win the title they still had to deliver the goods under extreme pressure, for the performance that clinched it was the equal of anything in the glorious past or the uncertain future. Sussex resisted to the bitter end at Hove, where, 97 behind on the first innings, they prolonged their second into the third afternoon. They led by 183 at lunch-time with three wickets in hand and their captain, Robin

Marlar, had no intention of declaring. He owed his first allegiance to the basic principles of the game which insisted that Yorkshire could be given no favours, so they had to work and scheme for all their gains.

They prised out those last three men in half an hour, Ray Illingworth and Don Wilson doing the damage, but, despite the spinners' break-through, the target had assumed monumental proportions – 218 runs in ninety-five minutes. Few would have complained had Yorkshire regarded the run-rate of more than two a minute as impossible. Instead, they hurled themselves into the chase with a violence that jerked the contest back to life.

Bryan Stott ensured the initial momentum – 15 from the first over by a startled Ian Thomson, including four overthrows as Sussex panicked. Seventeen spilled from that bowler's second over, with Stott and Brian Close hammering sixes. Yorkshire reached 50 in seventeen minutes and went past 100 in forty-five. The crucial partnership between Stott and Doug Padgett amounted to 141 runs in a fantasy of fast scoring which ensured the reality of the championship. Stott made 96 and Padgett 79, the priceless points being collected with five wickets in hand. At twenty-three minutes past four they had seven minutes to spare on a breathless afternoon.

Yorkshire had overcome a number of obstacles along the way, for Burnet fell into the sorry habit of losing the toss,

Bryan Stott, who played a dazzling innings at Hove in 1959 to help Yorkshire win the championship. (*Reuter*)

Back on the Mountain Top

being lucky only eight times in twenty-eight, so they usually had to contend with the worst of the wicket. They lost to Somerset for the first time since 1903, which hardly did their morale any good, and they succumbed to the lowest score of that otherwise glorious summer – 35 against Gloucestershire at Bristol, where the last six batsmen failed to score. Above all else, Yorkshire lost to Lancashire at Old Trafford for the first time in thirty-two years, a humbling experience which demanded either a blood sacrifice or the ultimate conquest.

The most glowing tribute to Burnet came at the Scarborough Festival, where, after being invited to join the MCC team, with Vic Wilson leading Yorkshire, the captain switched sides to accept the general acclaim. Yorkshire won that game and then really showed what they were made of by beating The Rest at the Oval after being forced to follow-on.

Bowled out for 160 in reply to 384, they amassed 425, thanks to a century from Wilson. Illingworth and Close then spun out the opposition with 66 runs to spare. The former was by now firmly established as a trusty all-rounder, while Don Wilson proved his value, too, having a hat-trick against Nottinghamshire at Middlesbrough to cheer him.

Burnet chose exactly the right moment to step down, handing over a side that was bubbling with enthusiasm and eager to get to grips with another challenge. His successor had much for which to thank him, and that man turned out to be Vic Wilson, the burly farmer from the Malton district, who had been senior professional and who had acted as Burnet's deputy.

The transfer from amateur to professional went smoothly and unopposed, for there was no other way. Wilson had far more friends than enemies and, without being of the highest class, had no trouble in commanding a regular place.

He received unswerving support as Yorkshire moved steadily to another championship with a comfortable margin over Lancashire and 137 runs too many for The Rest in the September trial of strength. The runners-up, though, were well pleased with their first double over the White Rose in sixty-seven years which took some of the icing off Yorkshire's celebration cake.

Trueman continued as a tower of strength, taking 132 wickets – over fifty more than anyone else. Although he experimented with a shorter run, relying from time to time on his natural ability to move the ball, no one faced him without some fear. Padgett, the most polished batsman, headed a list that had moments of failure. Yorkshire could never relax, but they made the best of what they had and Wilson handled his resources shrewdly. Without being carried away, the county had every reason to be contented.

The slip which allowed Hampshire their first title in 1961 came, therefore, as a disappointment, especially as Yorkshire had romped away in the first half of the summer with seven wins in eight games. Not one of the batsmen could lift his average to 40, but the bowling, with Trueman and Illingworth invariably to the fore, appeared strong enough.

This also proved to be the case in 1962, when Yorkshire regained their rightful place. Trueman and Illingworth still led the way among the bowlers and a freak of mathematics left Tony Nicholson, a seam bowler from Dewsbury and who came to county cricket via a spell

The likely lads of 1960. Ready for the pre-season nets at Headingley are (left to right): Binks, Sharpe, Birkenshaw, Bolus, Wilson, Bird, Pickles, Ryan and Padgett. (*Yorkshire Post*)

Back on the Mountain Top

in the Rhodesian police force, at the top of the batting averages – 98 runs for a figure of 49! Geoff Boycott also made his first appearance that summer, following John Hampshire, who had a couple of innings the previous year.

The competition reached a fascinating climax at Harrogate, where huge crowds turned up to watch Yorkshire beat Glamorgan by seven wickets to become champions. On a pitch that allowed some turn throughout, Glamorgan were dismissed for 65 and 101, but Yorkshire managed only 101 themselves in the first innings and the fact that all the second day was lost to rain added to the tension shared by 10,000 spectators. Over 5,000 sat through the downpour in the hope of being in at the kill, but they had to be patient. Jeff Jones completed an unusual hat-trick – the last two wickets of Yorkshire's first innings and the first of their second with successive deliveries – but in every other way Yorkshire had complete control.

Wilson, who was thirty-nine when appointed captain, went out at the top, leaving the honour of leading Yorkshire in 1963, their centenary year, to Brian Close, the multi-talented sportsman, who had it in his power to break almost every record in the game. Close, at 18 years and 149 days, had been the youngest player to win an England cap in 1949, and, in addition to his effortless all-round cricketing skill, he acquitted himself sufficiently well at soccer to be signed by both Leeds United and Arsenal, clubs not given to mistaking geese for swans. He reached low single-figure handicaps both left-handed and right-handed at golf and potted with profitable efficiency at snooker. Possibly because it all came so easily, he never quite directed his energies into the most productive channels.

He did the double twice, in 1949 and 1952, and opened the innings for England, but his horizons were limited by his approach which ignored personal gain and his complete disregard for individual statistics made him an excellent captain, ready to make sacrifices and lead from the front.

His promotion came as a matter of routine, but when a member sought confirmation at the annual meeting in January 1963, the president, Sir William Worsley, with a slip of the tongue, announced: 'It is a chap called Brian Sellers.'

Yorkshire celebrated their one hundredth birthday in the best possible way, defying injuries and England calls to remain champions. The outcome reflected credit on the old hands and the new recruits, for Boycott led the batsmen and Trueman the bowlers as the side papered over the cracks caused by the Test selection of

Close, Phil Sharpe and Trueman and the incapacity of Illingworth, Stott, Padgett and Ken Taylor.

Wilson, after losing his place in 1962, emerged as the leading wicket-taker, while Nicholson gave substance to the belief that Yorkshire had discovered another of the eternally accurate medium-paced seamers by whom they set such understandable store.

The summer of 1964 emerged as one of the finest, crowded with days of glorious sunshine, but Yorkshire had to make do with fifth place behind Worcestershire, who followed this first championship success with another the next year. Yorkshire finished fourth then, struggling all the while to link their batting and bowling effectively.

Illingworth and Trueman were, as ever, at the forefront of things, with the England pace man having quite admirable figures of 115 wickets for only 1,307 runs in 1965, but the lack of consistency dogged the team to an alarming extent.

Fortunes sank to a sickeningly low level at Middlesbrough on May 20, 1965, when Hampshire shot them out for 23 – their lowest total. There were, of course, excuses for this debacle, but they did not add up to justification for a spineless surrender. The ball swung appreciably in a damp atmosphere and the pitch was unreliable, permitting sharp lift or no bounce at all in unpredictable sequence, but Yorkshire, trailing by four runs on the first innings, made no noticeable attempt to improvise. When, for once, the rustic swing might have been worthwhile, a succession of batsmen pushed and prodded and edged catches into the slips. By one o'clock on the

Yorkshire	*second innings*	
Boycott	lbw b White	5
Hampshire	c Keith b Shackleton	2
Padgett	c Keith b Shackleton	0
Close	c Barnard b White	1
Sharpe	c Sainsbury b White	1
Illingworth	b White	0
Hutton	c Barnard b White	0
Binks	c Keith b White	0
Trueman	lbw b Cottam	3
Wilson	not out	7
Nicholson	c Livingstone b Cottam	0
extras		4
		23

Fall of wickets: 1–7, 2–7, 3–7, 4–7, 5–8, 6–8, 7–12, 8–13, 9–23.
Bowling: Shackleton 9-5-7-2; White 10-7-10-6; Cottam 1.4-0-2-2.

second day the issue had been settled and Yorkshire, having won the toss and gained the best of conditions, were in disgrace. Hampshire, as shocked as the stone-faced crowd, gathered in the 20 runs they needed to win as though in a trance.

Strangely enough, Yorkshire completed the first leg of another title hat-trick in 1966 against the unwelcome background of artificial limits to the first innings, for one hundred and two of the two hundred and thirty-eight championship fixtures were used in an experiment involving a maximum of sixty-five overs. This made a mockery of established batting practice and Yorkshire suffered along with the rest, for only the studious Boycott and the enterprising Close beat the 30 mark.

In going back to the top, Yorkshire lost six matches, but their bowling carried them through. Illingworth, Nicholson, Wilson and Trueman all averaged better than 20.

They also benefited from their usual self-sufficiency. They trusted each other so Close could take calculated risks, secure in the knowledge that the backing would be immediate and positive. His leadership was inspiring and he turned the rule books upside-down against Lancashire at Old Trafford, where Yorkshire won by 12 runs after forfeiting an innings. By introducing a new tactic into the game, Close set the scene for one of the most exciting of Roses conclusions. Heavy rain meant only ninety-five minutes' cricket on the first two days, during which Yorkshire made 50 for three.

A delayed start on the Tuesday hardly helped and Yorkshire batted quietly through to lunch before a stoical audience, who turned up out of habit and sat in sombre silence because there was nothing to shout about. It was a ritual that fitted into the pattern of the past, but Close was about to break the mould which shaped attitudes on these occasions. He declared during the interval at 146 for seven, leaving a maximum of 165 minutes, and Lancashire startled the spectators into life by declaring after four deliveries at 1 for none. Close promptly sent them in again while everyone with access to a copy of the regulations studied the legality of the proceedings.

Argument centred on the possibility of collusion, which was strongly denied by both parties and could not be countenanced officially, before Lancashire set about the job of making 146 to win. The advantage swung one way and then the other, but Yorkshire had the whip hand when Illingworth delivered the last possible over to Tommy Greenhough, a leg-spinner by trade who could never have dreamed of scoring the 17 Lancashire still wanted. His concern was solely with survival.

The first ball leapt past his hesitant prod forward and eluded wicket-keeper Jimmy Binks, dribbling through for four byes as Yorkshire opted to keep Greenhough down at the danger end. Four more defensive strokes punctuated the breathless tension, but Greenhough then missed as he played back and a full-throated appeal for lbw was upheld. Yorkshiremen acclaimed their heroes and Lancashiremen, swallowing their disappointment, could take satisfaction from their contribution to the day's entertainment.

Champions again in 1967, Yorkshire experienced all manner of difficulties, including some of their own making at Edgbaston, where Close put the England captaincy on the line in the county's cause. His team were accused of wasting time as they hung on for a draw and the captain shouldered the blame, being censured and replaced as Test skipper.

Yorkshire lost five championship games and had a mere ten points to spare at the end of an undistinguished race. For all the efforts of the legislators, the points system remained unacceptable, and in this season the awarding of two points for a draw persuaded many to follow negative policies. Matters came to an unpleasant head in Birmingham, where, whatever the explanations, Yorkshire stretched sportsmanship to the limits in preventing Warwickshire from scoring 142 for victory.

The cricket for two days was ordinary, with Warwickshire mustering 242 to gain a lead of four and then dismissing Yorkshire for 145. The home side reached the closing stages in a strong position so far as wickets were concerned, although requiring 54 from the last half hour. A steady drizzle made conditions difficult as Yorkshire fought to stave off defeat, and, with fifteen minutes to play, they complained that it was no longer fit. The umpires rejected this plea, but when heavy rain fell a general dash for cover ensued. Before they had cleared the playing area, however, the cloud passed over and Yorkshire bowled two more overs.

One by Trueman included two no-balls, three bouncers and the wicket of Dennis Amiss, who mis-hooked to offer a high return catch. Hutton bowled Alan Smith with a full toss and Warwickshire fell nine runs short of their target. Yorkshire, therefore, collected the two points that enabled them to share the leadership with Kent, but they ran the gauntlet of physical and verbal abuse on the ground, Trueman being struck by an umbrella. Some damage was also done

Back on the Mountain Top

September 1967 and Yorkshire have won the championship by beating Gloucestershire at Harrogate, but the tension rather than the joy shows in the faces as they leave the field. Left to right are: Trueman, Wilson, Close, Illingworth, Sharpe, Padgett and Taylor. (*Yorkshire Post*)

to their cars, by angry supporters who felt that Warwickshire had been cheated.

Close, steadfastly unrepentant, explained: 'The ball was wet throughout and it was necessary for the bowlers to dry it after every delivery. In the effort to save runs, it was also necessary for the fielders to go deeper than would normally be the case and so it took longer to cross over. Surely we could not be expected to run? In the last ten minutes Trueman, who can't get through an over in less than four minutes anyway, claimed a wicket and bowled two no-balls.

'The crowd made so much noise that I found it extremely hard to make my instructions known to the bowlers and the fielders. I could not carry on in those circumstances, so I walked over to the players to make myself heard.' That all sounded reasonable, but Yorkshire managed only twenty-four overs in 102 minutes – six in the last half-hour – and the County Advisory Committee, having studied the evidence, came down firmly against them.

Clearly shaken, Yorkshire contrived to lose their next engagement with Essex, who, after being bowled out for 87, recovered so well that they had nine runs to spare at Scarborough. Overall, it was very unsettling, but Yorkshire emerged relatively unscathed, for they finished first in 1968, fourteen points clear of Kent with eleven victories and four defeats.

They had reason for thinking that the future was assured, too, for the second team made it a splendid double as they headed the Minor Counties placings, but it was Trueman's swan song and the prospect of coping without him had to be faced. For all the promise of the slightly-built Middlesbrough seamer, Chris Old, who had made his debut in 1966, the departure of a truly superb fast bowler had to be viewed with some alarm.

Trueman had more victims in Test cricket than any other bowler and his 1,745 wickets for his county had cost a mere 17.13 runs each. With him went Illingworth, arguably the best day-in, day-out county all-rounder of the post-war period, although the road he took led to a quite brilliant phase of his career. Illingworth fell out with the committee over the question of security and the request for a contract which was not granted.

Speaking as captain of Leicestershire and England, he lifted a corner of the curtain that had separated Yorkshire from their public for so long. He also hinted at the areas of concern which existed just below the surface, even in a championship year. 'As a youngster your only ambition is to play for Yorkshire and unfortunately I believe the committee have traded on this,' he said. 'I knew that even in my best seasons some wanted to play Geoff Cope as off-spinner ahead of me, so I thought I'm going to be a fool if I hang on here for another year or two and then they tell me to clear off just when they feel like it.'

The breaking up of a capable well-balanced squad did not end there. Binks and Taylor directed their attentions elsewhere and the experience they took with them could not be replaced easily for league cricket was at a very low ebb, dominated by too many sub-standard paid players. In addition, Yorkshire had to face opposition increasingly strengthened by cricketing mercenaries.

Binks actually carried on through 1969, which brought a depress-

Yorkshire in 1969, the year of the second Gillette Cup victory. Left to right: back row – Balderstone, Hampshire, Nicholson, Hutton, Old, Boycott, Cope; front row – Sharpe, Binks, Close (captain), Padgett, Wilson. (*Yorkshire Post*)

ing joint twelfth place in the championship – in early June Yorkshire slumped to the foot of the table – and success in the Gillette Cup hardly disguised the limitations. Injury to Close, who missed most of the second half of the programme, created something of a crisis, accentuated by Nicholson's loss of form following a broken finger, and the county's single championship century was compiled by Boycott, who helped himself to 105 not out against Somerset.

Binks, the senior professional, took over as captain while he completed an unbroken run of 412 successive Championship matches before announcing his retirement. Old and Wilson encouraged thoughts of better days with some impressive bowling, but the more perceptive followers of the county's fortunes awaited the arrival of the 1970s with fears that had a logical foundation.

Superficially, there was an improvement as Yorkshire climbed to fourth in the table with eight victories and five defeats. Old, Richard Hutton, Cope and Wilson all worked hard and the batting carried a more dependable air, with six men averaging over 30. The committee drew attention to this in their annual report, adding: 'At the beginning of August the team had a good chance of being champions.' In the same breath, though, they announced they were sacking Close 'after long and careful consideration'.

During the year, David Bairstow, a stocky red-haired wicket-keeper from Bradford, made one of the busiest of debuts. Called up to Park Avenue, Bradford, for the fixture against Gloucestershire, he had to sit his A-level examination at Hanson Boys' Grammar School at seven in the morning to make himself available for the 11.30 start.

In his haste he failed to gain passes in English and economics, although he managed an O-level qualification in the latter, but his advance as a regular member of the county team pushed academic considerations into the background.

Chapter 11

IN THE WILDERNESS
(1971–1983)

The bitter, barren years of Geoff Boycott's captaincy were bracketed by the two biggest rows the county have known. Not surprisingly, therefore, the club had to live with the by-products of endless bickering and political manœuvring – poor results and lowly placings. Although the committee took most of the decisions and had created the climate in which he operated, Boycott was beaten with the stick of official displeasure, and the fact that he had constantly to defend himself did not help in the smooth running of the county machine.

The cavalier treatment of Close resulted in the formation of a vociferous Action Group, made up of members ready to campaign on his behalf, and this attracted distressing publicity. The first shots in the battle were fired at the annual meeting when the committee report and the statement of accounts were not accepted. Brian Sellers subsequently stood down as chairman of the cricket sub-committee and a peace formula was patched together, bringing some sort of order to Yorkshire's affairs, but the team stumbled through four disastrous seasons, finishing thirteenth, tenth, fourteenth and eleventh.

Alongside Boycott, Don Wilson served as vice-captain, an appointment sensibly made to cover the England opener's involvement with Test cricket, but an air of mystery settled over the arrangement.

Why had Phil Sharpe been overlooked for both the captaincy and the vice-captaincy? He had been named as deputy for Close and done nothing to blot his copybook, yet the committee downgraded him without offering an explanation. No one came up with a cast-iron theory as Yorkshire got off to a dismal start in 1971 without Boycott, who had broken his arm in Australia, and they never threatened to recover. The collective form contrasted sharply with Boycott's fluent progress on the way to becoming the first Englishman to average more than 100 – 100.12 to be exact – and in the championship his return of 109.85 was over three times better than that of Sharpe, the next man in the order.

This massive gap in ability between the captain and his crew, magnified by Boycott's unyielding dedication and refusal to understand those who could not match his sense of purpose, caused some friction. A handful of malcontents went so far as to complain about him to the committee, who could not bring themselves to deal decisively with the situation.

Despite a flying start on all fronts in 1972, when they got through to the knock-out stages of the new Benson and Hedges limited-overs competition and climbed to the top of the championship in early June, Yorkshire continued in the doldrums.

Injury to Boycott, whose finger was broken by Bob Willis of Warwickshire, in a Gillette Cup tie at Headingley, knocked away the cornerstone of their organisation and ruined any hopes of beating Leicestershire in the final of the Benson and Hedges Cup at Lord's, where the margin of defeat amounted to a comfortable five wickets. They fell woefully short of runs, reaching 136 and this one game emphasised the extent to which Yorkshire relied on Boycott. Altogether they won only one of the seventeen championship fixtures he missed in two years. He and John Hampshire pressed the Sunday League challenge without much support and when Boycott failed in the Gillette Cup at Harrogate in 1973 Yorkshire were shamed by Durham, an unconsidered Minor County, who beat them by five wickets.

One performance in 1973 from which Yorkshire emerged with great credit was their second tied game, for they achieved equality with Middlesex at Bradford with a patched-up side further crippled by a mystery virus. They were without Boycott, who nursed a strain, and Old, who was ill, and had only two capped batsmen in Sharpe and Hampshire.

For once shrugging off the doubts that so often handicapped them, they bowled accurately to restrict the visitors to 102, but then faltered in reply. They limped to 106 for nine by the close on the Saturday night and found that they could take their innings no further on the Monday morning. A doctor confined Howard Cooper to bed, while Arthur Robinson, after making his painful way to the ground, was promptly sent home as Middlesex batted a second time.

Yorkshire had not so much declared as suffered an enforced surrender and they had to make up their numbers with four substitutes as Graham Stevenson withdrew to his sick bed, too. Somehow they kept going as they bowled out Middlesex for 211 and set out to

In the Wilderness 113

climb the mountain towards the 208 they needed for victory. Colin Johnson produced one of his best displays to give their innings a solid foundation, but they were still 16 short when Cooper and Robinson came together – a shivering, unsteady pair who could hardly summon up the strength to stand at the crease.

Improbable strokes fashioned in a half-blind desperation narrowed the gap inch by wobbly inch until the scores were level. Sickeningly, Mike Selvey hurled a ball of full length and unerring aim through a weary lunge forward by Robinson and the spoils were shared.

In retrospect, we may wonder why Yorkshire could not produce these battling qualities on a more regular basis, for had they done so there is no doubt that much better results would have brought a welcome harmony into the club's activities. There is no easy answer, just a series of guesses – some informed, others based on prejudice or half-truths – but Yorkshire, whatever the reason, let themselves down more often than not by failing to play up to their potential.

The bowling seldom threatened, with Tony Nicholson bravely overcoming the effects of serious illness and Wilson, after losing the vice-captaincy, finding length and line elusive. Old was much the most likely to succeed, but he gained Test match recognition, while the luckless Cope busied himself in the nets, banned from the middle because of a suspect action.

This blow fell in late June 1972, and it sparked a chain reaction that strangled his prospects. Helped by the advice of Johnny Wardle, who accepted the job of guide and mentor, thus making his peace with the club, Cope managed to fight his way back into favour.

He was, though, forever dogged by the cameras and with a defiant flash of humour claimed that, on the basis of all the films in which he filled the central role, he possessed full qualification for election to the actors' union. Each season brought some ordeal, although he finally got his much-coveted England cap and, with it, a passing seal of approval. Despite all this, he was banned again in 1978 and trudged wearily back to the drawing board – to no avail.

A tentative return finished with more unfavourable reports from umpires and Yorkshire released him at the end of the 1980 season. Not the best of Yorkshire's bowlers, the thoughtful Cope featured as the most ill-used by fortune, for other players with slight flaws slipped through the net, and, as a spinner, he was never likely to hurt anyone.

As he dropped into the Bradford League and the Minor County

YORKSHIRE v MIDDLESEX
at Bradford
8–11 September 1973

Middlesex *first innings*   *second innings*

Smith	c Bairstow b Nicholson	10	c Wilson b Nicholson	23
Featherstone	c Hampshire b Nicholson	7	c Lumb b Stevenson	18
Brearley	c Bairstow b Stevenson	2	c Sharpe b Wilson	83
Radley	c Lumb b Stevenson	19	lbw b Bore	18
Gomes	lbw b Nicholson	12	lbw b Nicholson	0
Murray	c Stevenson b Nicholson	21	c and b Wilson	20
Edmonds	lbw b Cooper	2	c sub b Wilson	9
Titmus	b Cooper	0	run out	17
Jones	c Johnson b Cooper	4	c Sharpe b Nicholson	8
Black	lbw b Nicholson	10	c sub b Wilson	4
Selvey	not out	0	not out	0
	extras	15	extras	11
		102		211

Fall of wickets: 1–14, 2–19, 3–41, 4–44, 5–77, 6–82, 7–82, 8–92, 9–92.

Fall of wickets: 1–33, 2–51, 3–116, 4–117, 5–155, 6–171, 7–185, 8–190, 9–211.

Bowling: Nicholson 15.5–8–23–5; Cooper 17–9–20–3; Stevenson 9–3–23–2; Robinson 7–1–21–0.

Bowling: Nicholson 17.5–3–38–3; Stevenson 10–2–27–1; Wilson 19–5–67–4; Bore 25–9–51–1; Johnson 9–4–17–0.

Yorkshire *first innings*   *second innings*

Sharpe	c Edmonds b Black	19	c Featherstone b Selvey	4
Lumb	c Murray b Jones	0	c Jones b Selvey	0
Johnson	lbw b Gomes	33	c Radley b Selvey	78
Hampshire	b Gomes	21	b Titmus	12
Bairstow	c Selvey b Titmus	6	b Selvey	56
Stevenson	c Black b Titmus	7	b Selvey	1
Wilson	c Radley b Gomes	0	c Edmonds b Titmus	15
Cooper	not out	5	not out	10
Nicholson	lbw b Gomes	0	st Murray b Titmus	2
Bore	run out	5	b Titmus	9
Robinson	not out	0	b Selvey	6
	extras	10	extras	14
	(9 wkts)	106		207

Fall of wickets: 1–0, 2–32, 3–75, 4–88, 5–88, 6–95, 7–95, 8–95, 9–106.

Fall of wickets: 1–4, 2–18, 3–54, 4–134, 5–146, 6–170, 7–178, 8–186, 9–192.

Bowling: Selvey 13–6–16–0; Jones 12–4–26–1; Black 5–1–12–1; Edmonds 1–0–6–0; Gomes 18–9–22–4; Titmus 15–8–14–2.

Bowling: Selvey 25.5–5–74–6; Jones 7–3–19–0; Titmus 15–1–41–4; Gomes 15–4–39–0; Edmonds 8–4–20–0.

In the Wilderness

A guiding hand for Geoff Cope in 1972 from Johnny Wardle, who offered his services when the offspinner was banned because of his suspect action. (*Doncaster Newspapers*)

competition, where, ironically, he could wheel away without worry, Cope left Yorkshire with the inexperienced Peter Whiteley and the veteran Ray Illingworth as the offspinners and fate had big surprises in store for both of them. Those, and, indeed, Illingworth's return to the county of his birth were, however, a long way in the future in 1974, when Boycott fell out with England – or, to be more precise, with the system installed in the country's name – and went into voluntary exile from the international scene.

This raised the prospect of his day-to-day involvement with the county lifting general standards, especially as a number of influential critics were questioning the team spirit. The improvement, though, proved to be no more than slight – eleventh from fourteenth. Yet again the rumours of discontent in the dressing-room were broadcast and, since Yorkshire's three championship successes in 1973 had all been gained under the leadership of Sharpe, restored to favour without comment, the theory that the team did better without Boycott gained credence.

He had his brushes with injury, but he stood as the bulwark

against complete collapse. The club had little to cheer, but the Nottinghamshire game at Worksop in 1974 brought some relief. Victory by an innings and 69 runs ended a sequence of forty-three away matches in the championship without a win. It stretched back to July 28, 1970, when Essex were crushed by an innings and 101 runs at Colchester. Close had been captain in seven engagements, Boycott in twenty-one, Sharpe in nine and Wilson in six. The splendid Arthur Robinson, a burly, big-hearted, medium-paced left-arm seamer from Northallerton, celebrated with a hat-trick, but it was not a result that led on to anything else.

Faced with a testing start to the 1975 programme, Yorkshire concentrated on avoiding defeat on their first five championship outings. Steadily building on that, they went on to reach second place, giving Leicestershire a good run for their title money and their supporters a much appreciated lift. Boycott and Richard Lumb briefly rose to the heights of Holmes and Sutcliffe, fashioning six century partnerships and averaging slightly over 64 together for the first wicket.

The bowlers had to compensate for Nicholson's illness, which meant that he appeared on only five occasions and took six rather expensive wickets. Robinson and Howard Cooper, another steady rather than penetrative seamer, excelled themselves and in that year at least Cope and Phil Carrick, the slow left-armer, were as effective as any spin combination in the country. Yorkshire lost once in the championship, equalling the distinction of 1946, so spirits were reasonably high in the May of 1976. For once Yorkshire squared up to the challenge of a new season with justifiable optimism.

Sickeningly, Old broke down on the opening weekend with knee trouble that restricted him to 119 overs and seven wickets. Boycott promptly joined the sick parade after being hit on the right hand in the Sunday Roses clash at Old Trafford, standing down through nine successive matches at a time when he hoped to be consolidating the gains of the previous summer.

Eighth place, then, did not represent anything like a disaster and the patient public were ready to give the players another chance. This act of faith proved justified in the early stages of 1977, for Yorkshire got through twelve matches unbeaten, keeping in touch with the leaders in the championship and overcoming the lengthy loss of Old through injury after a burst which brought him sixteen wickets at 10.56 each in four outings.

After twelve games on the treatment table, Old made an explosive return, thrashing the second fastest century of all time in 37 minutes against Warwickshire at Edgbaston. Pride of place is accorded to Percy Fender, who, *Wisden* and contemporary reports tell us, reached three figures in 35 minutes for Surrey against Northants at Northampton in 1920.

There must, though, be some doubt about this matter, for the official scorebook contains a number of inconsistencies which raise questions about the accuracy of the timing associated with Fender's great effort. Yorkshire's scorer in 1977 was Ted Lester, a meticulous expert with a foolproof, double-check system far in advance of anything used over fifty years earlier, yet his considerable resources and those of Warwickshire's Charlie Groves were stretched to the limit by the Birmingham pantomime. They were, though, certain about the span of Old's assault and those who witnessed the proceedings, in the course of which fielders broke all records in getting the ball back to the bowler, were inclined to think that really this century could not have been beaten for time. The pitch offered little hope to the bowlers as the contest drifted along without serious shape, Warwickshire declaring at 204 for three in reply to Yorkshire's 353 for five. As Yorkshire helped themselves to batting practice, Warwickshire concentrated on improving a sagging over-rate. Leading fast bowler Bob Willis operated from four paces to hurry things along and, with Old at the wicket, Rohan Kanhai and John Whitehouse, much more in their element as batsmen, rushed through some gentle overs, Warwickshire managing to bowl forty-two in only ninety minutes – a hectic rate by any standards.

Indeed, the bowling never revealed more than mildly serious intent, but Old, for his part, hit hard and often. 'It was not my fault Warwickshire bowled so badly,' he said defensively in the face of unexpected complaints about the day's drama. 'When the ball was there to be hit, I hit it.' He used up a lot of time in getting to 50 and had been in for almost ten minutes when reaching double figures. Twenty-eight minutes elapsed before he passed the half-way stage. 'Once I had got to that point, Jim Love came down to my end and said I ought to be in line for the fastest hundred of the season, so I just kept going with that in mind,' added Old, who made 50 more from twenty-one deliveries in a brutal blitz.

Altogether he hit six sixes – one of them out of the ground – and thirteen fours in his 107 which occupied forty-one minutes and took in seventy-six balls. If that was remarkable, the subsequent effort by Lancashire's Steve O'Shaughnessy was more so. He equalled

Fender's thirty-five minute time in September 1983, making his runs against the casual bowling of David Gower (9-0-120-0) and James Whitaker (8-1-87-0) to defy cricketing logic.

Yorkshire's season fell into disarray once Boycott had come to terms again with the England selectors, returning to the fold in the third Test against Australia at Trent Bridge, where he put together a very slow but vital century. One fascinating aspect of their unbeaten sequence was that Yorkshire fielded first on each occasion – six times by choice – and when at last Boycott decided to bat on winning the toss they lost to Kent. Whether that decision or the one which had just brought the announcement of his renewed selection by England weighed the heavier in the balance is a matter of opinion, but the reawakening of his international ambitions had far-reaching consequences.

From that point, Yorkshire lost five out of nine matches and differences arose within the club.

These dragged on into a bitter winter, with Don Brennan, now a member of the cricket committee, calling for a change of captain and being rebuked in turn by the county chairman Arthur Connell. Brennan based his case on the claim that Boycott did not possess the qualities that inspired others and that it made more sense to have a man in charge who was more or less present all the time.

Brennan put forward Cope as the logical alternative in a local radio broadcast which publicised divisions within the ruling body and pushed a number of angry members into forming what they called the Reform Group. They campaigned on Boycott's behalf and demanded that Brennan be expelled. This was unconstitutional, but he did lose his place on the cricket sub-committee while the 'reformers' continued to challenge the committee as a whole.

For a while a sense of collective responsibility papered over the cracks, and the erratic nature of Yorkshire's cricket was illustrated by another upsurge which carried them to fourth in 1978. The revival did not save Boycott, who was replaced by Hampshire for the following year. The committee had acknowledged the need to modernise their administration by inviting Ray Illingworth to become team manager in 1979, neglecting to consult Boycott, and, without allowing the two an opportunity to work together, they went on to set up a new management team.

Mr Connell rubbed salt into an already substantial wound when he informed the world that the decision had been taken not so much

Bill Athey, who became the youngest player after Len Hutton to score a first-class century for Yorkshire, made his debut in 1976. (*Mike Brett*)

because of what Boycott had done but more because of what he was, although inconsistently he placed much emphasis on the offer of a further two-year contract as a player. As he pondered the pros and cons, Boycott had every reason to feel cheated.

Yorkshire had done well to overcome serious injury problems and Test calls. Most of the bowlers, including Graham Stevenson, a young seamer from Ackworth who had become a regular member of the senior squad without quite fulfilling his enormous potential, wrestled with a series of niggling strains, while Cope, under the throwing cloud again, went away to work on his action.

The team won ten of their twenty-two championship fixtures, losing three, and the results under Boycott and Hampshire, who deputised when the former represented England, were eagerly analysed. The figures were: Boycott P12, W5, D6, L1; Hampshire P10, W5, D3, L2 and they proved nothing. Boycott, throughout his years in charge, had been the most consistent scorer, while Hampshire had reliably backed him up at a slightly lower level. The latter had also figured at the centre of a controversy at Northampton, where he batted so slowly that the committee warned him that they would not tolerate a repetition.

Legal issues were raised by the Reform Group, who forced a special general meeting at Harrogate, where the cricket committee survived a vote of no confidence and the ship of state narrowly avoided capsizing in some decidedly rough waters before Hampshire and Illingworth got their hands on the helm. Hampshire had finally displaced Boycott at the top of the averages in that summer – 54.18 to 50.94 – the first change since 1963, but inevitable pressures checked his advance.

The new captain found that the worries of leadership affected his batting, and he stumbled slightly in 1979, when Yorkshire slipped down to seventh, for he failed to make a century for the first time since 1973. Boycott, having confirmed his loyalty by playing on, packed his infrequent appearance with runs – 1,160 in the championship for an incredible average of 116 – as he became the only man to beat the three-figure barrier twice. Bouncing briskly in, cap firmly squared up on his head, he led the bowlers, too, his nine wickets costing 9.33, and this double-linked him with George Hirst, who topped both sets of averages in 1910.

Boycott and Lumb claimed nine of the eleven centuries, while Carrick fitted in as a commanding all-rounder – 621 runs and fifty-one wickets – but Old was restricted by side muscle strains and Arnie Sidebottom, a hostile medium-paced seamer and neat batsman, could not command a reliable rhythm largely because he was distracted by soccer at which he was good enough to play for Manchester United at one stage.

Captaincy again became the focal point of heated discussions and thoughtful calculations in 1980, when Hampshire hurt his thumb and Lumb and Old each tried his hand to gain one win and two draws. The tip of a potentially dangerous iceberg bobbed above the surface over contracts.

Boycott, Hampshire and Old were made special cases in mid-season, being awarded further terms, and this caused some rumblings of discontent from others in the dressing room. Eventually, the club chairman, Michael Crawford, who had taken over from Mr Connell, travelled down to Sheffield to promise that in future all contracts would be discussed at the same time. This was a far cry from the days of Lord Hawke and Brian Sellers and the gesture, however well meaning, did not help to restore discipline which had become a bit ragged at the edges.

The batting in 1980 had a built-in reliability, with nine players averaging more than 30, but the bowling seldom did itself justice and Yorkshire had to settle for sixth place in the championship. As a sign of the times and an indication of the shortage of first-class talent, Yorkshire were able to field a full eleven of capped players against Derbyshire at Scarborough on September 3 for the first time since 1968.

Hampshire had had enough by the end of the summer. He resigned, making way for Old, who came into the job a little bit by the side door since Lumb had also been asked what he thought about leading the side. The tall, self-effacing opener opted for the quieter life and Yorkshire had reached a point at which every action came under the microscope of speculation about the motive behind it. The divisions created by the handling of Boycott grew wider for a variety of reasons, none of which helped the county to get back onto its feet.

Rapidly changing attitudes among the players and the supporters were not readily understood by some sections of the committee, with the result that misunderstandings occurred. As Yorkshire slipped back down to tenth in 1981, they struggled with a depressing catalogue of physical misfortune. They had all ten capped players available only once and even then – against Derbyshire at Chesterfield on August 22 – Old was less than one hundred per cent.

Hampshire and Bairstow did duty when Old dropped out before the uncapped Neil Hartley gained promotion – a unique honour for a professional – against Warwickshire at Scarborough on July 29. Illingworth, motivated by a desire to safeguard the future, took a calculated gamble, which flew in the face of tradition, but Hartley handled matters with unexpected maturity. He sensibly ignored disapproving murmurs and made light of the weakened sides which he inevitably had to lead.

During the days of the depression, as real to Yorkshire cricket as the industrial disasters were to an earlier generation, it became the habit to look back with enchantment to happier times and many youngsters found themselves weighed down with the matching millstones of a glorious past and continually high public expectation. The summer of 1981 was, however, illuminated by two Colts who promised to be very special.

Martyn Moxon came to the forefront in June, when he emulated

Neil Hartley, who had the distinction of captaining Yorkshire as an uncapped player in 1980. (*Mike Brett*)

Cecil Tyson by scoring a century on his debut. His 116 off the rampant Essex attack represented an innings of exceptional quality since it came as Yorkshire, following on, fought a long rearguard action to avoid defeat. The twenty-one-year-old Barnsley batsman permitted no flutter of nerves to mar his progress as he claimed another distinction by punishing Derbyshire at Sheffield, where he scored 111 to become the only Yorkshireman to record a century in each of his first two home matches.

Three months later Paul Jarvis, a well-built boy from Redcar, made his debut at the tender age of sixteen years and seventy-five days against Sussex at Hove – the youngest player to appear for Yorkshire in first-class cricket. Although he did not earn a wicket with his medium-paced seamers, he, like Moxon, confirmed that he had the temperament to make the most of his natural gifts.

Boycott could not escape the spotlight for long and an off-the-cuff comment in public about the policy of leaving him out of the Sunday League – Hampshire's age also counted against him in the

In the Wilderness

Celebration for Martyn Moxon, who became the second Yorkshire player to score a century on his debut when he made 116 against Essex at Headingley in June, 1981. Congratulating him are (left to right): Arnie Sidebottom, Peter Whiteley, Richard Lumb and Chris Old. (*Andrew Varley*)

same way – angered Illingworth, who suspended him from the last two championship matches. This storm broke at Scarborough, where a public demonstration in Boycott's favour fractionally delayed the start of play in the Northants fixture as complaining customers accompanied the umpires out into the middle.

Old sought to clear the air by conducting a poll which unearthed evidence that the England opener did not enjoy universal popularity among his colleagues, although subsequent events did not support that conclusion. As Yorkshire twisted and writhed on the horns of a monstrous dilemma, unsure whether to forgive Boycott or back Illingworth, they bought some breathing space by instituting an in-depth inquiry into all aspects of their operation. The aim, presumably, was to restore confidence in the ruling body, but not a lot emerged that was new, and the club wisely rejected a recommendation to dispense with Boycott, who gradually came to a better understanding with Illingworth.

In this respect Yorkshire were lucky, for the two of them provided

'Welcome to Headingley,' said the computerised scoreboard, but Chris Old had lost the captaincy and was on his way to Warwickshire seven months after this picture was taken on the the day the county reported back for training in 1982.
(*Yorkshire Post*)

the backbone of solid, professional experience, especially as Hampshire sought his release during the winter of 1981 and joined Derbyshire. Privately, Boycott and Illingworth each expressed admiration for the other's ability and by degrees the message got through. Boycott actually earned nomination as vice-captain for the championship, sharing the job with Hartley, who was given the task of understudying Old in the one-day games, but whichever way Yorkshire turned they ran head-first into crisis and another turmoil lurked around the corner in 1982.

The team went through the agonies of a dreadful run which culminated in a terrible hammering at the hands of the Northants batsmen at Middlesbrough in June. On the Saturday of the championship engagement and in the Sunday League, Northants amassed 664 runs for seven wickets from 121 inept overs and with morale at something below rock-bottom Yorkshire concocted a remedy that threatened to kill or cure. Two weeks after his fiftieth birthday Illingworth picked up the distant threads of his playing career.

He displaced the sacked Old after testing the waters by making what everyone had been led to believe was a 'one-off' appearance in a friendly game with Zimbabwe at Sheffield, where he convinced cricket chairman Ronnie Burnet and, more importantly, himself that he could defy the years to cope with the physical demands. 'I have looked after myself and stayed pretty fit,' he explained. 'In addition, I have taken part regularly in the nets, so if I am careful there is no reason why I should not come through all right.'

Obviously limited in the field, he nevertheless used his expertise to check the decline and Yorkshire hung on to tenth position, reaching the comparative calm of September with just one defeat. Gloucestershire inflicted this at Bradford, where by capricious coincidence Boycott captained the team for the first time since 1978 because Illingworth had a leg strain.

Old, understandably depressed, did not have a good time as a bowler, his short ration of forty-seven wickets costing 26.14 runs each, and, in the face of a substantial financial loss, Yorkshire cut their staff, releasing among others the man who had begun the season as captain. Illingworth sensed that Old had lost the yard of pace that made him a dangerous strike bowler and the county could hardly afford to retain him as a one-day seamer, but, however logical the thinking, someone had got something very wrong.

Sadly this feeling followed the club into 1983, when the celebration of the first-class game's 150th anniversary in the county proved distinctly muted. Indeed, complete disaster was averted only by success in the Sunday League which brought the first major trophy for fourteen years.

Illingworth could claim this as a personal triumph, for he enjoyed a remarkable run of luck with the toss, winning it on eleven out of fourteen occasions. Thus he could make the opposition bat first and organise an effective run-saving operation, usually assisted by slow pitches, in which he figured so prominently that at the age of fifty-one he headed the national averages for the Sunday competition.

Satisfaction in this direction contrasted sharply, however, with the misery of last place in the Championship for the first time, especially as Yorkshiremen have steadfastly and rightly continued to regard the three-day game as the true test of the age-old skills. The team achieved just one victory and, as this came against Hampshire at Southampton, they completed a home programme without winning a game – another unwanted record.

In one dismal spell in 1983 they lost four successive matches, the worst sequence since 1947, and in the shadow of all these disappointments there was further friction between Boycott and Illingworth, the leading personalities. Understandably, Ronnie Burnet, in his

The 1983 line-up (from left to right): back row – Colin Johnson, Jim Love, Arnie Sidebottom, Alan Ramage, Nick Taylor, Martyn Moxon, Simon Dennis, Paul Jarvis, Eric Brailsford (physiotherapist), Steven Rhodes; front row – Kevin Sharp, Phil Carrick, Bill Athey, Richard Lumb, Doug Padgett, Ray Illingworth, Geoff Boycott, Graham Stevenson, David Bairstow, Neil Hartley. (*Yorkshire Post*)

role as cricket chairman, had held them up at the pre-season luncheon as shining examples in terms of professionalism, but differences existed.

These centred largely on Boycott's scoring rate, which dropped some way below what the captain regarded as acceptable against Nottinghamshire at Worksop and subsequently Gloucestershire Cheltenham. As a matter of record, Boycott scored 140 not out, yet, while he did so, Yorkshire struggled to 297 for four from 100 overs and a close of play total of 344 for five, and he used up 247 deliveries in his six-and-a-half-hour innings. The pity of it all was that Boycott was otherwise busily putting together his second best season for Yorkshire, eventually scoring 1,941 runs, an aggregate he exceeded just once, in 1971, when he reached 2,221.

He came agonisingly close to 1,000 runs in August, reaching 984 and producing some remarkable statistics along the way. The most impressive of these were squeezed into the fixture with Nottinghamshire at Bradford, where Boycott gave another casual demonstration of his stamina by being on the field throughout the game.

In the Wilderness

On the last day, Boycott completed his second century of the match – the third occasion on which he had topped 100 in each innings in all matches and the second on which he had done it for Yorkshire. His unbeaten 141 included 103 runs between the start of play and lunch – a rare enough feat to provide the statisticians with much food for thought.

This is an area in which research involves a number of difficulties and the facts are not easily established. Thus no list is likely to be one hundred per cent accurate, for some instances may be missed through lack of definite information and others slipped in owing to misleading reports. Percy Holmes, for instance, is credited by many people with an actual century – that is beginning his innings at the start of play – before lunch against Northamptonshire at Harrogate in 1921, yet contemporary accounts indicate that he was 96 at the break and reached three figures immediately afterwards.

Bearing this in mind, it is reasonably safe to say that, so far as Yorkshire are concerned, Boycott joined a fairly select list of batsmen who have made one hundred runs in the first session. The men concerned are:

CENTURY BEFORE LUNCH

First day

J.T. Brown	107 *v* Nottinghamshire at Nottingham, 1896
D. Denton	100* *v* Somerset at Taunton, 1897
J.W. Rothery	118 *v* Hampshire at Bournemouth, 1905

Second day

W. Bates	108 *v* Kent at Maidstone, 1881
G.H. Hirst	106 *v* Gloucestershire at Dewsbury, 1900
D. Denton	101 *v* Cambridge University at Cambridge, 1903

Third day

G. Ulyett	107 *v* Middlesex at Sheffield, 1884
J.T. Brown	100* *v* Australians at Bradford, 1899
D. Denton	110 *v* Leicestershire at Sheffield, 1899
G.G. Hirst	108 *v* Surrey at the Oval, 1904
D. Denton	109* *v* MCC at Scarborough, 1908

100 RUNS ADDED TO OVERNIGHT SCORE BEFORE LUNCH

Second day

E. Wainwright	0 to 104	(104) v Sussex at Sheffield, 1892
J.T. Brown	116 to 233*	(117) v Sussex at Sheffield, 1897
G.H. Hirst	84 to 188	(104) v Surrey at the Oval, 1899
J.T. Brown	20 to 128	(108) v Leicestershire at Huddersfield, 1900
S. Haigh	4 to 104*	(100) v Nottinghamshire at Sheffield, 1901
G.H. Hirst	21 to 153	(132) v Leicestershire at Dewsbury, 1903
W. Rhodes	97 to 201	(104) v Somerset at Taunton, 1905
M.W. Booth	47 to 163*	(116) v Worcestershire at Worcester, 1911
D. Denton	5 to 120	(115) v Middlesex at Lords, 1919
D. Denton	26 to 149*	(123) v Worcestershire at Worcester, 1920
A. Wood	7 to 123*	(116) v Worcestershire at Sheffield, 1935
E.I. Lester	2 to 113*	(111) v Derbyshire at Scarborough, 1947
L. Hutton	2 to 102*	(100) v Somerset at Huddersfield, 1950
W.H.H. Sutcliffe	70 to 171*	(101) v Worcestershire at Worcester, 1952

Third day

G.H. Hirst	29 to 143*	(114) v Nottinghamshire at Scarborough, 1900
W. Rhodes	1 to 105	(104) v MCC at Scarborough, 1901
M. Leyland	52 to 153*	(101) v Hampshire at Bournemouth, 1932
G. Boycott	14 to 117*	(103) v Nottinghamshire at Bradford, 1983

The Nottinghamshire engagement also marked the sensational first appearance of Ashley Metcalfe, a nineteen-year-old from Farsley in the Bradford League. He stroked his way to a stylish 122, thus becoming the third and youngest Yorkshireman to score a century for the county on his first-class debut.

Alongside Moxon, Metcalfe offered hope for the future, despite the long-running arguments which brought the club into increasing ridicule. These hit the headlines again on October 3, when the committee decided by eighteen votes to seven not to give Boycott another contract. Inevitably the reaction from many members was both angry and immediate, forcing Yorkshire to reconsider although they came to the same conclusion by eighteen votes to eight. The winter was dominated by angry exchanges which involved barristers, the courts and considerable expense before, in the end, the committee were heavily defeated at a special meeting in Harrogate. Forced to resign they were routed at the subsequent polls as members turned to a new administration which included Boycott as the district representative for Wakefield and Close who, standing successfully in Bradford, became cricket chairman. The biggest revolution in the club's history brought a complete change of management.

Chapter 12

TACKLING THE TOURISTS

The Australians bowed to the might of Yorkshire in the course of their first visit to England in 1878 and since then they have more often than not found their regular appointments with the county something akin to an extra Test. That initial meeting staged at Huddersfield on May 30 and 31, drew large crowds to see the tourists win by six wickets, aided by some hostile bowling from 'The Demon' Frank Spofforth. Honours were even following the return at Sheffield, where Yorkshire tightened their fielding and had nine wickets to spare.

Oddly enough, the county did not beat Australia again until 1890, despite taking part in thirteen matches. Five games were arranged in 1882 – two at Bradford and one each at Sheffield, Dewsbury and Middlesbrough – with Australia winning three and drawing the other two, a sequence which, together with the associated familiarity, bred some contempt among the customers, who stayed away in financially worrying numbers.

Ted Wainwright made the first century for Yorkshire against the tourists – 105 in 1888 to help guarantee a draw – but Bobby Peel and George Ulyett shared the spoils in 1890 as Yorkshire completed their only double over them – by seven wickets at Sheffield and by eight wickets at Bradford. Peel's haul added up to 44 runs for once out and twelve wickets for 69 on the first occasion, while Ulyett's ten for 85 was decisive on the second.

Yorkshire added another victory in 1893 – by 64 runs at Sheffield, where their fielding accounted for the difference between the sides. The Australians dropped a host of catches – five in the second innings – and these proved expensive luxuries in a tight tussle. Yorkshire made 137 and 71 against 84 and 60, with Peel and Wainwright doing most of the damage. To balance this, the tourists compiled their biggest score against Yorkshire in the same year – 470 at Bradford, with George Giffen hitting 171. He had been thoughtlessly rested from the first match and was hastily called up when the Australians realised the strength of the county challenge.

Among the other notable performances were a return of eight for

Ted Wainwright – it was not uncommon for his fingers to bleed when he bowled.

78 by Schofield Haigh at Bradford in 1896, when Australia won by 140 runs, and splendid batting six years later by John Brown, whose innings of 84 and 167 enabled him to stand as the first player to aggregate over 250 in one of these fixtures.

The greatest drama unfolded at Leeds in 1902, when huge crowds witnessed one of Yorkshire's finest hours. On the first day 35,705 spectators poured through the turnstiles, stormed and captured the reserved seats and spread themselves around the boundaries. Many were drawn by the presence of Victor Trumper, an immortal among cricketers and a batsman with few if any peers.

They nodded knowingly when, opening for the Australians, he stroked his way to 38, the highest score in either first innings as Yorkshire replied with 107 to the visitors' 131. The pitch looked soft on the second morning and interest centred on Wilfred Rhodes, whose spin, the experts thought, would bite. Lord Hawke held a different view, however, preferring to use George Hirst and the Hon.

F. S. Jackson and he was brilliantly vindicated by this pair, who swept aside the cream of Australian batting for a mere 23 – their lowest total against Yorkshire. Hirst took five for nine and Jackson five for 12 and they received half of the ball each as a memento. The details of that famous innings were:

Australia	*second innings*	
Trumper	b Hirst	7
Duff	c Jackson b Hirst	0
Hill	st Hunter b Jackson	1
Gregory	not out	10
Darling	b Hirst	1
Noble	b Hirst	2
Armstrong	b Hirst	0
Hopkins	lbw b Jackson	0
Kelly	b Jackson	0
Jones	b Jackson	0
Howell	c Hunter b Jackson	0
extras		2
		23

Six of the batsmen were bowled, one lbw and one caught at the wicket and so commanding was the bowling that the ball barely cleared the square throughout the entire innings.

Yorkshire had to wait for sixty-six years for their next success, although only the weather robbed them at Hull in 1904, when they made 370 and, after dismissing the Australians for 148, had them at 158 for eight in the second innings.

The spread of cricket brought Yorkshire into contact with the South Africans as early as 1894, but the Springboks began with no more than an expensive exploratory expedition, losing to Leeds and District and Scarborough and District. They were not much better in 1901, when Yorkshire won by 151 runs at Harrogate, doing South Africa the honour of putting into the field a strong side when, as they pressed their championship challenge, they might have preferred to rest their senior players in the face of such weak opposition.

A cabman, perched outside the ground, was the victim of a notorious accident when a huge hit from one of the South African batsmen soared over the primitive fence and dislodged him from his seat. He sent a letter demanding damages which was ignored and finally dropped the case which he took up in the heat of the moment with his dignity at stake.

The South Africans gradually stiffened their resistance, eventually winning with quite a bit in hand at Bradford in 1907, which was not

The lazy, hazy days of summer at Headingley in 1959 – the major centre for Yorkshire cricket with which the tourists are most familiar.

altogether surprising since there had been a set-back against the West Indians a year earlier. Then Yorkshire paid the penalty for not employing their full resources and took a hiding, notably from a pace bowler called Ollivierre, who captured seven for 23 in a total of 50 as the West Indians won by the massive margin of 262 runs.

Yorkshire and Lancashire forged an unlikely alliance when the Australians returned in 1909, causing some puzzled and disturbed murmurings about the nature of things on both sides of the Pennines. The respective committees organised this joint representation to oppose the tourists at Hull and Old Trafford, but even the heavens wept at the sight, spoiling both matches and persuading officials to abandon an idea which literally flew in the face of reason.

One of the high points in the series between Yorkshire and the Australians came at Sheffield in 1930, when leg-spinner Clarrie Grimmett took all ten wickets. Grimmett, with 144 victims at 16.85 runs each, was easily the tourists' most potent force that summer, his importance in the Australian scheme of things being thrown into sharp focus at Bramall Lane.

Holmes and Sutcliffe put Yorkshire on a firm footing, the latter making 69 to dominate the exchanges until the total reached 120. A suitably imposing score brightened the horizon on a dull, overcast day, but Grimmett, who operated with controlled ingenuity, gathered up the remaining wickets with a mystifying mixture. Seven fell to him for 16 in one particularly destructive burst while his colleagues toiled away without threatening to interfere with his personal demolition job.

They sent down forty-three overs for 104 runs. Grimmett delivered twenty-two to collect his ten for 37, keeping the long procession of batsmen guessing with his low trajectory, curling breaks and top spinners. Three were stumped, far out of their ground, failing miserably to invent a stroke that might fit in with the position of their feet – a sure indication of utter bewilderment. Australia added to this by making 320 in their turn, but thanks to the weather Yorkshire did not have to face another trial by spin.

All India were added to the list of touring countries in 1911, when they tumbled to defeat by an innings and 43 runs at Hull, but while the strength of some parties has to be questioned, this international flavour added spice to the domestic dish and catered for growing appetites.

World-famous players offered a new challenge, something different, and Yorkshire relished the thought of testing their arms against the rest of the world. Victory, defeat and, albeit to a lesser degree, draws all in their own way brought a new dimension, being the by-product of some splendid cricket. A case in point brings us forward to 1938 and a drawn match with the Australians which all Yorkshire passionately believed must have been won but for rain on the third afternoon.

The advantage over the years had rested substantially with the Australians, much to Yorkshire's annoyance, so there was a good deal of excitement at Bramall Lane when Brian Sellers took the initiative by sending in the tourists on a soft pitch. A crowd in the region of 35,000 watched the grim struggle in which Yorkshire's eager attack was boldly resisted by Don Bradman, with 59, and Lindsay Hassett, with 94, the latter switching from defence to all-out assault as he recognised the danger of running out of support.

His last 44 occupied only twenty-five minutes, so the entertainment came as a consequence of keen tactical appreciation. Yorkshire's main thrust had been delivered by the offspin of Frank

Smailes, who claimed six for 92 in a total of 222, and his Australian counterpart Mervyn Waite took equal satisfaction in the conditions, taking seven for 101 as Yorkshire crumbled to 205, sustained that far by a brave stand of 42 for the eighth wicket between the redoubtable Emmott Robinson and the doughty Arthur Wood.

Batting conditions remained treacherous on the Monday, when Bill Bowes at his most aggressive would, with no more than the basic assistance from the field, have broken the back of the Australian resistance in the second innings. As it was, first Charlie Badcock and then Bradman survived chances to slip, but, putting those blemishes behind them, Yorkshire worked to a purpose, capturing six wickets for 32 as the tail folded, leaving a victory target of 150. Throughout the morning of the last day Yorkshire, with Sutcliffe and Hutton prominent, clawed their way to 83 for three, but heavy and persistent rain long into the afternoon ensured a damp anti-climax.

Sellers came close to victory again ten years later, this time at Bradford, where he deputised for Norman Yardley, who was ill. Most, if not all, the Yorkshire players on duty thought it the best match in which they had taken part and, although Bradman's all-conquering 1948 team eventually edged home by four wickets, they willingly conceded that they were more than a little relieved to escape defeat. Without hesitation they confessed fear on an otherwise untroubled progress around the country. Bradman stood down, conserving his energies, a slight, real or imagined, which Yorkshire took to heart. The Australians, planning for the Tests, also left out their offspinner Ian Johnson, thus putting themselves under some handicap in damp, cold conditions.

A start could not, in fact, be made until the early afternoon and it immediately became clear that, as in 1938, runs were to be at a premium. Yorkshire batted first and were all out for 71, with Keith Miller displaying his extraordinary range by bowling offspin skilfully enough to take six for 42. Hutton, with his limp-wristed facility for removing the venom from the rearing snake-like ball, occupied the crease for almost an hour, but he never suggested comfort and may have unnerved his colleagues, for Yorkshire fell short of their customary standards. Regrouping, they recovered in the field. Frank Smailes took six for 51 and Australia were once more grateful to Miller, who faced up to the crisis with some brave hitting that accounted for two sixes in 34 runs.

Facing a deficit of 30, Yorkshire groped their way to 89, Bill

Tackling the Tourists 135

Johnston mastering the art of spin bowling this time to emerge with six for 18 from fifteen overs. The batting continued to attract criticism, but the pitch was such that the county retained a finger-tip grip on the proceedings largely by dint of their bowling. Smailes and Johnny Wardle, pitchforked straight into the action, reduced Australia to 20 for five, breaking through at four and hurrying on amidst a catalogue of errors forced to some extent by the quality of Yorkshire's work and in part by draining confidence.

When a sixth wicket went down at 31, Yorkshire were being carried along by a partisan gathering of their clans buoyed up by the thought that Sam Loxton, nursing a pulled groin muscle, would not bat. The fatal lapse came from poor Hutton, of all people, for he could not quite hold a difficult chance offered to short fine leg by Neil Harvey; an eighteen-year-old on his first tour. Harvey went on to save the day, finishing the contest with a straight-driven six which instantly brought joy and despair to the rival camps.

Frank Smailes had some brilliant bowling performances against the Australian tourists. (*Yorkshire Post*)

Australia nonetheless were left with a healthy respect for Sellers, who by a quirk of coincidence had compiled the first of his four centuries for Yorkshire when taking 104 off the tourists at Sheffield in 1934.

Yorkshire, therefore, had not beaten the Australians since 1902 when they assembled in Sheffield in June 1968, and by local reckoning the time for attending to this omission was long overdue. The portents were not good, for Brian Close and Tony Nicholson were injury absentees, but 11,000 of the faithful gathered to lend weight to the effort, and Trueman, acting captain, won an important toss. The heavy sultry weather of that weekend suggested the ball might swing in the air, but Yorkshire knew considerably more about batting in those conditions than the tourists did about harnessing them to suit their bowling.

Geoff Boycott embarked on one of his scholarly exercises, dealing scornfully with the new ball and then settling to explore the skills of leg-spinner John Gleeson. He embarked on this exercise with the Tests in mind, dissecting the variations of his opponent through the microscope of the forward defensive push, taking meticulous care so that the rest of the match might have been going on in another place.

Yorkshire moved steadily along, calculating that runs in the bank could have extra value if the often threatened rain arrived, which it did on the Monday morning as a low, black, growling storm skirted the ground and cut fifty minutes out of the proceedings. Neither the players nor the supporters were exactly sure what they wanted, for time lost could be precious, but stormy circumstances had to work against the Australians. Trueman extended the innings as long as possible and then throughout the hot, steamy afternoon his bowlers whittled their way through half-formed opposition which leaned heavily on the broad bat and hunched shoulders of Bill Lawry. The tourists' skipper propped up the tattered shell of the Australian reply until easily caught by Trueman at slip as Illingworth made the ball lift and turn sharply. Australia followed on.

They fared no better. Richard Hutton, slinging in a delivery of low full length, yorked the weary Lawry for nought and the flood gates fell open. The visitors' dressing-room in the old Bramall Lane pavilion was situated on the ground floor with a large window looking out onto the rows of seats. The Australians had left it slightly open to allow the passage of essential fresh air and as their leader marched slowly and sadly back to rejoin them it was hurled violently up by a splendidly leering Yorkshireman, who pushed a hawk-like nose into the room and shouted jubilantly: 'Tha's had it now. T' job's over.'

To their credit, the Australians accepted the verdict with good grace, bowing to the truth with half-hearted grins and limp promises of what the rest would do. In reality, only the weather caused any concern. The hovering thunderstorm delayed Tuesday's resumption by twenty minutes and in the growing darkness after lunch Trueman had to use Illingworth and Don Wilson to keep things going as the batsmen asked searching questions about the light.

When the skies brightened briefly, he came back to speed things

The most famous of Yorkshire's father-and-son combinations. Len Hutton and Richard, who both played for England, the former as one of the all-time great batsmen and the latter as a lively all-rounder. Both also had special moments against the Australians. (*Yorkshire Post*)

up in more ways than one and Yorkshire completed one of the greatest performances against any opposition with an innings and 69 runs to spare. Heavy drops of rain sploshed on the excited crocodile which wound its way back into Sheffield city centre, and in surrounding towns and cities drains were blocked and manholes raised by the torrents which swept through streets echoing with the news of the county's doings. Nature composed a fitting symphony to honour the occasion.

In modern terms, of course, the men from Down Under were supplanted at the top of the tree by the upsurge in the Caribbean cavaliers, whose colourful representation provided another facet of the domestic scene and presented new fields for Yorkshire to conquer. The distinction of being the only county to beat the 1963 West Indians in a first-class match was, therefore, keenly appreciated.

The universally popular tourists otherwise bowed the knee only

YORKSHIRE v AUSTRALIANS
at Sheffield
29 June–2 July 1968

Yorkshire *first innings*
Boycott	c Taber b Chappell	86
Sharpe	c Lawry b Gleeson	47
Padgett	st Taber b Gleeson	56
Hampshire	c Lawry b Gleeson	33
Taylor	c Taber b McKenzie	24
Illingworth	not out	69
Binks	c Taber b McKenzie	0
Hutton	c Walters b McKenzie	2
Trueman	c Sheahan b Gleeson	13
Wilson	c Redpath b McKenzie	0
Stringer	not out	12
extras		13
	(for 9 wkts dec.)	355

Fall of wickets: 1–105, 2–162, 3–219, 4–230, 5–287, 6–287, 7–297, 8–330, 9–330.

Bowling: McKenzie 27-7-73-4; Renneberg 19-2-58-0; Connolly 32-16-49-0; Gleeson 47-12-123-4; Chappell 6-0-33-1; Walters 7-5-6-0.

Australians *first innings*
Lawry	c Trueman b Illingworth	58
Redpath	c Binks b Trueman	12
Walters	c Trueman b Hutton	4
Sheahan	c Trueman b Hutton	10
I. Chappell	run out	18
Inverarity	c Stringer b Illingworth	2
Taber	b Illingworth	9
McKenzie	c Hutton b Illingworth	6
Gleeson	b Trueman	4
Connolly	b Trueman	20
Renneberg	not out	0
extras		5
		148

Fall of wickets: 1–26, 2–36, 3–50, 4–97, 5–99, 6–113, 7–119, 8–123, 9–147.

Bowling: Trueman 10.2-2-32-3; Hutton 12-3-37-2; Stringer 4-2-6-0; Illingworth 17-3-44-4; Wilson 9-1-20-0; Taylor 1-0-4-0.

second innings
b Hutton		0
lbw b Hutton		12
c Illingworth b Trueman		62
b Trueman		17
c Hutton b Illingworth		26
lbw b Illingworth		1
st Binks b Illingworth		0
c Binks b Trueman		0
b Illingworth		12
run out		0
not out		4
extras		4
		138

Fall of wickets: 1–8, 2–21, 3–61, 4–111, 5–112, 6–112, 7–113, 8–130, 9–134.

Bowling: Trueman 19-4-51-3; Hutton 12-5-35-2; Illingworth 22-12-23-4; Wilson 13.1-7-25-0; Boycott 1-1-0-0.

YORKSHIRE v WEST INDIES
at Middlesbrough
15–17 May 1963

Yorkshire	*first innings*		*second innings*	
Padgett	c Allan b King	5	retired hurt	2
Hampshire	b King	19	c Solomon b Worrell	25
Sharpe	lbw b Griffith	20	lbw b King	10
Close	b Griffith	23	lbw b Worrell	23
Taylor	lbw b Griffith	10	c Allan b Worrell	13
Stott	c Kanhai b Valentine	65	b Griffith	8
Illingworth	c Allan b King	1	c King b Worrell	28
Trueman	c Allan b Griffith	55	not out	20
Wilson	b Sobers	4	did not bat	
Binks	b Griffith	14	not out	13
Ryan	not out	5	did not bat	
extras		5	extras	3
		226	(6 wkts)	145

Fall of wickets: 1–13, 2–50, 3–61, 4–66, 5–85, 6–95, 7–173, 8–187, 9–219.

Bowling: Griffith 22.2-7-37-5; King 22-4-67-3; Worrell 9-1-19-0; Valentine 17-3-48-1; Sobers 8-1-50-1.

Fall of Wickets: 1–32, 2–50, 3–72, 4–77, 5–105, 6–119.

Bowling: Griffith 19-9-33-1; King 20-3-47-1; Worrell 20-3-62-4.

West Indies	*first innings*		*second innings*	
Worrell	c Close b Ryan	22	b Trueman	18
Carew	c Taylor b Ryan	8	c Illingworth b Ryan	3
Kanhai	b Trueman	19	b Trueman	9
Nurse	c Binks b Trueman	7	b Illingworth	26
Sobers	c Trueman b Taylor	17	b Taylor	29
Butcher	c Binks b Taylor	13	not out	46
Solomon	c Sharpe b Taylor	4	c Hampshire b Trueman	12
Allan	not out	16	c Trueman b Ryan	0
Griffith	hit wkt b Trueman	2	c Binks b Trueman	4
King	c Taylor b Trueman	0	b Trueman	4
Valentine	c Close b Trueman	0	absent hurt	
extras		1	extras	0
		109		151

Fall of wickets: 1–20, 2–37, 3–56, 4–57, 5–75, 6–79, 7–100, 8–103, 9–103.

Bowling: Trueman 20-5-38-5; Ryan 25-11-32-2; Taylor 26-12-33-3; Illingworth 2-1-4-0; Close 1-0-1-0.

Fall of wickets: 1–1, 2–6, 3–8, 4–26, 5–71, 6–71, 7–110, 8–147, 9–151.

Bowling: Trueman 13.3-5-43-5; Ryan 14-3-52-2; Illingworth 12-4-42-1; Taylor 11-5-14-1.

to England in a Test and to Sussex in a one-day challenge game. In the final analysis, Brian Close, in winning the toss and giving his men first use of a covered but variable pitch at Acklam Park, Middlesbrough, gained a vital advantage, while grey skies and cool winds obviously did not suit the West Indians.

The occasion brought a rare instance of Trueman figuring as top scorer in a completed match, his 75 runs for once out being quite remarkable, while his ten wickets for 81 were also easily the best bowling figures. Yorkshire required plenty of courage in the face of hostility from Charlie Griffith and Lance King, for they lost their first six wickets for 95 and John Hampshire with a bruised cheek before a 7,000-strong crowd had settled into their damp seats.

Hampshire was hurt through his own misjudgment. No more than half way towards preparing for the hook, he found a ball from Griffith rising into his face and he turned away to suffer an agonising blow on the side of the head. He recovered to resume his innings in the afternoon, but it was Bryan Stott, surviving a series of edges which sent the ball flying into and through the slips and aided by the belligerent Trueman, who turned the tide. The latter, under the terms of the unwritten agreement between fast bowlers, was spared the pounding to which his team-mates had been subjected and struck some powerful blows.

Yorkshire also kept the batsmen in a constant state of apprehension, avoiding unforced errors both in the field and in the business of tactics to prise out a lead of 117. Immediately, however, Doug Padgett suffered a similar fate to Hampshire. With three added, he shaped to play back to Griffith, failed to accurately assess the pace of the ball, and took it on the cheekbone. The damage, although not so serious as was first thought, prevented his taking any further part in a contest that gripped players and spectators alike.

Close, tightening the screw, sacrificed the potential of his last four wickets, even though Trueman and Jimmy Binks were busily widening the gap. Declaring in the gloom of the early evening, he set a target of 263 in four hours and forty minutes and the tourists demonstrated their concern by promoting first David Allen and then Griffith to partner luckless opener Michael Carew and by appealing vainly against the light.

They lost two quick wickets and under the slate-coloured skies of the last morning, duly folded. Seymour Nurse and Gary Sobers perished bravely on the bayonet of Yorkshire's attacking thrust, adding 45 in fifty frantic minutes, but the swinging ball exposed frailty which magnificent stroke-play could not disguise as the West Indians asked too much of themselves. At twenty past one, Yorkshire were lunching and savouring triumph by the decisive margin of 111 runs. Not even defeat by an innings and two runs in the return at Sheffield could take away the glow of that marvellous occasion.

It is part of the price cricket has paid for re-organisation that touring games have lost some of their fascination. Undoubtedly television has over-exposed the leading figures and, at the same time, destroyed the magic once associated with the progress around the country of the overseas caravan. Too often the visitors give the impression of being preoccupied and, with everything revolving around the Tests and one-day internationals, the sense of occasion which once drew inquisitive and expectant audiences to the county matches has been replaced by a thinly disguised indifference. In the average county versus tourists fixture both parties often have other things on their minds, while Yorkshire no longer get a place in the schedule because the major games at Headingley serve as the county's share of overseas entertainment. Progress does not invariably mean improvement and in losing touch with the values of the past, cricket has sacrificed part of its heritage.

Chapter 13

THE RUN-MAKERS

One of Yorkshire's enduring strengths – and, therefore, one of England's – has been the quality of their openers. Just as Kent have, season after season, cornered the market in exceptional wicket-keepers, Yorkshire continue to unearth batsmen whose character and temperament fit them for the most demanding of roles.

Those who believe that going in first imposes no particular strain should reflect on the shortage of volunteers in those periods when county and country have wrestled with the built-in handicap of uncertain starts to their innings. Yorkshire have served the national cause faithfully to an impressively high standard, and their three best first-wicket players have definitely been Herbert Sutcliffe, Len Hutton and Geoff Boycott, with Percy Holmes only a little behind on the basis of figures.

Each stood as champion in his own generation, although Sutcliffe, the only batsman to complete one hundred centuries for the county, had to operate alongside Jack Hobbs, with whom he figured in many wonderful partnerships for England. Comparison in their case may, indeed, be odious, but at a safe distance we might say that their skills were complementary, making it unnecessary to put one on a higher pedestal than the other.

At the same time, the human being is the most competitive of animals and it is the way of things for one man to be set against another. Sutcliffe, Hutton and Boycott have, therefore, been the subject of much statistical research by amateurs as well as professionals who all find fascination in the relative facts and figures. One line of investigation has taken in the percentage of Yorkshire's runs, including extras, scored by Boycott up to 1981.

In matches won, Boycott scored 23.3 per cent of the total, while his share was 23.7 per cent in drawn games. He made 20.3 per cent of the runs in matches lost, from all of which we get a fair indication of his value.

A similar trend of thought has unearthed the comparative championship figures for Sutcliffe, Hutton and Boycott, although, in the latter's case, the mathematics take us only to 1979. This little table, nonetheless, is still instructive.

	Sutcliffe	Hutton	Boycott
Percentage of team runs	18.3	19.4	23.3
Percentage of times top scorer in an innings	27.3	30.6	38.2

The most important inference we can draw from this is that Sutcliffe and Hutton played in stronger teams than Boycott, which is something we really knew anyway, and we have to look at the men as individuals and personalities.

Sutcliffe became a great player because, like Boycott, he did not ignore weaknesses and, by dealing with them, he transformed them into strengths. He admitted that he lacked the natural grace of Hutton, Hobbs, Wally Hammond or Holmes, but he harnessed his skills in ramrod straight shafts of concentration and had few peers on a difficult pitch. One of the secrets of his on-going success concerned the refusal to be disturbed by a mistake and, having played and missed or after being given a 'life' in the field, he would invariably lean on the bat and survey the scene as if everything was going exactly to plan.

Strangely, well-meaning friends in the Pudsey Britannia club, when he set about the task of extending and perfecting his range, advised Sutcliffe to stick to league cricket. 'You are all right in the nets, but you haven't got the temperament out in the middle,' they told him. Mental toughness that manifested itself endlessly in the most demanding situations also enabled him to ignore such foolishness. He drew strength from an inner certainty, practising, like Boycott, with such determination that the exercise became an end in itself. While his Bradford League colleagues used the nets in a casual way, Sutcliffe would bat, bowl and field as though in a match, calculating each run that had been scored or conceded.

Having paid so much attention to the groundwork, he knew where he stood and he acquired so much confidence in himself that he gave the distinct impression of being haughty. This was accentuated by his fastidious attention to detail in dress and behaviour as he earned recognition for his immaculate turn-out. After the longest of innings, he returned to the pavilion literally without a hair out of place. Bill Bowes, who played with him for many years, recalled: 'No innings ever left him jittery or nervy. Unlike some batsmen whose hands trembled so badly after scoring a century that they could not sign autographs, Herbert would shower, dress in a quiet

A boyhood picture of Herbert Sutcliffe (centre) at the Pudsey Manual Training School, where he was taught the basics of woodworking. (*Fox Photos*)

corner of the dressing-room and then settle down to answer letters or deal with business.'

Sutcliffe also retained a fierce pride in his professional calling, which explains why the ridiculous idea of his becoming an amateur to captain Yorkshire had to be abandoned. As he saw it, professionals had to do everything better than the amateurs, whether in playing or conducting themselves socially, and, as a senior member of the dressing-room, he insisted on the strict observation of a recognised code of conduct.

Character expressed through cricket was never better illustrated and Sutcliffe knew failure only by the standards that he set himself. To others he had an infallibility.

His artistry and dependability became recognised through innings after innings which had as their common starting point a defensive patience, but he could also attack with rare gusto when the opportunity presented itself or the occasion demanded. In his famous assault on the Essex bowlers in company with Morris Leyland at Scarborough in 1932, Sutcliffe advanced his own score from 100 to 194 in forty minutes, while his one hundredth century was a spirited dash to 132 in less than two hours as Yorkshire beat the clock and Gloucestershire at Bradford in the same year.

On another occasion, when trapped on a sticky wicket by Northants at Kettering, Sutcliffe struck ten sixes in 113, although no one else could survive for more than a few desperate overs. When a new scoreboard was erected at Edgbaston in the early 1930s, the fund-raising activities were supervised by a good friend of the Yorkshire team and, at his request, the official opening coincided with Warwickshire's game against the county. During the ceremony the benefactor modestly expressed the hope that a Yorkshireman might record the first century on the board. Sutcliffe quietly said: 'Right, I'll do it.' There was no bravado, just a whispered promise, and Sutcliffe proved as good as his word.

The First World War delayed his entry into the first-class game until he was twenty-four, but in those days there were fewer teenage prodigies and maturity had its place in the order of things. Sutcliffe benefited to an extent for he looked the complete batsman when he began his association with Holmes, eight years his senior, in 1919. The two met for the first time in Leeds while waiting for the tram to Headingley for the nets, so they were by no means strangers when they came together as Yorkshire's opening pair, going on to share in seventy-four century stands together.

Their understanding became instinctive as their running between the wickets confounded the most carefully laid plans of the opposition. They stole singles with absolute certainty to undermine fielding resolve, and extensive research reveals few instances of their running out each other. An average of two mistakes a season can be accepted.

Holmes, because of his age, had his prospects more seriously affected in the conflict between Britain and the Kaiser, but for a long time he and Sutcliffe shared the same birthday – November 24 – although it eventually transpired that Holmes had been mistaken, having been born on November 25. He grew up at Oakes, just outside Huddersfield, learning his cricket in the asphalted schoolyard which today stands empty.

Teachers at the turn of the century had clearly defined ideas about cowardice and often fastened the back legs of the boys to the side of the wicket chalked on the wall, thus ensuring that no one could back away from the short ball. It is doubtful whether this restraint was needed for Holmes, who competed with older pupils on merit, for he remained particularly fluent on the leg side, proclaiming in later years that he would have 'given a tanner a time' for deliveries which batsmen tried to avoid altogether.

Holmes, in company with Andy Sandham, of Surrey, found himself pushed into the Test background because Sutcliffe and Hobbs were so successful and he grew to resent the situation. In 1928 he said: 'I am tired of continual disappointment. I have felt sure that someone with influence is keeping me out of the honours. I have never complained before, but I have decided to refuse any further invitations to play in representative games. I shall be quite content to play with Yorkshire.'

Either the authorities overlooked these remarks, which would hardly have been appreciated by either the MCC or the Yorkshire committee, or they accepted the merit of Holmes's argument, for he did get one more Test cap – against India in 1932 and he showed no reluctance to turn out.

His outburst was an isolated incident, for Holmes remained a cheerful member of the first-class 'club' throughout. He always wore pumps in the field and maintained a lively, bouncy presence whatever his position. Eager and speedy in the deep, he could also catch well enough in the slips and he added just as much, if in a different manner, as Sutcliffe to the team. Opponents in some cases feared him more than his famous partner, because he 'scored so quickly,' but Sutcliffe never lingered far behind and sometimes galloped ahead when acceleration was the order of the day.

Sutcliffe was the first Yorkshireman to complete a century of centuries, followed by Hutton and Boycott, but neither of these two completed the feat for the county. Hutton emulated Sutcliffe as a product of Pudsey, progressing to the Yorkshire and England teams, serving his turn as apprentice alongside the master before the Second World War and losing little by comparison.

How many runs he would have scored had there been cricket between 1940 and 1944 is a matter of conjecture, but while the conflict raged on he had to cope with serious injury and once peace came he found himself as the backbone of the England innings. Most of all, the war years denied him the benefits that would have accrued from playing with a really strong side. Instead, he had to shape his cricketing attitudes to suit the needs of others.

When he might have been storming the ramparts he found it necessary to take charge of building them. Hutton's dismissal as often as not signalled a general collapse in the Test arenas of the world, so he resorted to stern self-discipline. The glory of his cover drive remained, which made it all the more a pity that he unfolded it less regularly than either he or the public would have wished.

Hutton, first attending the Yorkshire nets early in 1930 as a mere stripling of fourteen, already understood the fundamentals of batting so well that George Hirst, the finest of coaches, merely said, as an aside: 'There is nothing we can teach this lad,' and the old soldier let nature take its obvious course. Too many alleged experts tamper with youngsters' styles to the detriment of individuality and Yorkshire have been accused of destroying the seeds of ability by seeking to transplant them without sufficient thought.

In that sense Hutton was lucky. Fate did not smile on him all that often afterwards, notwithstanding his promotion as England's first professional captain in 1952. That honour was double-edged in that it carried a heavy price for a man already well aware of how much depended on him. Towards the end of his career, it was suggested that he received preferential treatment within the county and if that is the case, no one had more right.

Only briefly could he indulge himself and give full rein to his classic strokes – usually relaxing in the county fixtures of no championship significance – but for the most part his runs mattered more than the manner in which he gathered them. Although a prisoner of circumstance, Hutton still delighted the eye and for whose who loved the game for itself he illuminated the scene by simply negotiating a maiden over from Ray Lindwall, the superb Australian fast bowler, or from a high-class spinner on a turning pitch.

Ray Illingworth has been in the game longer than most and has seen and understood more than anyone in around thirty years. Having studied the world's best run-makers from the vantage point of bowler, fielder and cricket manager, he still treasures a distant memory of Hutton frustrating bowling intent by the precise placing of his cover drive.

The object lesson came at Scarborough in the carefree atmosphere of the Festival and he stood in awed respect at the non-striker's end while Hutton calmly stroked Peter Sainsbury to the cover boundary time and time again. The Hampshire left-arm spinner, a seasoned campaigner, could, as Illingworth says, 'bowl a bit,' but he was destroyed. 'He finished up with seven men in the covers, but Len, who didn't always enjoy batting, took up the challenge and beat the field almost at will. It may have been Festival entertainment for the spectators, but the battle out in the middle was real enough and the stroke-play was as good as anything I've seen.'

Despite the growth of the one-day game with its instant attraction and run-saving theories, there is still fascination in the battle between bat and ball. Hutton's finest innings, therefore, could well have been no more than 30. He claimed these out of a miserable England total of 52 at the Oval in 1948, when Don Bradman's Australians – candidates for the title of all-time invincibles – were crushing all resistance.

Incredibly he had been omitted from one Test in that summer, the excuse apparently being that he had lost his nerve against Lindwall and Keith Miller, who did not hesitate to use the bouncer when it had the desired effect. At the Oval, Hutton played them with fearless authority before falling to a catch that bordered on the miraculous.

He survived because he managed to minimise the possibility of error and he did not require a second chance, for no false stroke marred his innings as he proved his superiority in unmistakable fashion.

The same qualities were Boycott's hallmark. The most controversial of all Yorkshire cricketers, he, more than Hutton, stood out alone as the outstanding player in a desperately poor Yorkshire team, hemmed in and harassed on all sides by the influx of overseas talent to other counties. He is the one man in over a decade who merits consideration with the best. Boycott, too, has handled severe pressure, for, notably during his term as captain, he represented more than half the side.

An inability to win anything fuelled the flames of argument to an unacceptable extent and Boycott's value has been obscured by the smokescreen that drifted across the club's affairs throughout the 1970s. The popular line of criticism, based on his reputedly slow scoring, insisted that he operated entirely with his own interests uppermost in mind. Thus he averaged over one hundred twice without convincing the doubters that his intentions were honourable. When he did it for the first time in 1971 sinister motives were

OPPOSITE A touch of class from the master – Geoff Boycott in forceful action. (*Tony Edenden*)

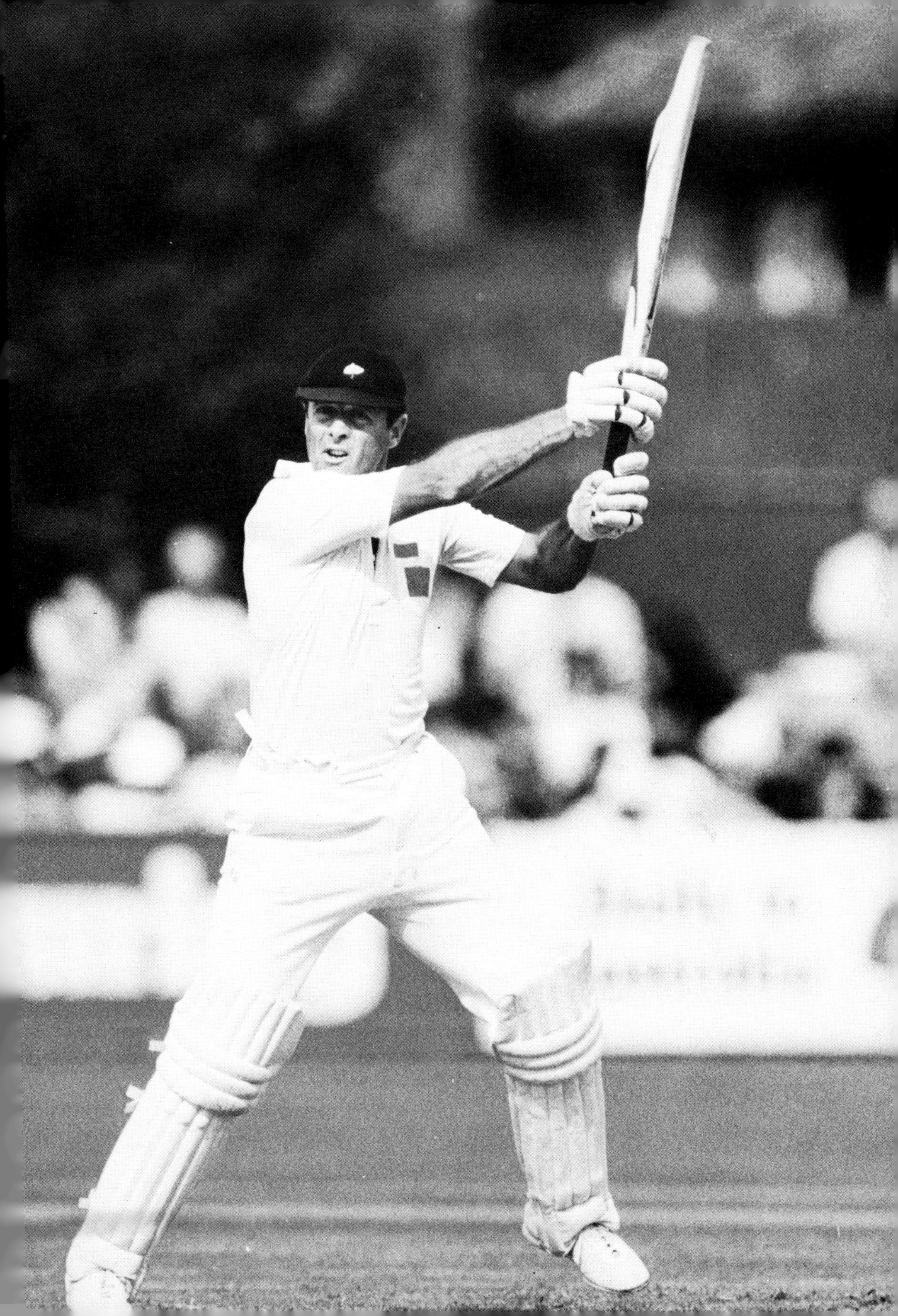

attached to his co-incidental declaration in the final fixture with Northants at Harrogate.

Boycott demonstrated with monotonous regularity that he could score quickly, for there are many examples of match-winning sprints on his part, but, as with Hutton, he experienced few relatively easy moments when he could relax and let others worry. 'I just go out and do my best for the team,' he would say when his detractors grabbed the headlines, 'but many people just do not understand the game. They blame me because I am an easy target as the best batsman.'

Judged on figures, he stands comfortably alongside Sutcliffe and Hutton. The half-remembered, occasionally imagined and usually exaggerated differences of the bar-room debate may separate them, but the statistics are a much more reliable guide.

All three are part of a great tradition to which lesser known Yorkshiremen have also contributed. Among the most important were Jack Brown, from Driffield, and 'Long John' Tunnicliffe, of Pudsey. They combined in a number of prolific partnerships, the highest being 554 at Chesterfield in 1898 and 378 against Sussex in the previous year. Brown died at the tragically early age of thirty-five from congestion of the brain and heart failure. His share of the 554 was exactly 300 and he deliberately broke his wicket to improve the county's chances of victory since there were strictly limited provisions for a declaration in those days.

He had two favourite strokes, the late cut and the hook, which Holmes also used profitably. Brown perfected the hook when opposing counties went to great pains to restrict scoring on the offside and he had some success as a bowler, lobbing up 'donkey drops', which surprised one or two batsmen when well set.

Tunnicliffe gained a world-wide reputation as a slip catcher with 678 victims, while as an emergency wicket-keeper in six matches he stumped nine and caught seven to indicate that this was another area in which he might have made a name for himself. Pudsey Britannia was his first senior club and he caused something of a sensation, for they had to hold a special meeting to admit him as a sixteen-year-old as their rules debarred anyone under eighteen. The biggest hitter in the district, he never lost his enthusiasm for giving the bat a full swing.

Tunnicliffe played his part in the Chesterfield stand – then, of course, the biggest for the first wicket – on an empty stomach. Having spent a virtually sleepless night due to some minor but

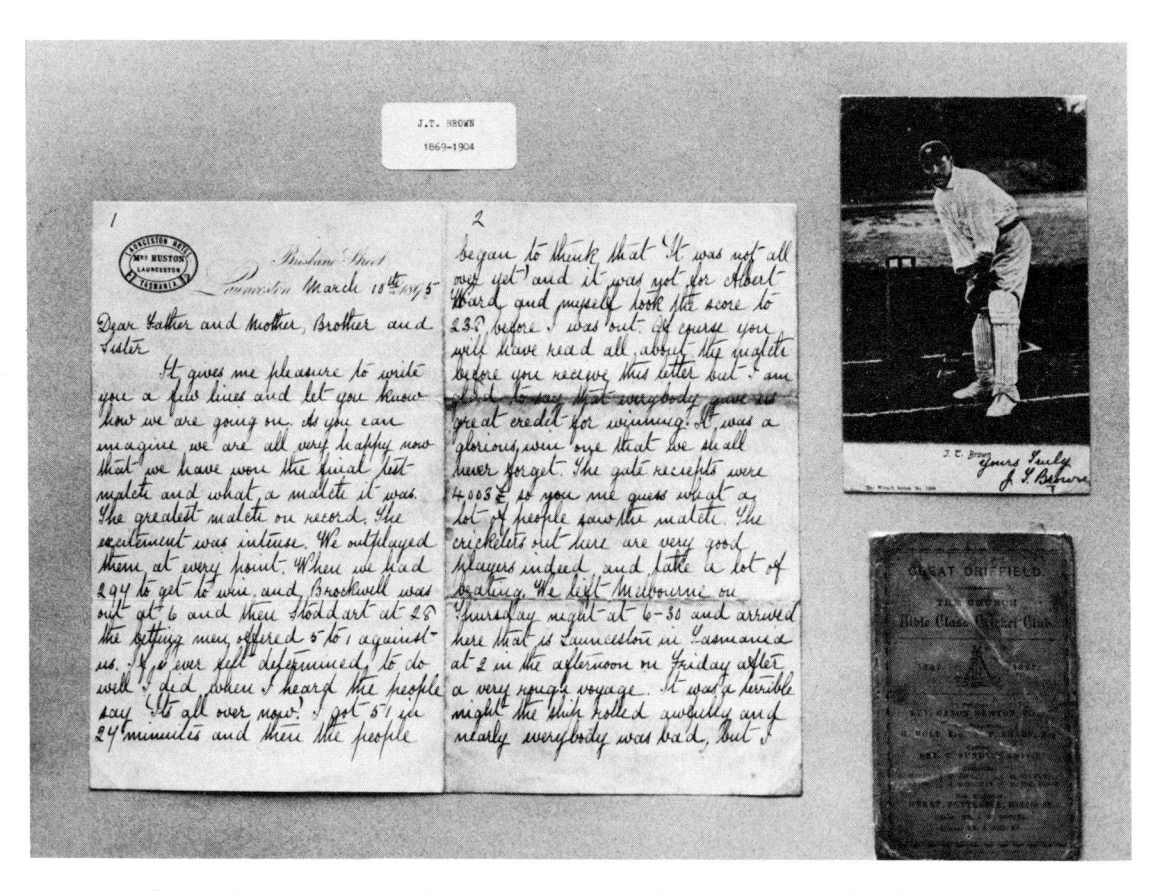

A famous letter home from Tasmania, written by John Brown in 1895 after England had beaten Australia 3–2 in the Ashes series 'Down Under'. There is also a signed picture of the Driffield batsman, together with the 1887 fixture list of the club with which he learned the game. (*Yorkshire Post*)

painful ailment, he had to miss breakfast in order to catch his train. Understandably, therefore, he waited for the luncheon interval with impatience, but a large and hungry crowd overwhelmed the caterers, leaving the players to do the best they could. All Tunnicliffe managed was a twopenny sandwich.

As he and Brown flogged the hapless bowling long into the afternoon, Tunnicliffe observed: 'I didn't know how to keep up my end and I felt I would like to get out and go in search of food.' He stuck to his post to the close, though, with Yorkshire on 480, the remaining runs coming in a hurry under Lord Hawke's instructions. A keen student of cricket, Tunnicliffe developed into Lord Hawke's right-hand man until leaving in 1907 to take up a coaching engagement at Clifton College, where he helped to polish the gifts nature had bestowed on Walter Hammond, who served under him.

Earlier Ephraim Lockwood and John Thewliss had set the pattern, while Louis Hall and George Ulyett formed a famous firm at the head of the Yorkshire innings. The latter pair were nicely balanced, with Hall notorious for his caution and Ulyett much livelier. W.G. Grace, however, observed about Hall: 'He could hit when he had a mind to, but these occurrences were few and far between.' The Batley giant concentrated on giving the county a solid backbone, realising almost from the outset that 'while the public do not readily appreciate the fact, a sticker can be very useful'.

This was certainly true with 'Happy Jack' at the other end. Ulyett's nickname had been coined because of his jovial appearance in the Yorkshire dressing-room on his debut and he gave no reason for anyone to advocate a change. His nature made him into an attacker of the bowling whatever the state of the contest.

Thus he cheerfully ignored the persistant entreaties of his captain, Lord Harris, during a tour to Australia in 1879. With the 'Demon Spofforth on the rampage, Lord Harris urged: 'George, do play steady, we want to win this match.' Apparently deaf, Ulyett, who 'had a hitting fit on', slogged his first three deliveries for four, four and three. Continuing along his merry way, Ulyett savaged the Australians and responded to the advice by explaining: 'I'm sorry, my lord, but I rather feel like hitting them.' Lord Harris gave in. 'All right, damn you, go your own way,' he shouted and then stood back while his partner hit up 55 in half an hour and had 'a rare good time'.

Another dashing stroke-maker, David Denton, followed Ulyett into the Yorkshire side, but many regarded him as being too rash for his own good, despite his excellent figures. They called him 'Lucky Denton', but he always argued that he suffered his share of misfortune without making too much of it by grumbling. For a man who made over 33,000 runs, he opened his account in a lowly position, appearing at number ten on the card in 1894 against Warwickshire at Sheffield. He relied on his instincts with regard to style and did not bother with coaching, putting his faith instead in constant practice in his youth.

'I worked for a soap works and used to go straight to the cricket field, where I practised until nine or ten o'clock at night without thinking of going home for tea. I was generally first there and last away.' Denton excelled in the field as well and his running catches featured prominently in Yorkshire's performances.

He also brought off a coup that George Hirst could not manage

George 'Happy Jack' Ulyett, from Sheffield, who worried Lord Harris when he had one of his 'hitting fits'.

for all his brilliance, for Denton captured the prized wicket of W.G. Grace and, in doing so, caused much merriment in the dressing-room. He gained an lbw decision against the great man with a fairly gentle delivery that simply looked too easy to hit. 'A nonsense ball,' Grace said, seeing nothing to laugh at in the incident, but Denton could turn his arm over to respectable effect, going out of the game with thirty-seven wickets to his name.

Edgar Oldroyd, from Healey, near Batley, was another early order batsman to find himself out of favour for his slow scoring, but to the more discerning observers he, like Hall, sought to serve the collective cause. He adapted his methods on request, for in club cricket he had been regarded as a phenomenon for the rapidity and consistency of his scoring.

He was another member of the short-trousered brigade of precocious youngsters, and, as a thirteen-year-old member of Staincliffe first team in the Spen Valley League, used to give the spectators 'a rare laugh because the pads almost covered my legs'. He began as a medium-paced off-break bowler, but made 50 for Staincliffe against Gomersal when fourteen and got a collection of seven shillings and sixpence, which was a considerable sum in 1903. 'I paid a lot of attention to batting after that,' he recalled.

Making his debut at Hull against Sussex in 1910 as a twenty-one-year-old, Oldroyd was in and out of the side up to the outbreak of war. His average in 1913 was an unsatisfactory 14.03, but the committee did not lose heart when it crept disappointingly up to 15.57 in the following year. In the same way they backed their judgment over Morris Leyland, one of the most fluent and certainly the best loved of the middle-order men, whose christian name was spelled that unusual way on his birth certificate but 'Maurice' on his death certificate. Oldroyd justified their faith with his solid dependability, Leyland advanced much further, and it is a constant theme in the story of Yorkshire cricket that the slow developers have often drawn strength from deep roots.

Oldroyd is credited with an innings of 103 not out against Hampshire at Sheffield in 1921, but in reality he actually scored 99 not out, and the story behind those additional four runs is another warning about taking the statistics from the past at face value.

Yorkshire had to work unexpectedly hard to win their first home match of the championship programme, needing 263 in their second innings. They achieved their target for the loss of four wickets, indebted largely to Oldroyd, who played with great resolution and skill. Unfortunately, he could not get the strike when it mattered most and found himself on 99 as his captain, Derek Burton, made the winning hit.

The umpires duly took off the bails and prepared to pull up the stumps before the Hampshire captain, the Hon. Lionel Tennyson, took a hand. 'Your innings was well worth a century,' he said to the disappointed Oldroyd. He then ordered the game to continue while he bowled a gentle delivery which was gratefully struck to the boundary technically after the game had been completed.

Leyland did not come easily into the team, so he required all his obvious enthusiasm and ready wit, together with brilliant fielding on the boundary edge, to compensate for an early shortage of runs.

Happily he got the time in which to become accustomed to the keen demands of the county circuit and once he had come to terms with them he stood at the heart of the Yorkshire side for many years. A hard-hitting, left-hand batsman, with a flowing drive wide

The Run-Makers

of extra cover, he revelled in the big occasion and scored 1,705 runs against Australia for an average of 56.83.

Pencilled in at number five, when crisis loomed he would say: 'Put me in now, skipper, I'll stop them if I can't score off them!' More than once he went in when England lost an early wicket and rarely did he fail. Bill O'Reilly, the fierce, competitive Australian bowler, rated by the majority of sound judges as among the best two or three of all time, admitted he would give away 70 runs any time to avoid having to bowl at Leyland.

In addition to his 26,180 runs for Yorkshire, Leyland took 409 wickets and his contemporaries advanced the soundly based argument that he would have become a very fine left-arm spinner but for the presence of Wilfred Rhodes and Roy Kilner. Not content to remain in their shadow for ever, Leyland experimented and began delivering the occasional wristy, left-hander's off-break to the right-hand batsman, a style which Johnny Wardle, among others, perfected.

Whenever two batsmen were frustrating Yorkshire or play had declined into dull stalemate, someone in the team would suggest: 'Put Morris on with some of his Chinese torture.' As Roy Kilner explained: 'It's foreign stuff and you can't call it anything else.' On this basis, Leyland took credit for inventing the term 'Chinaman', which has described the left-hander's googly ever since.

Probably Wilf Barber and Arthur Mitchell together illustrate the strength of Yorkshire cricket in the 1920s, for they knew better than most the heartbreak of endless twelfth-man duties when they would have been welcomed into immediate active service by every other county. Both went on to play for England, so they were very good, but not good enough for Yorkshire for a long time.

Barber's claims included a well-recognised brilliance in the field, mostly on the square-leg boundary at a time when it was common practice for batsmen to take up the challenge of short-pitched bowling by hooking. He held dozens of spectacular catches, helped by a keen memory which reminded him whether a particular batsman generally put the ball in front or behind square. He stuck closely to the text book, swinging the bat straight back and maintaining the sweet swing of the pendulum up and down the line until finally trouble with his feet caused him to seek less exacting employment in the Bradford League.

Mitchell had more in common with Hall and Oldroyd than Leyland or Barber, but that was not in itself a bad thing, and he had a key function within the framework of a magnificent squad. 'I give nowt and expect nowt,' he growled and a legion of young hopefuls were to learn that he felt just the same about life when he became the county coach. Any boy who could survive a net session with 'Ticker' Mitchell had nothing to fear on the field.

Among the amateurs, another Mitchell, Frank, demands attention. He had an irregular association with Yorkshire between 1894 and 1904, by which time his business interests had taken him to South Africa. He led Cambridge University in 1896 and assisted them notably in 1894, when his innings of 75 and 92 brought victory by 117 runs over Yorkshire. Mitchell focussed attention on another loophole in the laws against Oxford at Lord's. The regulations demanded that if the side batting second were 120 behind they had to follow on and it was not until 1900 that the fielding captain enjoyed the option of batting again himself. Mitchell did not want Oxford to follow on and when they stood in danger of doing so he instructed E.B. Shine to deliver two no-balls, raising quite a storm. Much-needed change, however, followed his decision.

Mitchell, a fine all-round sportsman, qualified for rugby and cricket Blues as a freshman at Cambridge, where his straight-driving drew favourable comment, and he had the distinction of returning to England in 1912 as captain of the South African tourists.

In more modern times, the stylish Willie Watson followed Holmes from Paddock in the Huddersfield League, while Frank Lowson made his runs so gracefully that the public were apt to mistake him for Hutton when they were partners in the 1950s.

Throughout the 1970s and into the 80s, only John Hampshire came anywhere near keeping up with Boycott, and the Thurnscoe batsman gathered his runs in a robust manner that added welcome acceleration to the middle of many an innings.

Bill Athey, the youngest player after Hutton to make a century for Yorkshire, came from Middlesbrough to brighten the horizons as the county sought to escape from the gloom of so much disappointment under Boycott. His slightly-built frame carried the unexpected power delivered by the fine timer of the ball but he lacked consistency, became disillusioned and departed for Gloucestershire. There remained, however, the glittering promise of Martyn Moxon and Ashley Metcalfe, whose instinctive ability must have drawn a few approving nods from the ghosts of the past keeping a protective eye on their legacy to the world.

YORKSHIRE'S LEADING BATSMEN

	Completed innings	Runs	Average
G. Boycott (1962–83)	499	28,456	57.02
L. Hutton (1934–55)	465	24,807	53.34
H. Sutcliffe (1919–45)	768	38,561	50.20
P. Holmes (1913–33)	625	26,220	41.95
M. Leyland (1920–47)	638	26,180	41.03
W. Watson (1939–57)	367	14,049	38.28
A. Mitchell (1922–45)	479	18,034	37.64
F.A. Lowson (1949–58)	373	13,897	37.25
T.L. Taylor (1899–1906)	112	3,951	35.27
E. Oldroyd (1910–31)	458	15,876	34.66
J.H. Hampshire (1961–81)	635	21,979	34.61
W. Barber (1926–47)	443	15,289	34.51
F. Mitchell (1894–1904)	119	4,090	34.36
E.I. Lester (1945–56)	312	10,616	34.02
G.H. Hirst (1891–1929)	949	32,232	33.96
F.S. Jackson (1890–1907)	308	10,405	33.78
D. Denton (1884–1920)	1,010	33,608	33.27
P.A. Gibb (1935–46)	47	1,545	32.87
M.D. Moxon (1981–83)	46	1,495	32.50
K.R. Davidson (1933–45)	41	1,331	32.46
H. Halliday (1938–53)	261	8,361	32.03
N.W.D. Yardley (1936–55)	364	11,632	31.95
D.B. Close (1949–70)	709	22,650	31.94
W.B. Stott (1952–63)	290	9,168	31.61
J.D. Love (1975–83)	198	6,237	31.50
R.G. Lumb (1970–83)	350	10,991	31.40
J.V. Wilson (1946–62)	658	20,539	31.21
W. Rhodes (1898–1930)	1,035	31,156	30.10
R. Kilner (1911–27)	435	13,014	29.91
P.J. Sharpe (1958–74)	595	17,685	29.72
J.T. Brown (1889–1904)	559	16,380	29.30
J.B. Bolus (1956–62)	161	4,712	29.26
D.E.V. Padgett (1951–71)	711	20,306	28.55
C.W.J. Athey (1976–83)	225	6,320	28.08
R. Illingworth (1951–83)	537	14,986	27.90
K. Sharp (1976–83)	121	3,291	27.19
J. Tunnicliffe (1891–1907)	749	20,109	26.84
K. Taylor (1953–68)	480	12,864	26.80
W.G. Keighley (1947–51)	46	1,227	26.67
H.D. Bird (1956–59)	23	613	26.65
G. Smithson (1946–50)	55	1,449	26.34
C. Turner (1925–46)	234	6,117	26.14
W.H.H. Sutcliffe (1948–57)	239	6,247	26.13
F.E. Greenwood (1929–32)	58	1,458	25.13
B. Leadbeater (1966–79)	209	5,247	25.10

BATSMEN WHO HAVE SCORED 2,000 RUNS IN A SEASON

G. Boycott	2,221 in 1971
D. Denton	2,272 in 1905
	2,223 in 1911
	2,088 in 1912
G.H. Hirst	2,257 in 1904
	2,164 in 1906
P. Holmes	2,144 in 1920
	2,351 in 1925
	2,093 in 1928
L. Hutton	2,448 in 1937
	2,316 in 1939
	2,068 in 1947
	2,640 in 1949
M. Leyland	2,196 in 1933
F.A. Lowson	2,067 in 1950
A. Mitchell	2,100 in 1933
D.E.V. Padgett	2,158 in 1959
P.J. Sharpe	2,201 in 1962
W.B. Stott	2,034 in 1959
H. Sutcliffe	2,236 in 1925
	2,418 in 1928
	2,351 in 1931
	2,883 in 1932
	2,183 in 1935
	2,054 in 1937

TWO CENTURIES IN ONE MATCH

G. Boycott	*v* Nottinghamshire 103 and 105 in 1966
	v Nottingham 163 and 141 not out in 1983
D. Denton	*v* Nottinghamshire 107 and 109 not out in 1906
	v MCC 133 and 121 in 1908
G.H. Hirst	*v* Somerset 111 and 117 not out in 1906
P. Holmes	*v* Lancashire 126 and 111 not out in 1920
L. Hutton	*v* Essex 197 and 104 in 1947
	v Sussex 165 and 100 in 1949
	v MCC 103 and 137 in 1952
E.I. Lester	*v* Northants 126 and 142 in 1947
	v Lancashire 125 not out and 132 in 1948
W. Rhodes	*v* MCC 128 and 115 in 1911
H. Sutcliffe	*v* MCC 107 and 109 not out in 1926
	v Nottinghamshire 111 and 100 not out in 1928

The Run-Makers

BATSMEN WHO HAVE PLAYED THROUGH A COMPLETED INNINGS

G. Atkinson	*v* Nottinghamshire (30) in 1865
G. Boycott	*v* Leicestershire (114) in 1968
	v Warwickshire (53) in 1969
	v Warwickshire (138) in 1971
	v Middlesex (182) in 1971
	v Nottinghamshire (175) in 1979
	v Derbyshire (112) in 1983
T. Darnton	*v* All England (81) in 1865
I. Grimshaw	*v* Kent (36) in 1881
L. Hall	*v* Sussex (31) in 1878
	v Sussex (124) in 1883
	v Sussex (128) in 1884
	v Kent (32) in 1885
	v Surrey (79) in 1885
	v Derbyshire (37) in 1885
	v Sussex (50) in 1886
	v Kent (74) in 1886
	v Gloucestershire (119) in 1887
	v Sussex (82) in 1887
	v Surrey (34) in 1888
	v Gloucestershire (129) in 1888
	v Middlesex (85) in 1889
	v Nottinghamshire (41) in 1891
P. Holmes	*v* Northants (145) in 1920
	v New Zealanders (175) in 1927
	v Northants (110) in 1929
L. Hutton	*v* Leicestershire (99) in 1948
	v Worcestershire (78) in 1949
F.S. Jackson	*v* Cambridge University (59) in 1897
F.A. Lowson	*v* MCC (76) in 1951
D.E.V. Padgett	*v* Gloucestershire (115) in 1962
W. Rhodes	*v* MCC (98) in 1903
	v Essex (85) in 1910
J.W. Rothery	*v* Worcestershire (53) in 1907
W.B. Stott	*v* Worcestershire (144) in 1959
H. Sutcliffe	*v* Essex (125) in 1920
	v Hampshire (104) in 1932
	v Rest of England (114) in 1933
	v Worcestershire (187) in 1934
	v Glamorgan (135) in 1935
	v Oxford University (125) in 1939
G. Ulyett	*v* MCC (146) in 1884
	v Derbyshire (199) in 1887

Chapter 14

THE ALL-ROUNDERS

The enduring genius of Yorkshire's two outstanding all-rounders is measured in the breadth of their accomplishments. Garfield Sobers certainly, Keith Miller possibly, reached similar heights, but nobody sustained brilliance over so long a period in the day-to-day routine of county cricket. Wilfred Rhodes did the double of 1,000 runs and 100 wickets sixteen times between 1898 and 1930; George Herbert Hirst, in addition to his unapproachable double double, managed the more human feat fourteen times in thirty-one years. Rhodes scored 31,156 runs and took 3,608 wickets for Yorkshire; Hirst had 32,232 runs and 2,569 wickets.

An innings of 341 by Hirst against Leicestershire at Leicester in May 1905 is the highest for the county, while the greatest number of wickets in a season – 261 – were taken by Rhodes in 1900. The two were quite simply in a world of their own, so it must be regarded as something of a miracle that they should both be born in Kirkheaton, a tiny village sitting proudly on the outskirts of Huddersfield.

They had to be superbly fit, and Hirst, talking about his fantastic season of 1906, remembered: 'The effect on my legs was so severe that I really feared in August that I might not last out the course. Each day provided a new trial. My legs became like iron and had to be rubbed with oils to get the muscles supple again. It no doubt seems fine to have a record such as that to your credit, but in the physical sense I can say it was not worth it.'

He meant this in the personal sense; for there never has been a better, more genuine team man, nor a kindlier soul. Hirst had his heart in Yorkshire cricket and never neglected his obligations. He learnt all his cricket out in the middle and perfected his skills by constant application – 'there will never be any other road that leads to success' – as he found his feet.

The most devastating weapon in his considerable armoury eventually became swerve. With this he destroyed batsmen, for, as one downcast victim ruefully complained: 'I don't know how you can be expected to play a ball that appears to be coming straight but when it reaches the wickets is like a very fast throw from cover point.'

Hirst, in his thoughtful way, noticed that occasionally the yorker, which he used to great purpose, would swerve in the air, so he set out to investigate. 'Experience showed me that in certain circumstances the ball will swerve quite clearly,' he said. 'The most favourable conditions are where the ground is surrounded by trees and there is a nice soft breeze with a little moisture in the atmosphere. The best wind, in my view, is the half head wind – in my case, as a left-arm bowler, from third man. I held the ball with the seam straight between first and second fingers, with the thumb and third finger supporting the ball.'

He considered that the flattening of the seam accounted for the disappearance of swing after nine or ten overs, adding: 'There is something about a new cricket ball I could never fully understand or explain.' He could, though, answer any questions about his batting. 'I have been told I have a two-eyed stance, but I must confess that I never felt uncomfortable, which is the real test.' This philosophy made him so good as a coach. 'Unless I saw a batsman was obviously uncomfortable, I never interfered,' he said. Quick footwork, he would patiently point out, is more than half the basis of sound batsmanship, while in bowling he placed the emphasis on the follow-through.

He avoided the pitfall of conceit as though it did not exist, retaining a keen sense of humour which guarded against an inflated sense of self-importance. In a match against Derbyshire at Glossop, he failed to get a run or a wicket in the first innings and fell asleep with his pads on in Yorkshire's second effort. Brought sharply back to the land of the living by the fall of a wicket, he scrambled up and broke the seat on which he had been slumped. He was promptly bowled by a ball that snapped a stump and observed, as he regained the shelter of the pavilion, that all he had to do to complete a perfect match was to drop a catch.

Sure enough, he managed to make a hash of 'a chance I should have made nineteen times out of twenty', and got home very relieved to have suffered no further disaster.

Everyone who came under the influence of Hirst in the county nets has steadfastly held the opinion that there could never have been a better coach. His naturally understanding and gentle nature helped boys to show off what skills they had, untroubled by the fear of scorn or anger, and he possessed the most marvellous insight into the techniques which set him as a man apart from the mere experts of the approved methods.

Ted Lester, who brightened many an afternoon with his powerful hitting in the late 1940s and early 1950s, remembers with respect and admiration his first experience of Hirst's instinctive knowledge of what was right and what was wrong. 'I was batting in the nets one day when George came up and quietly asked me how many times I had been out lbw in that season's league matches. I thought about it and told him that it had not happened very often. George just smiled and said "That's all right, lad, just carry on." It was years later that I finally worked out what he had noticed about how

George Hirst, the most respected of all cricket coaches, passes on a few tips to a group of Yorkshire Colts. The young man second from the right in a blazer is Ted Lester, who had a successful career as a hard-hitting batsman, while second from the left is a youthful Johnny Wardle. (*Yorkshire Post*)

I played on the leg side. I am certain that if I had been getting out lbw he would have changed me in some way, but he was ready to let me stick to my particular style when it did not cause problems. That is what I believe to be marvellous coaching.'

Hirst took care, too, with the failures. 'You've done well tonight, son,' he would say to a boy he knew had no hopes of going any further, sending him home happy and, perhaps, a shade better equipped to handle the crushing disappointment of rejection.

Rhodes, with 881, made most appearances for Yorkshire and in virtually every one of them both imparted and acquired knowledge. His concentration was intense, his attention to detail incredible. As a boy he worked away quietly on his own, exploring the arts of spin by putting chalk marks on the ball to study its flight path more accurately.

In refreshing contrast to the instant experts of an age that worships theory and finds complexity in almost everything, he admitted that he never knew when his most dangerous delivery was going to manifest itself. 'It was a swinger that dipped near the end, pitching around leg-stump and breaking back sharply to the off, but though I could bowl it I could not explain how I did it,' he said. He also stood fairly square as a batsman, believing that 'By facing the bowler I can see the ball better and judge the flight more accurately, so my left foot gets moving quicker and the stroke can be more carefully calculated.' He knew that he found himself challenging the accepted tenets, 'but I speak from experience, which is all I can do'.

Bearing all this in mind, we may marvel to learn that the toss of a coin gave Rhodes his first chance. Lord Hawke had it in mind to choose a left-arm spinner called Albert Cordingley, who, six years older, made the bigger impact in a trial game. Both players went with the party on the journey south which marked the opening of the 1898 season and the official expectation was that Cordingley would be called upon initially at least. Stanley Jackson must have seen something special in the quiet young man from Kirkheaton, however, for he championed his cause to Lord Hawke, who settled the issue in the time-honoured method. Jackson guessed right and Rhodes never looked back, being selected as one of *Wisden*'s five cricketers of the year in his first season.

Poor Cordingley sat and watched Rhodes throughout those early fixtures, congratulated his rival with good grace and went back to the anonymity of league cricket. It is tempting to argue that Rhodes would have made his way whatever the outcome of that fateful toss, but no one remembers just how good Cordingley was and it is just possible that Rhodes might never have settled into first-class cricket if the coin had fallen the other way. What is known is the influence Rhodes exerted on the Yorkshire players with whom he came into contact.

Most of the younger men who had the privilege of crossing his path learned something and the up-and-coming representatives of several generations underwent the ritual of reporting to him each evening to review the progress of the day's play. Constructive criticism flowed, while praise came in much smaller doses, although when it was given it had been thoroughly earned. All the same, Rhodes did not enjoy coaching. He operated at too advanced a level for mere mortals who populated the ranks of the pupils at Harrow, where he took up duties after his retirement.

Basically, in any case, he had no liking for teaching cricket, being utterly self taught himself. 'What can you do by coaching?' he would ask. 'Pluck, footwork, judgment and concentration are the foundations of good batsmanship and you either have these qualities or you haven't.' He also scoffed at the popular conviction that he could pitch the ball on a sixpence. 'On a newspaper, perhaps,' he said, 'but a good length is not the same thing at all to different batsmen. You have to note how each man plays, how far forward he comes naturally before you can test him with length bowling.'

The most popular and for some strange reason readily accepted story concerning Rhodes centred on his match-winning last-wicket stand with Hirst at the Oval in 1902, when England beat Australia by the narrowest of margins. When Rhodes, as a slim young man of twenty-four, marched forward to join his county colleague 15 runs were still needed towards a target of 263 and the pair duly collected them carefully, one at a time. Out of this grew the legend that Hirst had instructed his young partner 'We'll get them in singles.' In later years Rhodes became rather annoyed at the constant references to this bit of nonsense. 'I don't particularly recall that either of us said anything,' he complained, 'but I do know that if we had received a poor ball we would have hit it for four if possible. It would not have made any cricketing sense to ignore the possibility of a boundary, although it is true that we took no chance at all and that we had to get the singles as best we could.'

Everything Rhodes did on the field had an absolute sense of purpose. Thus when Bill Bowes made his debut, Rhodes stationed him precisely at mid-on, marking the point with his foot on the ground. Sure enough almost at once Bowes caught a flashing drive largely as an act of self-preservation. 'That,' observed his mentor, 'should be a lesson. Always go where you are put.' As Bowes, with stinging palms, reflected, a yard either way and the ball would have whistled past him for four. 'I always paid great attention to what Wilfred said,' he added.

There have been many ready to witness his greatness, but the most impressive demonstration of his unique gifts came when he was sixty-five, dogged by failing eyesight and handicapped by creaking limbs that were reluctant to respond to a still nimble mind.

He graciously agreed to bowl the first over at the opening of a new cricket ground near Wakefield, with Brian Sellers batting. The former captain recalled: 'Wilfred couldn't see the stumps at my end. I could have been no more than a blurred and distant image, yet, bowling from memory, with his arm upright, he flighted the ball beautifully and dropped on a good length six times out of six. I played through a maiden over on merit and was glad enough to survive it.'

Rhodes became completely blind but continued to attend matches. 'I see they've taken the new ball,' he commented on one visit. Smiling at the complete confusion this remark caused, he added: 'I can tell it's the new ball because it makes a different sound on the bat.' He played with W.G. Grace and with Don Bradman, spreading his genius thickly across the years.

True to the essential nature of his background and upbringing, Rhodes remained as careful with money as he was, indeed, with everything in his daily routine. His family were farmers, which is probably why he expected life to be hard and adjusted accordingly and he would, no doubt, have been satisfied to leave some £50,000, a tidy sum for a man who lived for ninety-five years. It represented a solid achievement to set alongside his batting and bowling.

Once a return journey to Lascelles Hall, no more than a stone's throw from his birthplace, to play in a benefit match involved a long and tedious journey to Huddersfield by train. Arriving at the station with George Hirst, he secured the assistance of a porter, who pushed a handcart bearing their equipment up the long hill towards Lepton while the two players followed on behind at more leisurely pace. Rhodes paused at the entrance to the ground to renew some old acquaintance and was eventually approached by the porter, by now red-faced with his exertions but clearly confident of well-earned reward.

The year is 1949 and Wilfred Rhodes, almost blind, is seventy-two, but the classic action had survived the passage of time when he bowled an accurate over to mark the opening of a new cricket ground at Wakefield. (*Yorkshire Post*)

'I've put all your cricket things in the corner of the dressing-room, Mr Rhodes,' he said, touching his cap.

'Oh aye, thank you,' replied Rhodes.

'I've kept everything tidy,' persisted the porter.

'That's good of you.'

'It's been a long hard walk.'

Rhodes finally appeared to give in. 'Hasn't Mr Hirst given you anything?'

'Oh yes, sir, he gave me sixpence,' replied the porter, happier now that he had made his point to profitable effect.

'Aye,' said Rhodes, walking on, 'well that'll be for both of us.'

Schofield Haigh did the double only once – in 1904 – so in comparison with Rhodes might easily be mistaken for a makeweight, but he scored 11,000 runs in addition to collecting one hundred wickets or more on nine occasions, becoming linked with his Huddersfield colleagues in a dynamic combination. Legend has adorned him with a perpetual smile and he was in reality a humorous man who took his cricket seriously without letting it become an obsession.

He could even raise a chuckle when he 'lost' a wicket after bowling Surrey's Tom Hayward at the Oval in the record-breaking encounter of 1899, when Yorkshire took a fearful pounding. It had been a tiring day, but in the last over he summoned up sufficient strength to hit Hayward's stumps only to find, after some discussion, that the decision had been given against him, the umpires ruling that the ball had rebounded from the wicket-keeper's pads.

Haigh often headed the county's bowling averages, operating

The All-Rounders

from a long run before exchanging out-and-out speed for finger spin and introducing a slower ball which spread uncertainty around the circuit as it arrived at the wicket long after the crestfallen batsman had completed a stroke formed in the confident expectation of greater pace.

His best performance in figures was nine for 25, but he had highest regard for an eight for 78 against the Australians in 1896 on a good wicket at Bradford. His readiness to see the funny side of life survived into his spell as an umpire in the Scarborough Festival. There he gave John Tunnicliffe out to a dubious catch at the wicket.

'Were you sure that I played the ball?' asked the batsman.

'Not really,' replied Haigh.

'Then why on earth did you give me out?'

'Well, I noted the expression on your face and thought you looked very guilty,' said Haigh.

Character undoubtedly has always been a major element in the make-up of the typical Yorkshire cricketer and while playing similarities made them so formidable as opponents most had little personal habits. Thus, Roy Kilner could usually be distinguished among his fellow professionals by his cap, which he wore with such a distinct tilt to the left that it rested on his ear. Originally introduced into the side as a batsman, he became a bowler out of necessity.

When the county lost Alonzo Drake and Major Booth and George Hirst retired, another bowler was needed, so Kilner dutifully concentrated on the role. He took one for 305 runs in 1914 but

The ever cheerful Schofield Haigh, who never lost his sense of humour and figured prominently alongside his great contemporaries, Hirst and Rhodes. He headed the county bowling averages on ten occasions.

improved to such an extent that in 1923 he had 143 victims at a cost of 12 runs each – the reward for hours of thoughtful application. He also benefited from an optimistic nature that sustained him whatever difficulties he came across as he experimented.

Amateurs generally reserved their energies for batting, which was regarded as the more gentlemanly pursuit, but the Hon. Francis Stanley Jackson fits into the same category, in terms of attitude, as Grace. He applied himself vigorously as an all-rounder, completing the double once in the course of averaging 33.78 with the bat and 19.18 with the ball. A classic stroke-player, Jackson bowled at a fast medium and could be relied upon to hit an accurate rhythm under any pressure.

His most spectacular success came in helping to dismiss the Australians for 23, accounting for four of his victims with the last five balls of the match. Jackson captained England in 1905, winning the toss in all five Tests against Australia, and became president of the MCC in 1921.

Emmott Robinson qualifies as an all-rounder on more than statistics, admirable though these were. He had few equals as a team man, while his eccentricities, which included a sort of dog kick at the start of his run-up, caught the public imagination. He hardly looked athletic with his diminutive frame, bandy legs, greying hair and peculiar crouching walk, yet he was quick over the ground and possessed a keen understanding of the game.

Bill Bowes was one of many with reason to be grateful to Robinson, who advised him early in his career to 'get a note-book and make sure that every day you write down what you have learned – where batsmen have got runs and how they have got out. Every day you'll discover something new and after ten years you will remember something you had forgotten.' Robinson also set great store by the weatherglass, explaining: 'It's always nice to know when there is a sticky wicket in the offing.'

Robinson, coming to Yorkshire after Major Booth had been killed in the First World War, had been a leading performer in the Bradford League for many years.

He immediately felt at home, 'getting his feet under the table' he called it, and he stood out with bat, ball and in the field with his fearless agility. He stationed himself in such apparent peril at silly mid-on that the more sensitive among the opposition were moved to suggest he might retreat a little, if only as an act of self-preservation. His reply never varied. 'Never mind me, thee get on wi' thi' laikin.' He bowled unchanged throughout a match three times – with Abe Waddington against Northamptonshire in 1920 and 1921 and with George Macaulay against Worcestershire in 1927.

Like many with the same sort of background, he kept his financial affairs under close scrutiny and his eagerness to stay 'straight' featured in an amusing incident at Leyton, where the ground was a penny tram ride from the station. Bowes followed Robinson and Edgar Oldroyd upstairs to the top deck and instinctively bought tickets for all three when the conductor came along. That evening the trio travelled by chance together again and Robinson did the honours. Turning to Oldroyd, he said: 'Now then, you give Bill a penny and you'll be level. We can settle up later.'

He hadn't a lot of money but always said that he did the best with what he had, and his cricket trousers had a roll up at the bottom instead of a turn up – 'To allow for shrinkage.' On his retirement, he took his wisdom and experience to Repton, where he coached shrewdly in a genial understanding way until a rheumatic shoulder forced him out of active service and onto the umpires' list.

The *Yorkshire Year Book* indicates that Robinson made his last appearance in 1931, which is accurate so far as it goes. He did, however, make an unscheduled return in the Headingley Roses fixture of 1933. In the first place, Robinson turned up on the Monday, with Wilfred Rhodes and George Hirst, to watch and, no doubt, talk over old times.

The county were, however, in desperate trouble. Percy Holmes was in bed with lumbago and Hedley Verity could not play because his arm was stiff and sore, the legacy of vaccination a week earlier. Yorkshire had only one twelfth man available, but Robinson answered the call, going out to field in borrowed kit and displaying 'the same old eagerness and keen eye for every move'.

Lancashire batted with all the tenacity traditionally associated with the occasion, grinding out 431 runs and forcing Yorkshire to take the second new ball. 'I bet you would have liked to take that second new ball,' observed a friend, having noted Robinson's frustration at being part of the action without being centrally involved. 'I'd much rather have taken the first, you can do a lot more with that,' replied Robinson, who, nevertheless, admitted that 'the exercise was very welcome'.

Among his most memorable performances was a nine-for-36 return in the 1920 Roses clash at Park Avenue, where Lancashire, only 52 short of victory with six wickets in hand at lunch on the last day, lost by 22. Their last wicket fell to Kilner, who took it with what would otherwise have been a wide, bowled in an attempt to ensure that Robinson took all ten. The batsman, however, jumping out to make the most of what looked a loose delivery, missed and was stumped. In the circumstances, it is impossible to accept that Robinson actually meant it when he said: 'If I had to live my life over I would go into business. I have enjoyed every minute of my cricket, but I would not recommend it as a career.'

Raymond Illingworth, in fact, became the living proof that Robinson was wrong. The model Yorkshire player – a top quality craftsman who put in the time and hard work to 'bottom' the job – Illingworth's day-by-day reliability became a by-word over thirty years and his ability to come back at fifty and compete seriously paid tribute to the grounding he received and to which he responded. For him, cricket really was a career.

There have been flashier all-rounders, some of whom have been idolised out of all proportion to their skill, but most teams would prefer the solid dependability of Illingworth.

Ted Lester, who in becoming scorer to Yorkshire saw more of the team than anyone in two decades, summed up the Pudsey product succinctly. 'In all the time I have watched him, I have never known Illingworth to let the side down. If you looked at a pitch and thought Ray should be a match-winner on it, he invariably was. When you saw a crisis on the horizon and thought he might patch things up, he always chipped in with a few runs.'

Despite his unobtrusive manner, Illingworth stood out as well above average from childhood. Playing against Wyther Park School in a challenge match, for example, he took five wickets for 11 runs and scored 52 of the 64 that brought victory. He had to compete for attention with Bob Appleyard and Brian Close, but long spells as twelfth man made him all the keener to progress. In looking ahead, he had to weigh up well-meant advice which advocated that he should concentrate on bowling and then that batting might be his forte. He soldiered on doing both, thinking shrewdly that two strings to his bow gave him more fire power, and finally he mastered both trades.

OPPOSITE Ray Illingworth's expertise as a captain was based on a deep knowledge of the groundsman's art. Here he is discussing a few points with George Cawthray, who was in charge of the square at Headingley for many years. (*Yorkshire Post*)

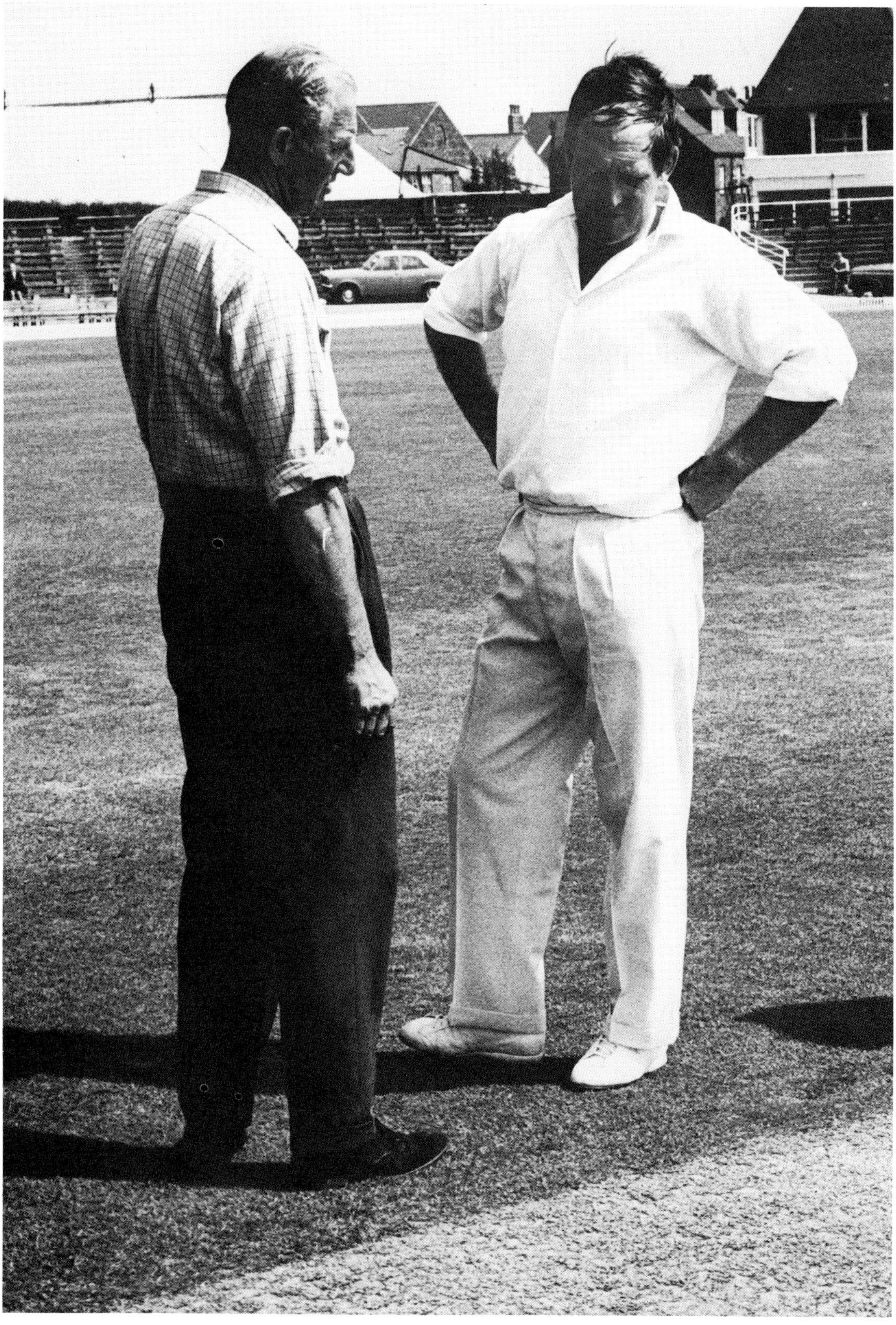

'Being a bowler and not having to worry about how many runs I made, it often happened that I could relax and play a few shots while the specialists worried about getting out,' he said. 'Similarly, a lean spell with the ball did not mean the end of the world, for I usually got some runs to compensate.'

He revealed his true colours at Harrogate in 1967, when Yorkshire wanted at least first innings points against Gloucestershire to be sure of the championship. They dealt capably with a drying pitch to score 309, prolonging their first innings into the second day. Illingworth then set about the visiting batsmen to take seven for 58 and make sure of that key first place in the table.

By no means satisfied, he spun the ball more viciously in the second innings as Gloucestershire followed on to be dismissed for 99, beaten by an innings and 76 runs in the fading light of 6.45.

Illingworth's spell added up to 13-9-6-7 – six caught and one stumped – as he conjured sharp turn out of the responsive turf. While the celebrations gently shook the foundations of the pavilion, he was asked his thoughts by the representatives of the Press. Turning his back on the champagne and the roars of jubilation, he gazed wistfully out onto the ground, by then shrouded in darkness. 'Well,' he said, 'it would have been nice if they could have batted again.' With the true artist's appreciation, he was reluctant to leave a canvas on which he found it easy to express himself so clearly. He is without question the leading cricket thinker of his generation and it was fitting that the most Yorkshire of post-war Yorkshiremen should have been in charge of the county side on the field in 1983 – the 150th anniversary of that first competitive venture.

Chapter 15

THE DESTROYERS

From the beginning Yorkshire have been blessed with bowlers suited to every occasion which goes a long way towards explaining their success. It is no use scoring heavily if runs merely lead down the blind alley of drawn games, which are the bane of cricket, and Yorkshire's prosperity depended heavily on standards set by Alan Hill, Tom Emmett and Edmund Peate being maintained by a succession of men who mastered length and line before adding extensive wicket-taking refinements.

Emmett is an outstanding personality and, together with George Freeman, formed one of the earliest fast-bowling partnerships of note. Referring to Freeman, W.G. Grace admitted: 'I have had occasional balls from him that would have beaten any batsman, his best one pitching between the legs and the wicket with sufficient break and rise to hit the off bail. When he and Emmett were together, I thought a hundred runs was something to be very proud of.'

Freeman came to prominence as a sixteen-year-old, grabbing fifteen wickets for 38 runs to help Boroughbridge beat Knaresborough and, as he grew in stature, relied on no more than three or four strides to speed the ball on its way with enough force to bruise and blacken a few forearms.

His successor, Hill, was renowned for his accuracy. He claimed a hat-trick which included Grace and thought himself to be 'a natural-born bowler, because I always preferred to have a ball in my hand rather than a bat'.

The three Yorkshiremen whose names appear in the brief list of those who have taken all ten wickets in an innings – Alonzo Drake, Hedley Verity and Frank Smailes – could most accurately be described as slow, and the other man who went straight through a completed innings was Ted Wainwright, the offspinner from Tinsley, near Sheffield. He had figures of 22.4-6-31-10 for Yorkshire against Staffordshire on August 4, 1890, in an engagement which did not qualify as first-class.

Wainwright also had nine Middlesex wickets at Sheffield four years later, but F.S. Jackson stepped in to break the sequence. He held the ball between thumb and first finger, which he pressed so hard against the seam that the skin often broke. This caused him much pain and it was not uncommon for his finger to bleed while he 'went about his business'.

His shining hour arrived at Dewsbury in June 1894, when he completed an all-bowled hat-trick on the way to removing five Sussex batsmen in seven balls. Wainwright, as he proved by making the first century for Yorkshire against Australia, could bat more than a little, which is the case with a lot of Yorkshire bowlers.

A famous exception to this comforting rule, Bill Bowes, had to overcome the bitter disappointment of rejection to justify his place among the leading bowlers. After his first trials with the county as a twenty-year-old, he became surplus to requirements. Going down to Lord's he secured a contract to serve on the MCC groundstaff, which became a blessing in disguise. As a net bowler he had to meet a demand for all types of delivery as a succession of batsmen sought to iron a fault or perfect a particular stroke and in doing so he expanded his own repertoire.

Observing the virtues of length and line religiously, he returned a much more accomplished seamer when the county had inevitable second thoughts. He never quite came into the category of fast bowler, but using his 6 feet 4 inches to full effect, he could make the ball lift unpleasantly enough to remind many batsmen that they had something they wished to communicate to the square-leg umpire. From time to time he faced the accusation that he overdid the short ball, and he did not hesitate to test the opposition's courage, but he seldom wasted his energies and the deliberate long hop, rising chest high and more, was used strictly to a purpose.

'There was a lot more effort involved in bowling a bumper, so I had to employ them only at the right time or I would have been burned out and no use to the team,' he said.

He had to excel in his specialised role, for despite non-productive batting and fielding that left him runner-up as often as not to the ball in any race, he held his place unchallenged for many years in as good a county team as there has ever been. Bowes is, in fact, unique among the world-class Yorkshire players in taking more wickets – 1,351 – for the county than he scored runs – 1,251. It is a distinction, if indeed that is the word, that Arthur Booth (122 wickets and 114 runs) and Mike Cowan (263 wickets and 170 runs) share, but neither approaches Bowes in length or quality of service. Not only did he take wickets with impressive regularity, he usually cut into the top half of the opposition order, spearheading the Yorkshire thrust and grimly matching his mettle against the leading batsmen of his time.

As a guide to his control we should note that he bowled Don Bradman four times in Tests, yet the most successful of all run-makers suffered this indignity only eleven times before the Second World War. Those who were lucky enough to be present at Sheffield in 1938 came away from Bramall Lane convinced that a maiden over from Bowes to Bradman had demonstrated the art of bowling at the highest level. Six times Bradman played and six times he missed, a ratio of failure that normally represented the Australian's ration for at least a couple of seasons.

While surviving the hardships of imprisonment during the war, Bowes became a good conjuror – some thought he had been one all the time with the cricket ball – and he qualified for membership of the Magic Circle. He broadcast on the game and covered Yorkshire's activities firstly for the *Yorkshire Evening News* and later for the *Yorkshire Evening Post*, retaining an amiable presence, although he never lost the stubborn streak that made him so fine a cricketer.

His long-standing companion in arms was Hedley Verity, whose death dealt the biggest single blow to Yorkshire. At least those closely concerned with the club felt that to be the case when the left-arm spinner became a casualty in the Second World War. Arthur Mitchell, whose prehensile close-catching aided Verity so importantly, echoed the thoughts of the majority when he said: 'I really thought that Hedley would play on until at least fifty and I reckoned that he and Len Hutton would make the foundations on which a superb Yorkshire side could be built. It would have been a fair old start with those two together.'

Mitchell, crouching close in on the offside, stood as the focal point of Verity's bowling on many a turning pitch, and, all around him, was a keen supporting ring. 'Hedley bowled such a marvellous direction that we felt absolutely safe,' said Mitchell.

'His height was so important because it enabled him to put the ball just where he wanted and he made it lift more than anyone of his type. He didn't spin it a lot, but the combination of bounce and some turn did the trick. Hedley studied his man, so he knew what each batsman could and could not do and what they might attempt. Every ball had a purpose. Even on a good batting wicket when he could look forward only to a hard day's work he kept the batsmen at it and I've heard them say how hard it was to get at him. Some of his best bowling was done on pitches that gave him so little help.'

His career record is a hall of fame in itself – all ten wickets twice, nine in an innings on seven occasions and seventeen wickets for 91 to destroy Essex at Leyton in 1933, which is the best return by any Yorkshire bowler.

It would, however, be difficult – if not exactly impossible – to argue that Verity was a more determined attacker of batsmen than George Macaulay, who injected a note of discernible hatred into the proceedings whenever he played.

It might even be that this animosity to all opponents cost him a notable Test run. He took a wicket with his first ball for England against South Africa at Capetown and also made the winning hit, yet still won only eight 'caps'. When he first turned out for Yorkshire in 1920, Macaulay planned to be a fast bowler, but George Hirst and Wilfred Rhodes appreciated that he was straining to maintain a pace that stretched him too much physically.

They persuaded him that his future lay in concentrating on his natural facility for spinning the ball. Hour after hour he would drop the ball on the spot from his rather ungainly approach to the wicket. Survival by the batsman provoked a venomous glare down the pitch which upset the rhythm of all but the stoutest hearts and ritual was repeated until Macaulay had his way or was removed from the attack, which did not happen all that often.

He never gave up, his persistence being much feared as well as respected, and every scrap of guile and effort went into each delivery so that an error from him attracted immmediate comment. Once he did bowl a full toss which was despatched to the boundary by the grateful batsman, who remarked cheerfully: 'It's a long time since I had one of those from you, Mac.' The response cut through the niceties of casual conversation between sporting adversaries. 'Aye and it'll be a long time before you get another,' snarled Macaulay.

His passion for getting to the bottom of things took him into the world of patent medicine after his retirement with unfortunate consequences. Towards the end of his playing days, he suffered considerably from rheumatism. The pain persuaded him to test an old-fashioned remedy sent to him by a Cumberland woman whose family had preserved the prescription from generation to generation. In ten weeks he was completely cured.

He subsequently went into partnership with the woman, opening an office in Wakefield to market the cure and had plans to branch out in Harley Street, but the venture failed and Macaulay appeared at a bankruptcy examination in 1937. Surviving this blow, he fell victim of the Second World War, being killed on active service in December 1940. Nothing, however, could dim the memory of his great bowling feats which included a hat-trick for Yorkshire on four occasions, an achievement equalled by another forceful character in Fred Trueman.

Trueman, too, stamped his personality on events, leaping out of thousands of headlines and hundreds of caricatures in the guise of Fiery Fred. He hated batsmen and showed it by perfecting the short rising delivery so that he worried the best and terrified the less accomplished or the more faint-hearted.

Through performance, attitude and character, he imprinted himself indelibly on the first-class scene. One of a miner's family of seven, he managed with little or no influential backing to escape from a demanding environment to become the world's leading Test wicket-taker and to prove himself as the modern fast bowling equivalent of Hill and Freeman.

He bowled quickly by instinct, fired by strength of limb and co-ordination of muscular movement. He inherited a natural grace, without which it is impossible to produce real pace, and he used it with the ferocity of youth.

Gradually, however, he grew to appreciate that the true art of bowling takes in a degree of subtlety and the quality he maintained brought confirmation of his ability. Trueman revelled in the power generated by the smoothly accelerating approach to the wicket and the perfect cartwheel action from which he could deliver the bouncer, yorker, outswinger or inswinger. This well-oiled action enabled him to continue long past the normal span allotted to truly fast bowlers, although he made some concession to the passing years with cutters and little seamers that kept the opposition under agitated pressure.

He strode the stage to the same commanding effect as the most dynamic Shakespearian actor and his routine owed much to the theatre. He went back to his mark purposefully rolling up his right shirt sleeve, which by accident or design always finished flapping about his wrist. He tossed back the perpetually unruly lock of black hair and swept forward like a tidal wave, swelling to a destructive peak and crashing through with appeals that were as much a statement as a question to the umpire.

Trueman could be difficult both on and off the field, running the

Fred Trueman – the most successful and possibly the quickest of Yorkshire's pace bowlers. (*Press Association*)

gauntlet of official disapproval here and there, yet this, in a sense, served as an advantage, for it built his reputation and made him all the more an attraction with a public that never lost interest in his activities.

Trueman, though, had another side to his nature, one which only those inside the dressing-room saw. Brian Close, who knew him better than anyone, said: 'He developed an image which betrayed him. He was a bit rough and forthright and strong willed as a young man, but he took the blame for a lot of things done by other folk. You had to sense his moods. Sometimes you needed to get at him. Then he would work himself up and play magnificently. Other days a bit of leg-pulling did the trick. We had rows, but they were rows between two self-respecting men. Not many cricket followers will realise that Fred suffered disappointments with great sensitivity. If he went through a bad spell it meant personal failure to him and he felt things very deeply.

'If the boys were feeling a bit low, however, he had the knack of lifting them. He had a great heart and could sense the moment in a big match when to unleash something really exceptional.'

Trueman earned admiration for his more spectacular feats which sent stumps flying and had batsmen dancing apprehensively out of line, but he also revealed to the thoughtful followers the possibilities that exist for the more skilful seamers. At times he carried the Yorkshire attack on his broad shoulders, and his sturdy legs never let him down. 'Do you know,' he asked at the height of his fame, 'I reckon I have had twenty-seven partners opening the bowling with me.'

Ranking alongside Trueman in volume of work, Johnny Wardle filled a variety of roles, switching from stock to shock bowler with ease and doing it all with a highly-developed sense of humour which made his bitter departure all the more distasteful. Wardle, again like Trueman, possessed in-born ball skill which enabled him to shine at most games. Trueman flirted briefly with the Football League and Wardle might have been a professional with Wolverhampton Wanderers, but he rejected an approach by Major Frank Buckley, the Midlands club manager, on the grounds that he was better off working as an apprentice fitter at Hickleton Main Colliery and taking the money offered by the queue of local league clubs willing to sign him on professional terms.

Orthodox left-arm spin bowling mixed with back-of-the-hand stuff made him a dangerous operator and there is reason to think that he would have been more successful in a stronger side that could have used him sparingly and in suitable circumstances. He communicated with the public to an extent that has never been surpassed, for whatever he was doing he conveyed the distinct impression that the spectators were part of the act.

Thus when brilliantly fielding a fierce drive or a flashing edge, he would pocket the ball with an impressive sleight of hand and peer into the distance to ask his audience where it had gone.

His arrival as a batsman brought an air of expectancy, for he timed his strokes sweetly enough to send the ball surprising distances and again he played to the crowd. A miscue over the slips would mean the appearance of the invisible chalk 'for the end of his cue' and even his own downfall did not dampen his spirits. Having been comprehensively bowled, he surveyed the wreckage of his stumps

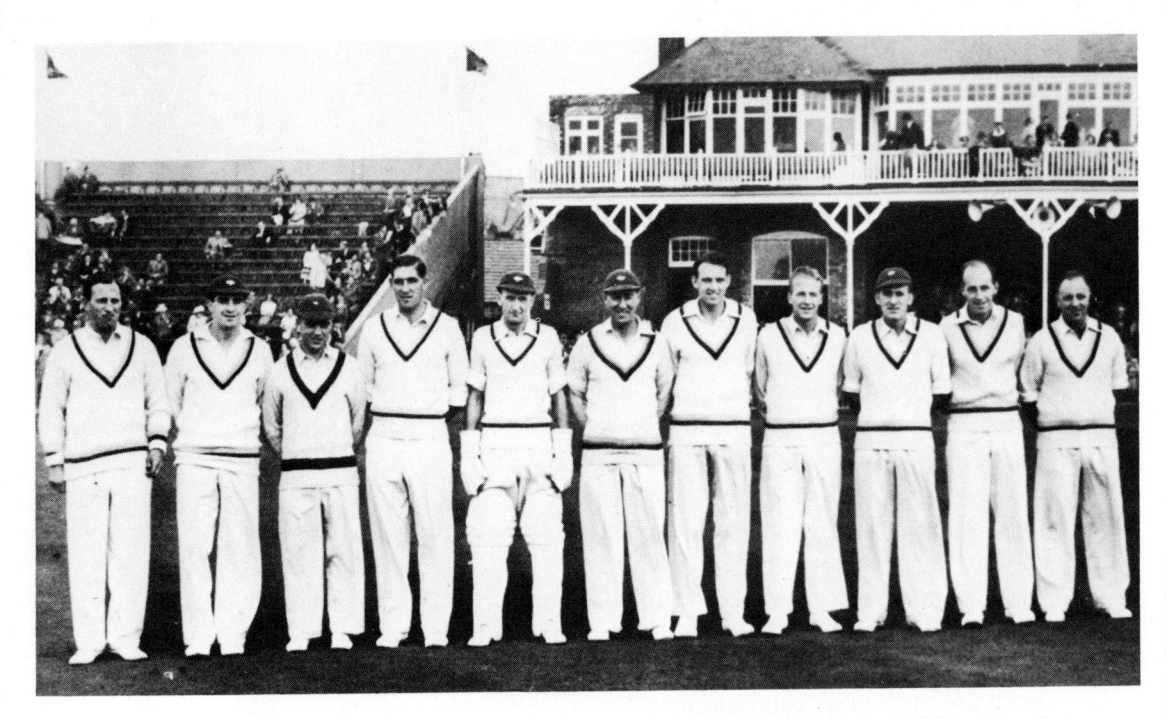

The line-up at Scarborough in 1951 when Bob Appleyard took his 200th wicket of the season. Left to right: Len Hutton, Fred Trueman, Eddie Leadbeater, Vic Wilson, Don Brennan, Norman Yardley, Appleyard, Willie Watson, Johnny Wardle, Ted Lester and Harry Halliday.

before marching back to the pavilion, pausing to enquire, 'Did it look out from here?' as he passed through the customers near the players' gate.

Bob Appleyard, in contrast, came to cricket late in life and rarely found much to laugh about as he battled with the spectre of ill-health. He could, however, use the new ball, which he swung into the bat at a lively medium-pace, and he also got a fair amount of spin from the off.

At twenty-seven, therefore, he emerged from the Bradford League as a ready-made replacement for Alex Coxon, who had left the county, and for offspinner Close, who was on National Service. He took two hundred wickets in 1951, his first full season, breaking the record of 154 set by Wilfred Rhodes, and, despite illness which kept him out of the game for two years and necessitated a lung operation, he continued to reap a rich harvest.

Appleyard confessed that he found the hard, unrelenting grind of county cricket something of a trial, but applied himself diligently as he acquired mastery of pace and flight. He also had a secret weapon which came into being by chance. This was a fast leg-break which suddenly materialised as he bowled a normal off-cutter and he had the good sense to leave well alone, letting it happen whenever the fates decreed. After all, he thought, if he did not know it was going to come the batsmen had no hope.

Whether he would have been so devastating in modern times, with a limitation on leg-side placings is another question. Like Verity he used his height to make the ball lift into the batsman's body, forcing catches around the corner, so restrictions must have handicapped him, but the odds are that he would have found an answer in another direction of attack.

He played, of course, at the same time as Wardle and Trueman, which must have helped, and no Yorkshire bowler can have ploughed so lonely a furrow as Chris Old, who would have been a magnificent foil for Trueman but who largely had to lead the strike force and do some of the donkey work. Although dogged by injury, Old had genuine class and could reflect on the problems of being born at the wrong time.

YORKSHIRE'S LEADING BOWLERS

	Runs	*Wickets*	*Average*
G. Freeman (1865–80)	2,187	218	10.03
E. Peate (1879–87)	10,286	819	12.55
T. Emmett (1866–88)	16,100	1,269	12.68
A. Hill (1871–82)	7,151	563	12.70
H. Verity (1930–39)	21,366	1,558	13.71
A. Booth (1931–47)	1,684	122	13.80
T. Armitage (1872–78)	1,676	119	14.08
G.P. Harrison (1883–92)	4,272	295	14.48
R. Iddison (1863–76)	1,570	106	14.81
R. Peel (1882–97)	23,398	1,550	15.09
R. Appleyard (1950–58)	9,813	637	15.40
S. Haigh (1895–1913)	29,546	1,916	15.42
W.E. Bowes (1929–47)	21,191	1,351	15.68
R. Wilson (1899–1923)	3,078	196	15.70
I. Hodgson (1863–66)	1,400	88	15.90
W. Rhodes (1898–1930)	57,732	3,608	16.00
E. Lockwood (1868–84)	2,273	141	16.12
T.W. Foster (1894–95)	1,105	68	16.25
S. Wade (1886–90)	3,392	207	16.38
R.O. Clayton (1870–79)	2,528	154	16.41
W. Bates (1877–87)	11,024	660	16.70
J.M. Preston (1885–89)	3,872	228	16.98
G. Macaulay (1920–35)	30,292	1,773	17.08
F.S. Trueman (1949–68)	29,890	1,745	17.13

	Runs	Wickets	Average
E. Wainwright (1888–1902)	20,230	1,173	17.24
R. Kilner (1911–27)	14,873	858	17.33
J.H. Wardle (1946–58)	27,163	1,537	17.67
G.H. Hirst (1891–1929)	45,903	2,569	17.86
A. Drake (1909–14)	8,626	482	17.89
L. Greenwood (1863–74)	1,537	85	18.08
G. Ulyett (1873–93)	8,801	484	18.18
R. Illingworth (1951–83)	26,219	1,422	18.43
J.T. Newstead (1903–13)	5,555	297	18.70
M. Booth (1908–14)	10,632	558	19.05
F.S. Jackson (1890–1907)	9,708	506	19.18
A. Waddington (1919–27)	16,095	831	19.36
A.G. Nicholson (1962–75)	17,296	876	19.74
A. Coxon (1945–50)	9,428	464	20.31
R. Aspinall (1946–50)	2,670	131	20.38
D. Wilson (1957–74)	22,626	1,104	20.49
E.P. Robinson (1934–49)	15,135	735	20.59
T.F. Smailes (1932–48)	16,622	802	20.72
C.M. Old (1966–82)	13,409	647	20.72
W. Ringrose (1901–06)	3,224	155	20.80
J.T. Brown, Darfield (1897–1903)	2,141	102	20.99

BOWLERS WHO HAVE TAKEN 200 WICKETS IN A SEASON

R. Appleyard   200 wickets, average 14.14 in 1951
G.H. Hirst   201 wickets, average 15.36 in 1906
G. Macaulay   200 wickets, average 14.93 in 1925
W. Rhodes   240 wickets, average 12.72 in 1900
               233 wickets, average 15.00 in 1901

MOST WICKETS IN A MATCH

17 for 91 H. Verity v Essex at Leyton in 1933
16 for 35 W.E. Bowes v Northants at Kettering in 1935
   for 38 T. Emmett v Cambridgeshire at Hunslet in 1869
   for 112 J.H. Wardle v Sussex at Hull in 1954
15 for 38 H. Verity v Kent at Sheffield in 1936
   for 50 R. Peel v Somerset at Leeds in 1895
   for 51 A. Drake v Somerset at Weston-Super-Mare in 1914
   for 56 W. Rhodes v Essex at Leyton in 1899
   for 63 G.H. Hirst v Leicestershire at Hull in 1907
   for 100 H. Verity v Essex at Westcliff in 1936
   for 123 R. Illingworth v Glamorgan at Swansea in 1960
   for 129 H. Verity v Oxford University at Oxford in 1936

OPPOSITE Tony Nicholson, his accurate medium-paced seam bowling made him one of Yorkshire's best limited-overs players. (*Yorkshire Post*)

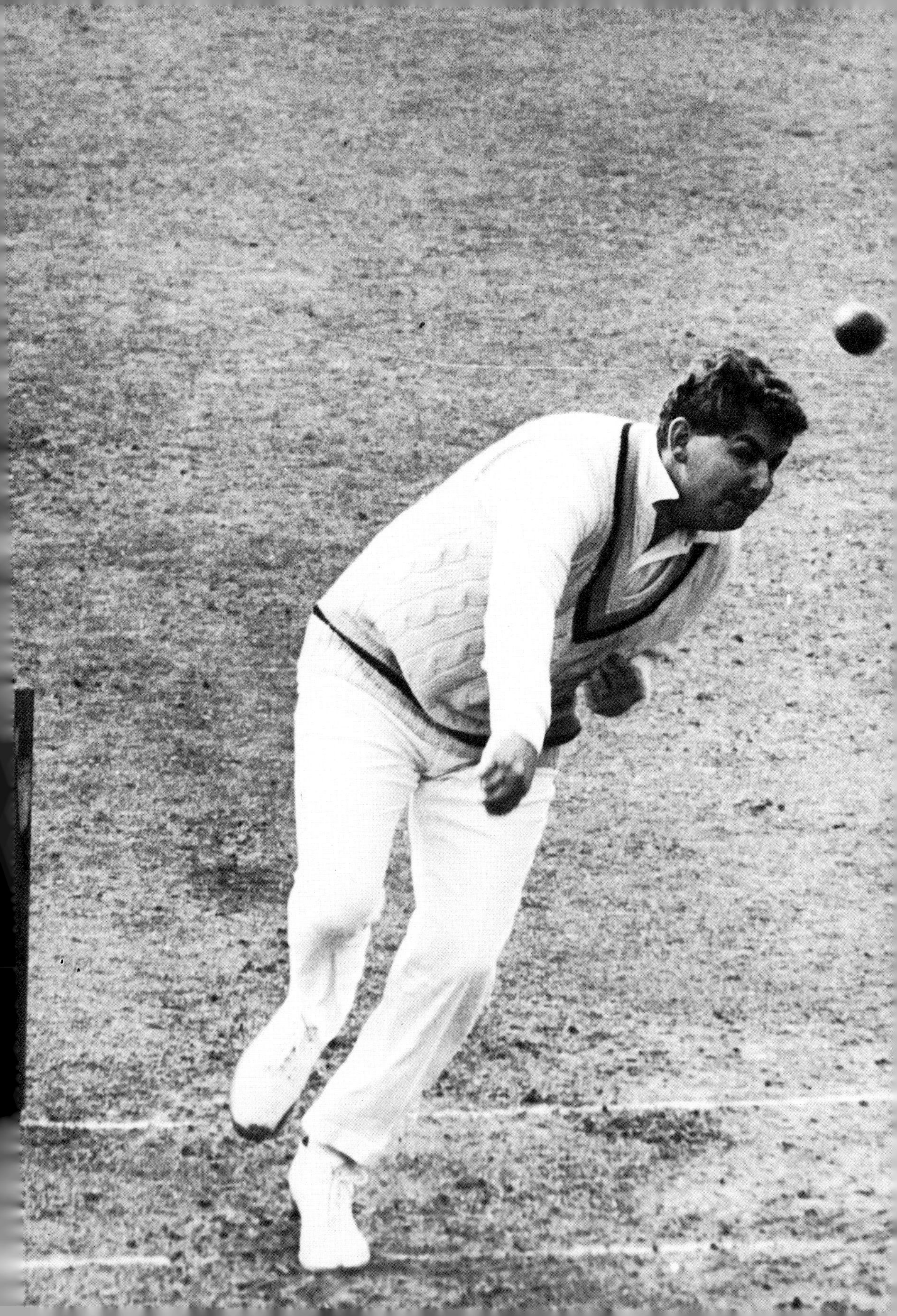

NINE WICKETS IN AN INNINGS

W.E. Bowes	for 121 *v* Essex at Scarborough in 1932
M.J. Cowan	for 43 *v* Warwickshire at Birmingham in 1960
T. Emmett	for 34 *v* Nottinghamshire at Dewsbury in 1868
	for 23 *v* Cambridgeshire at Hunslet in 1869
T. Foster	for 59 *v* MCC at Lord's in 1894
S. Haigh	for 25 *v* Gloucestershire at Leeds in 1912
G.H. Hirst	for 45 *v* Middlesex at Sheffield in 1907
	for 23 *v* Lancashire at Leeds in 1910
	for 41 *v* Worcestershire at Worcester in 1911
	for 69 *v* MCC at Lord's in 1912
R. Illingworth	for 42 *v* Worcestershire at Worcester in 1957
A.G. Nicholson	for 62 *v* Sussex at Eastbourne in 1967
R. Peel	for 22 *v* Somerset at Leeds in 1895
J.M. Preston	for 28 *v* MCC at Scarborough in 1888
W. Rhodes	for 28 *v* Essex at Leyton in 1899
	for 39 *v* Essex at Leyton in 1929
W. Ringrose	for 76 *v* Australians at Bradford in 1905
E. Robinson	for 36 *v* Lancashire at Bradford in 1920
H. Verity	for 60 *v* Glamorgan at Swansea in 1930
	for 44 *v* Essex at Leyton in 1933
	for 59 *v* Kent at Dover in 1933
	for 12 *v* Kent at Sheffield in 1936
	for 48 *v* Essex at Westcliff in 1936
	for 43 *v* Warwickshire at Leeds in 1937
	for 62 *v* MCC at Lord's in 1939
E. Wainwright	for 66 *v* Middlesex at Sheffield in 1894
J.H. Wardle	for 48 *v* Sussex at Hull in 1954
	for 25 *v* Lancashire at Old Trafford in 1954
A.C. Williams	for 29 *v* Hampshire at Dewsbury in 1919

BOWLERS WHO HAVE PERFORMED THE HAT-TRICK

R. Appleyard	*v* Gloucestershire in 1956
M.W. Booth	*v* Worcestershire in 1911
	v Essex in 1912
J.T. Brown (Sen.)	*v* Derbyshire in 1896
G.A. Cope	*v* Essex in 1970
A. Coxon	*v* Worcestershire in 1946
G. Deyes	*v* Gentlemen of Ireland in 1907
A. Drake	*v* Essex in 1912
H. Fisher	*v* Somerset in 1932
W. Fletcher	*v* MCC in 1892
G. Freeman	*v* Lancashire in 1868
S. Haigh	*v* Derbyshire in 1897
	v Somerset in 1902
	v Lancashire in 1909
A. Hill	*v* United South in 1874
	v Surrey in 1880
G.H. Hirst	*v* Leicestershire in 1895
	v Leicestershire in 1907

The Destroyers

M. Leyland	*v* Surrey in 1935
G. Macaulay	*v* Warwickshire in 1923
	v Leicestershire in 1930
	v Glamorgan in 1933
	v Lancashire in 1933
J.T. Newstead	*v* Worcestershire in 1907
E. Peate	*v* Kent in 1882
	v Gloucestershire in 1884
R. Peel	*v* Kent in 1897
W. Rhodes	*v* Derbyshire in 1920
A.L. Robinson	*v* Nottinghamshire in 1974
E. Robinson	*v* Sussex in 1928
	v Kent in 1930
E.P. Robinson	*v* Kent in 1939
H. Sedgewick	*v* Worcestershire in 1906
F.S. Trueman	*v* Nottinghamshire in 1951
	v Nottinghamshire in 1955
	v MCC in 1958
	v Nottinghamshire in 1963
G. Ulyett	*v* Lancashire in 1883
H. Verity	*v* Nottinghamshire in 1932
A. Waddington	*v* Northants in 1920
E. Wainwright	*v* Sussex in 1894
D. Wilson	*v* Nottinghamshire in 1959
	v Nottinghamshire in 1966
	v Kent in 1966

Chapter 16

THE MEN BEHIND THE STUMPS

For some reason completely beyond the comprehension of their colleagues and supporters, Yorkshire wicket-keepers have persistently failed to catch the selector's eye, yet this is a department in which the county have been marvellously well served from the days of George Pinder. He was living proof that wicket-keepers are born not made, for accident brought to official attention his exceptional talents at a time when he had no real interest in the position. He considered himself to be a run-of-the-mill bowler and had given no thought to the techniques of the job, simply enjoying the game as an eighteen-year-old with St Mary's in Sheffield. When the club's regular wicket-keeper failed to arrive for a match against Hull, he volunteered to stand in, as much to see what it was like as to fulfil any ambition. He acquitted himself so well that he never thought again of being a bowler and nor did anyone else.

Another example of the inbred nature of wicket-keeping is provided by the Hunter family, from Scarborough. The most famous branch of this sturdy East Coast tree was, of course, David, who served Yorkshire for twenty-two years, but his elder brother, Joe, earned one England 'cap' before dying at the tragically early age of thirty-five, while William, another brother, would have been the best of the three had he bothered to take up the game professionally. That, at least, was the considered opinion of David.

David Hunter is the county's most successful wicket-keeper with 1,327 victims in all matches and a handsomely high proportion of those – 372 – were stumped. He preferred to stand up to the fastest bowling, but by the 1890s – he began in 1888 – he agreed to move back, admitting: 'I found it better, especially for taking sharp catches.'

That most celebrated of cricket experts, Charles Burgess Fry, the Olympian all-rounder, observed about Hunter: 'He has the mark of the really great wicket-keeper in that he does not appear to do anything wonderful and yet is doing all that is required.' His hands paid adequate tribute to his reflexes and certainty of judgment in taking the ball, for they bore none of the tell-tale marks which

The Men Behind the Stumps

expose those who have to make late adjustments. He had neither swollen joints nor twisted fingers.

Twice Hunter had six wickets in an innings and four times he stumped five men in a match. He revealed a welcome tenacity as a batsman and, recognising his limitations, could be trusted to hold up his end in a crisis, most importantly in the last-wicket stand of 148 with Lord Hawke against Kent in Sheffield in 1898 which stood as the best for Yorkshire until Geoff Boycott and Graham Stevenson beat it at Edgbaston in 1982. Hunter and his captain had possibly the most complete understanding in running between the wickets of any pair.

'We never used to need to call to each other when we set off,' he explained. 'We saw where the ball was and if there was a run in it we ran and said nothing about it at all.' Hunter had two of the most difficult bowlers in the world to keep to in Hirst and Haigh. He regarded the latter as the more testing because of his sharp break-back, while he had to contend with Hirst's phenomenal swing – 'I have seen him swerve it wicket to wicket fully four feet time and again,' but Hunter never asked for any of the signals which have been employed in later years. He dealt with whatever came in a calm unhurried way.

His opinion offers an informed insight into the relative merits of Edmund Peate, Bobby Peel and Wilfred Rhodes, the left-arm spinners with whom he came into serious contact, and he rated them in that order, primarily using accuracy as his yardstick. Hunter's interests took in the breeding of canaries and pigeons, while he was a much admired clog dancer, an able concertina player and handbell ringer. Finally, lest anyone had any doubts about his masculinity, he was a more than punishing boxer.

Reversing roles with Hunter, George Macaulay, who made concessions to nothing and nobody, put Arthur Dolphin at the head of the wicket-keepers in his experience, 'Because I never saw a man with such quick hands.'

This was by no means idle praise – such a pointless exercise would never have appealed to the fiery Macaulay – and Dolphin had an incredibly high proportion of stumpings for the county – 260 against a total of 568 catches over seventeen years. Although he first appeared in 1905, he had to wait until 1910 before becoming established, but from that point he had no serious rival.

One of his outstanding achievements came in 1921, when he conceded only two byes in a Hampshire total of 456 for two at

Arthur Dolphin – one of the great line of Yorkshire wicket-keepers.

Headingley, where the ball got past the bat rather more often than might be imagined. Also a brave and resolute batsman, Dolphin went on to become a much respected umpire, standing several times in Tests – always bareheaded, however hot the day. He found a lot of pleasure in umpiring, for his own Test career was limited to one game – at Melbourne in February 1921 – largely by the presence of Herbert Strudwick, the great Surrey wicket-keeper.

An undemonstrative man, he had a commanding presence which came in handy in a rough and ready public house in the Midlands. The Yorkshire party, taking refreshment and minding their own business, attracted some unwelcome and threatening attention from local ruffians until Dolphin sat down and simply placed his hands, knuckles up, on the table. One look at the gnarled joints convinced the trouble-makers that he must be a celebrated bare-knuckle fighter and they quickly departed.

It says much for Arthur Wood that, following such as Hunter and Dolphin, he managed to set new standards, not least of which concerned consistency. He became the first Yorkshire wicket-keeper to top 1,000 runs in a season, while, remarkably free from injury, he got through 222 consecutive appearances before a casual remark gave him an unwanted break. Brian Sellers heard him talking about his unbroken run and, typically, brought him down to earth with a bang. 'You deserve a rest if you've played in all those games,' said the captain. 'You can be twelfth man and I'll give Paul Gibb a game.'

Wood could adapt readily to most sports, playing golf to a low single-figure handicap, being offered terms by Bradford Park Avenue at soccer and making a few useful breaks at billiards and snooker. Although his batting had uneven patches and he occasionally lost confidence, he displayed a neat, well-organised style when at his best.

He had a flair for lifting bowlers and a ready wit which he delivered with a deadpan expression. Hedley Verity, in one of his rare moments of helpless embarrassment, watched miserably as Kent's Frank Wolley drove a barrage of sixes onto the roof of the stand which used to separate the football and cricket grounds at Bradford.

'You know,' Wood told him as they crossed over at the end of another expensive over, 'it's just like having a boy scout band on the field going rat-a-ta-tat, rat-a-ta-tat.' He also christened himself 'Rhubarb' because he felt that he so often had to go in and sacrifice his wicket to 'force' the pace.

Wood's record run of appearances did not survive long, but the man who broke it can expect to retain his distinction for a long time. Jimmy Binks, a native of Hull, which has not sent forward many of its sons to serve the county, played in 412 matches in an unbroken sequence, a fact which says everything about his facility for taking the ball. He handled Fred Trueman's thunderbolts and stood up without too much trouble to Bob Appleyard and Tony Nicholson, who both did enough with the ball at sufficient pace to test his grasp of the sixth sense which all wicket-keepers have.

He is credited with the season's best haul for Yorkshire – 107 wickets in 1960 – and for fifteen years he became part of the furnishings. 'Lack of confidence was my greatest weakness,' he admitted in his formative days. 'I used to be more concerned about dropping a catch than actually holding one, which meant I was too nervous to relax.' He did not, however, miss many chances down the years and an excess of modesty persuaded him to say: 'The Yorkshire bowlers are so good that I always know where the ball is going to be.' The bowlers knew where he was going to be – exactly in the right place.

His decision to turn to industry, therefore, left a sizeable gap in the operation which Neil Smith filled briefly before giving way to the most ebullient of characters, David Bairstow, another Bradford man, who climbed out of his school desk and defied the risk of injury week after week, season after season – a solid rock in a sea of more than passing confusion.

Bairstow's acrobatic qualities made him particularly valuable in the one-day competitions, where he managed somehow to cover sufficient ground to fill in for leg slip on the one side and first slip on the other, thus giving his side an extra fielder. A variable spin attack created problems when he had to stand up, but his athletic catching to the quicker bowlers can never have been bettered.

Like Pinder, he escaped the confines of his specialist role to whip down a respectable medium-pace in the nets, earning a competitive chance in a Benson and Hedges Cup tie at Trent Bridge. He did not neglect his batting, which sprang strongly out of crude roots, his unyielding spirit enabling him to refine his style and follow Wood as a more than capable late-order run-maker. He completed 1,000 runs in a season twice with fewer matches at his disposal and his 145 off a strong Middlesex attack at Scarborough in 1980 is the highest innings by any Yorkshire wicket-keeper.

The popular east coast resort has another prominent place in the Bairstow file, for at North Marine Road in September 1982 he established a Yorkshire record with seven catches in an innings against Derbyshire, going on to equal the world record for catches in a match – eleven.

Bairstow is reluctant to discuss the relative merit of his catches and stumpings. 'It all happens so quickly that you can't honestly say that one is better than another,' he insists. 'Obviously some are straightforward, but one of those might be quite good because you have kept your concentration for a long time when the ball hardly got past the bat. Others you dive for and either get there or just miss out. You don't think about it, you just go. If you get the ball and catch it you are a hero, but if you drop it you are a fool, or so some people think.'

In the hurly-burly of limited-overs competition, Bairstow put a real sting in the tail. There can have been no more courageous efforts than his 103 not out to bemuse Derbyshire at Derby in the 1981 Benson and Hedges qualifying group. Chasing 203 for victory,

The Men Behind the Stumps

LEFT Jimmy Binks, who established a record with his run of 412 consecutive county championship matches.

RIGHT A study in concentration as David Bairstow polishes the skills that made him an outstanding member of the Yorkshire team in difficult times. Without doubt, he proved the most accomplished of wicket-keeper/batsmen. (*Yorkshire Post*)

Yorkshire collapsed to 123 for nine, but Bairstow refused to accept defeat. Mark Johnson, a medium-paced seamer on debut, contributed four to a last-wicket stand of 80 as his partner slaughtered the bowling. Bairstow made 50 from six overs at one stage, 26 coming from an over by left-arm spinner David Steele.

His enthusiasm is boundless. As a net bowler he will wheel away with unlimited energy and thus is in great demand. At the end of a hectic spell, Bairstow attempted to snatch a few minutes' rest in the dressing-room. 'Bowl me a few in the nets,' asked a batting colleague, throwing a box of balls casually in Bairstow's direction. 'Aye,' said Bairstow, in mock resignation, 'if you fetch me a bucket of sand I'll sing you *The Desert Song* at the same time.'

He is a fitting member of a very elite club.

WICKET-KEEPING RECORDS

	Caught	Stumped	Total
D. Hunter (1888–1909)	861	328	1,189
J.G. Binks (1955–69)	872	172	1,044
A. Wood (1927–46)	612	243	855
A. Dolphin (1905–27)	568	260	828
D.L. Bairstow (1970–83)	680	103	783

MOST DISMISSALS IN AN INNINGS

7 – D.L. Bairstow v Derbyshire at Scarborough in 1982
6 – J. Hunter v Gloucestershire at Gloucester in 1887
    D. Hunter v Surrey at Sheffield in 1891 (one stumped)
    D. Hunter v Middlesex at Leeds in 1909
    W.R. Allen v Sussex at Hove in 1921 (four stumped)
    J.G. Binks v Lancashire at Leeds in 1962 (one stumped)
    D.L. Bairstow v Lancashire at Manchester in 1971
    D.L. Bairstow v Warwickshire at Bradford in 1978
    D.L. Bairstow v Lancashire at Leeds in 1980

MOST DISMISSALS IN A MATCH

11 – D.L. Bairstow v Derbyshire at Scarborough in 1982
 9 – J. Hunter v Gloucestershire at Gloucester in 1887
     A. Dolphin v Derbyshire at Bradford in 1919
     D.L. Bairstow v Lancashire at Manchester in 1971

Chapter 17

RECORD STANDS

First wicket – 555 by Herbert Sutcliffe and Percy Holmes *v* Essex at Leyton, 15–16 June 1932

It is ironic that the meticulous Herbert Sutcliffe, of all people, should have been guilty of a careless act that has for more than fifty years caused a question mark to curl tantalisingly around his brilliant partnership with Holmes. The figure of 555 has been established in the record books and will not now be removed, but the facts indicate that the Yorkshire pair actually finished on 554, level with John Brown and John Tunnicliffe.

When the scoreboard rolled up to 555, Sutcliffe, in his own words, 'simply forgot about everything to lash out in the best country style'. As a consequence, he played on to Lawrence Eastman and Brian Sellers promptly declared.

The players left the field, but when Holmes and Sutcliffe returned to be photographed under the board, it obstinately clanked back to 554 and consternation reigned. Sutcliffe, justifiably annoyed, said that had he known the declaration was coming he would have tried to carry his bat and at least another couple of runs would have left no room for error. On the other hand, he had played long enough to know that his captain would not want to go on much longer once the record had been broken and, in any case, the board had been wrong several times on the second morning.

That was often the case at Leyton, where the scorers sat underneath and could not check visually on the information displayed, so that matters were left in the hands of the groundstaff – a situation not exactly unfamiliar in certain outposts today. This flaw in the system was exaggerated by the fact that Billy Ringrose, the Yorkshire scorer, apparently dealt with both books for a spell when the Essex representative, Charles McGahey, took a toilet break. The official version of the story brings in a business-like clergyman, who, busily keeping his own account of the proceedings, drew attention to the possibility that a no-ball might have been missed from the first ball of the second day. The umpire, Tiger Smith, of Warwickshire fame, conveniently recalled receiving a signal from Ringrose, labouring singlehanded at the time, but neither book had a note of this occurrence. The mystery of the extra delivery which should, of course, have been bowled, did not receive a mention and not everyone by any means accepted the justice of the final decision, which brought an alteration in the official record to raise the total by that vital single.

As *Wisden* shrewdly noted: 'Some of the circumstances surrounding this Leyton achievement were not quite desirable.' The Essex captain, Charles Bray, later admitted that there had been some collusion.

In his account, which carries an authentic ring, McGahey came to him as he lay resting in the Essex dressing-room to say that he and Ringrose were under pressure to find an extra run as their entries added up to 554. Tired and depressed, Bray gave his consent, bearing in mind that the faulty Essex board had misled the principals, but he came to regret this generous act, recognising that however much Holmes and Sutcliffe might have deserved the distinction and however certain they appeared to get it, the mathematics of the game are too important to be trifled with, whatever the excuse.

The quality of the performance is in no way diminished by the hubbub which followed. Holmes, like Tunnicliffe at Chesterfield, came to glory under a substantial handicap – in his case lumbago. He had been suffering for a little while and escaped almost at once when the wicket-keeper got both hands to a difficult chance without being able to make the catch stick. Holmes, understandably, lingered in the wake of his partner and felt that he might easily get out at any moment. Indeed, dismissal would not have been all that unwelcome since it promised relief from the nagging torment in his back. Gradually, though, the rhythm of the innings swept him up into its lengthening stride and the runs flowed, 423 coming in the first day.

The landmarks came and went – 100 runs in one hour and forty-five minutes; 200 in three hours and twenty minutes; 300 in four hours and thirty-five minutes; 400 in five hours and fifty-five minutes. Holmes spent a fitful night with his lumbago exacting full price for his endeavours and he seriously considered retiring. 'I would not,' he said, 'have given twopence for our chances of putting another 25 onto the overnight score.' The enthusiasts, presumably unaware of this difficulty, turned up in vast numbers to watch history unfold before their eyes and at 12.50 Sutcliffe imperiously

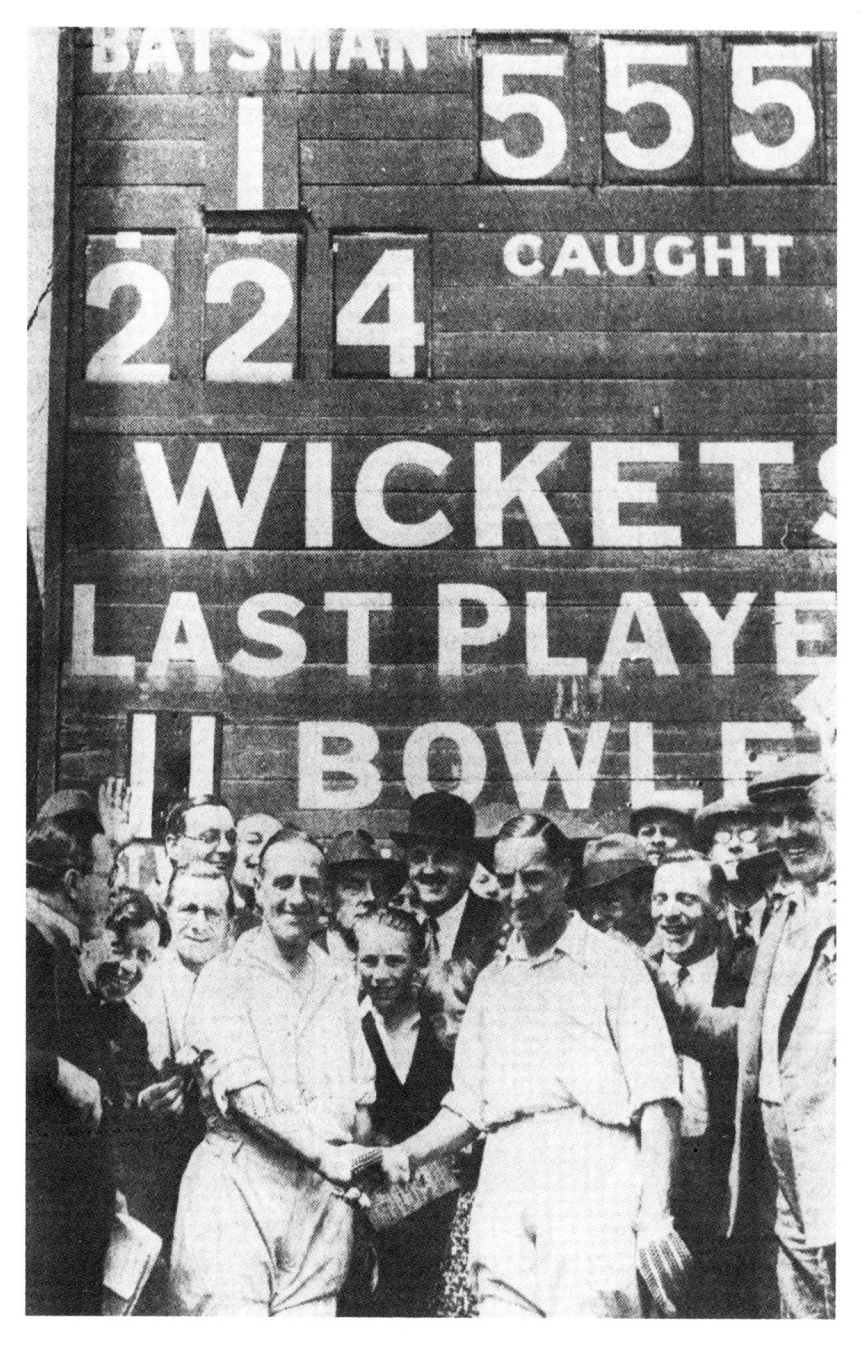

A golden moment on June 16, 1932. Percy Holmes (left) and Herbert Sutcliffe are pictured under the Leyton scoreboard showing their record 555 partnership, but there is some argument about the actual total.

struck two boundaries, the second of which took them past Brown and Tunnicliffe – or so they thought.

All, in the end, turned out for the best and Essex, who had also endured the back-breaking toil of fielding out to a huge Surrey score of 252 for one on the last day of the previous match, capitulated. The home side had no spirit for the fight, being bowled out for 78 and 164 to lose by an innings and 313.

Holmes was, incidentally, presented with a large photograph of himself and Sutcliffe, taken with the scoreboard as a background. It had been autographed and used as an advertisement for raincoats. The modest Holmes found a suitable use for what might, in the hands of some men, have become a major feature of the home. 'It comes in useful to cover up the fireplace in summer,' he said.

YORKSHIRE *v* ESSEX
at Leyton 15-17 June 1932

Yorkshire   *first innings*
Holmes   not out   224
Sutcliffe   b Eastman   313
extras   18
(one wkt dec)   555

Bowling: Nichols 13-4-105-0; Daer 40-8-106-0; Smith (P) 46-10-128-0; O'Connor 23-5-73-0; Eastman 22.4-2-97-1; Crawley 3-0-7-0; Taylor 4-0-14-0; Bray 1-0-7-0.

Essex

	first innings		*second innings*	
Crawley	b Bowes	0	c Sutcliffe b Bowes	27
Pope	c Rhodes b Bowes	6	c Mitchell b Bowes	9
O'Connor	b Bowes	20	c Rhodes b Bowes	7
Cutmore	lbw b Bowes	0	b Verity	1
Nichols	b Verity	25	not out	59
Eastman	c Sutcliffe b Macaulay	16	c Barber b Verity	19
Bray	c and b Verity	1	st Wood b Verity	6
Taylor	c Macaulay b Verity	5	c Macaulay b Verity	13
Sheffield	c and b Verity	0	c Sutcliffe b Verity	5
Daer	c and b Verity	0	c Verity b Bowes	0
Smith (P.)	not out	2	c Rhodes b Bowes	0
extras		3	extras	18
		78		164

Fall of wickets: 1-0, 2-19, 3-19, 4-48, 5-59, 6-60, 7-66, 8-72, 9-74.

Fall of wickets: 1-38, 2-47, 3-50, 4-50, 5-92, 6-128, 7-148, 8-162, 9-164.

Bowling: Bowes 12-1-38-4; A.C. Rhodes 10-5-15-0; Macaulay 7.1-2-14-1; Verity 7-3-8-5.

Bowling: Bowes 23.4-5-47-5; A.C. Rhodes 9-5-23-0; Verity 30-12-45-5; Macaulay 16-5-31-0.

Record Stands

Second wicket – 346 by Wilf Barber and Morris Leyland *v* Middlesex at Sheffield, 27 June 1932

Yorkshire found themselves playing second fiddle to Middlesex at Bramall Lane, where Patsy Hendren's century gave the visitors a sound first innings' score. In the absence of Sutcliffe, Holmes and Bill Bowes, who were on duty against All India, the county were

YORKSHIRE *v* MIDDLESEX
at Sheffield 25–28 June 1932

Middlesex	*first innings*		*second innings*	
Stevens	c Wood b Hall	5		
Allen	c Wood b Hall	57	lbw b Rhodes	15
Hearne	c Macaulay b Verity	29		
Hendren	c and b Macaulay	123		
Lee	c Rhodes b Macaulay	13	c Dennis b Rhodes	0
Hulme	c Dennis b Hall	29	not out	114
Haigh	b Hall	1		
Sims	c Wood b Hall	29	c Wood b Barber	49
Hart	c Macaulay b Hall	30	lbw b Rhodes	0
Price	c Sellers b Verity	6	b Sellers	7
Durston	not out	2		
extras		16	extras	11
		340	(5 wkts)	196

Fall of wickets: 1–8, 2–75, 3–105, 4–143, 5–231, 6–237, 7–287, 8–327, 9–336.

Bowling: Hall 40.2-15-71-6; Rhodes 27-7-58-0; Dennis 11-1-34-0; Verity 42-11-100-2; Macaulay 19-5-45-2; Turner 9-2-16-0.

Fall of wickets: 1–5, 2–28, 3–28, 4–177, 5–196.

Bowling: Hall 6-3-8-0; Rhodes 15-6-18-3; Verity 17-4-45-0; Turner 5-2-7-0; Dennis 3-0-18-0; Macaulay 7-1-16-0; Mitchell 8-2-25-0; Barber 10-0-25-1; Sellers 3.5-0-23-1.

Yorkshire	*first innings*	
Mitchell	b Allen	3
Barber	c Price b Allen	162
Leyland	c Durston b Sims	189
Turner	b Sims	5
Sellers	not out	61
Dennis	c Allen b Haigh	23
Wood	b Allen	7
Verity	c Hearne b Stevens	8
Macaulay	not out	3
extras		20
	(7 wkts dec.)	481

Fall of wickets: 1–9, 2–355, 3–371, 4–371, 5–411, 6–432, 7–458.

Bowling: Allen 34-8-115-3; Durston 23-6-58-0; Hearne 19-2-46-0; Stevens 13-3-34-1; Haig 19-4-40-1; Hulme 5-0-18-0; Sims 30-7-78-2; Lee 10-2-37-0; Hart 6-0-35-0.

obviously weakened and when Arthur Mitchell got out at nine the spectre of defeat arose. Morris Leyland, troubled by a leg strain suffered in pursuit of a quick single in the previous match with Sussex, was not at his best, while Barber also had his moments of uncertainty, so that Yorkshire lunched uneasily on 45 for one.

The uphill struggle continued throughout the afternoon, with the batsmen wresting the advantage inch by inch from the bowlers on an admittedly friendly pitch which allowed neither deviation nor variety of bounce. By tea the total had increased to 178 and appetites around the ground were all the keener for that. Yorkshire had also come to terms with another problem, for, at 53, playing back to Greville Stevens, Leyland aggravated his injury and had to call for a runner – Mitchell, who took his share of the hard work without hope of personal reward or recognition.

Far from being restrained, Leyland, wanting to be as little trouble as possible, hit the ball hard and often, reaching his century out of 202 in three hours. Barber needed another thirty minutes to complete three figures, but Middlesex were by then more interested in saving runs than taking wickets, so the balance of power lay with Yorkshire. In a glorious spurt towards the close, 135 runs came in only eighty minutes before Leyland finally edged to slip. He hit twenty-eight boundaries to Barber's fourteen, but the latter's elegance also illuminated the scene.

Third wicket – 323 unfinished by Herbert Sutcliffe and Morris Leyland *v* Glamorgan at Huddersfield, 27 June 1928

The month of June in 1928 did not encourage cricket, for the weather interrupted the proceedings too often to permit a reasonable rhythm. Huddersfield did not escape the deluge, but squeezed in between the showers came some brilliant batting which punished pretty poor bowling. The Glamorgan attack was handicapped by the wet ball, but the ground also devalued some of the stroke-play. Holmes and Edgar Oldroyd were the two who missed out before Sutcliffe and Leyland got into their stride. Rain caused a hold-up for fifteen minutes at one o'clock and a heavier downpour prevented the resumption after lunch until twenty-five past three, so that altogether there was no more than four and a half hours' playing time.

Sutcliffe, making the most of two 'lives', pressed on briskly, but Leyland pulled back up to lunch, which came with Yorkshire on 123 for two (Sutcliffe 47, Leyland 33). After that the left-hander increased the tempo, making up for time lost in the pavilion with 50 runs of his own in fifty-three minutes. At tea, therefore, he led by 91 to 69, and his century arrived out of 165 added in two hours. He, too, was missed twice while Sutcliffe, whose hundred occupied three hours and forty minutes, gave another unaccepted chance to slip.

Despite the delays and the slow outfield, Sutcliffe and Leyland averaged 90 an hour and the pity was that the last two days had to be abandoned, although Glamorgan could not have shared that view. Among the toiling ranks of the Welsh county on that day was Jack Mercer, whose association with the game stretched on into the 1980s as scorer with Northamptonshire. He looked back often with admiration to that feat. 'They played with such certainty that at times we barely knew where to try and keep them quiet. They simply gave us no respite and I wasn't sorry to see it rain,' he admitted.

YORKSHIRE v GLAMORGAN
at Huddersfield 27-29 June 1928

Yorkshire	*first innings*	
Holmes	c Walters b Davies (E.)	20
Sutcliffe	not out	147
Oldroyd	c Hills b Smart	11
Leyland	not out	189
extras		20
	(2 wkts)	387

Fall of wickets: 1-29, 2-64.
Bowling: Mercer 26-3-87-0; Arnott 22-1-88-0; Davies (E.) 17-5-49-1; Smart 11-0-64-1; Ryan 12-0-46-0; Davies (D.) 10-1-33-0.

Fourth wicket – 312 by David Denton and George Hirst v Hampshire at Southampton, 21-22 May 1914

Yorkshire charted an unusually erratic course as war clouds gathered on the horizon in 1914. They opened their account with three victories by an innings, but at Southampton they faltered badly. Inspired by the brilliance of Phil Mead, who played a typically sturdy innings of 213, Hampshire gained a first-innings' lead of 184 and made early inroads into Yorkshire's second attempt.

At 114 for three, the White Rose looked distinctly wind blown and Hirst joined Denton to negotiate a tricky last quarter of an hour on the second day. Continuing their resistance, the pair defied Hampshire until tea-time, ensuring against defeat and by degree taking command of the situation. They had, as a foundation-laying

YORKSHIRE v HAMPSHIRE
at Southampton 20-22 May 1914

Yorkshire

	first innings			second innings	
Rhodes	b Remnant	24		c Livsey b Brown	28
Wilson (B.)	c Livsey b Brown	56		b Remnant	19
Denton	c Mead b Brown	17		not out	168
Kilner	c Kennedy b Jacques	24		c Remnant b Smith	33
Hirst	c Mead b Jacques	17		c Kennedy b Newman	146
Burton	c Livsey b Remnant	15			
Drake	b Jacques	36			
Booth	b Kennedy	18			
Holmes	c Smith b Jacques	0			
Sir A. White	b Kennedy	1			
Dolphin	not out	4			
extras		20		extras	32
		232		(4 wkts dec.)	426

Fall of wickets: 1-62, 2-99, 3-107, 4-143, 5-152, 6-180, 7-227, 8-227, 9-228.

Bowling: Jacques 22.1-6-52-4; Kennedy 26-4-67-2; Brown 19-5-45-2; Smith 2-0-10-0; Remnant 9-1-29-2.

Fall of wickets: 1-45, 2-47, 3-114, 4-426.

Bowling: Jacques 26-6-56-0; Kennedy 45-17-104-0; Brown 19-5-70-1; Remnant 13-3-27-1; Newman 21.1-6-54-1; Smith 12-1-51-1; Bowell 12-1-32-0.

Hampshire

	first innings			second innings	
Stone	c Denton b Hirst	8		lbw b Drake	7
Bowell	c Hirst b Booth	2		not out	20
Remnant	b Rhodes	46		c Rhodes b Drake	0
Mead	c White b Hirst	213			
Brown	b Drake	24		not out	17
Newman	c Kilner b Rhodes	21		c Dolphin b Rhodes	26
Harrison	st Dolphin b Rhodes	76			
Kennedy	c Dolphin b Booth	4			
Jacques	lbw b Booth	3			
Smith	c White b Booth	1			
Livsey	not out	0			
extras		18		extras	7
		416		(3 wkts)	77

Fall of wickets: 1-8, 2-16, 3-93, 4-134, 5-189, 6-359, 7-406, 8-414, 9-416.

Bowling: Hirst 29.1-6-90-2; Booth 31-2-113-4; Drake 17-1-82-1; Rhodes 27-6-75-3; Kilner 10-0-38-0.

Fall of wickets: 1-22, 2-32, 3-40.

Bowling: Booth 5-2-6-0; Drake 16-7-19-2; Rhodes 12-4-23-1; Kilner 4-1-13-0; Wilson 3-0-9-0.

exercise, to keep a wary eye on defence so that in two hours up to lunch they scraped only 99, raising the total from 139 to 238, and the innings had been in progress for five hours and twenty minutes when the 300 was signalled.

Having made their point and rescued their side, Denton and Hirst could proceed to enjoy themselves, which they did, throwing off all restraint to hammer 100 in fifty minutes.

Denton completed his first century of the summer and hit twenty-seven boundaries, while Hirst had nineteen fours and one six, and it is significant that for all their caution they averaged seventy an hour throughout their association, a rate of progress that would now be admired in the most favourable of circumstances. Cricket surely was a better game when the fielding side put the emphasis largely, if not entirely, on taking wickets. Containment is a wearisome exercise.

Fifth wicket – 340 by Ted Wainwright and George Hirst *v* Surrey at the Oval, 10–11 August 1899

In many ways the season of 1899 turned into a disaster with Hirst fighting his way out of a frustrating and dispiriting spell with the ball. He had to consider whether to give up his bowling to concentrate on his batting, which remained thoroughly reliable, and it was felt in some official quarters that too much use was being made of him albeit that he was 'as strong as a lion and a glutton for work'. The thought that he could prosper as a specialist batsman gained substance from three consecutive centuries – a sequence never previously achieved – the first of which came at the Oval as Yorkshire made their highest score against Surrey.

As a contest the fixture never got off the ground, for the wicket remained perfect from a batsman's point of view and horrendous so far as the bowlers were concerned. Under a burning sun Surrey toiled for five hours and twenty minutes on the first day to keep Yorkshire down to 478 for four, with Wainwright and Hirst helping themselves to 176 in one hundred minutes. The remaining 164 runs in their partnership used up no more than one hour and fifty minutes so that they rushed along at 97 runs an hour.

Wainwright needed a little luck along the road to his career best 228, being dropped on nine, 28 and 188, but Hirst offered no semblance of a chance. Surrey's reply brought heartache for the Yorkshire bowlers, with Bobby Abel and Tom Hayward putting on

448, and it was in this match that Schofield Haigh thought he had bowled Hayward only for the umpires to rule that the ball had rebounded from David Hunter's pads.

Over eighty years later, we are still subjected to pitches that ensure stalemate and it remains one of cricket's quirks that conditions in which the bowlers have no real prospect of success are invariably described as 'good' while those which favour them are usually marked down as 'unfit'.

YORKSHIRE v SURREY
at the Oval
10–12 August 1899

Yorkshire	first innings	
Jackson	c Richardson b Brockwell	18
Tunnicliffe	c Hayes b Richardson	50
Denton	c Pretty b Brockwell	47
Mitchell	b Jephson	87
Wainwright	c Hayward b Lockwood	228
Hirst	b Richardson	186
Smith	c Jephson b Lockwood	8
Haigh	not out	24
Lord Hawke	b Richardson	13
Rhodes	b Richardson	8
Hunter	b Richardson	0
extras		35
		704

Fall of wickets: 1-67, 2-104, 3-142, 4-302, 5-642, 6-650, 7-660, 8-678, 9-700.
Bowling: Lockwood 39-9-146-2; Richardson 53.1-15-152-5; Brockwell 49-12-144-2; Hayward 14-4-56-0; Jephson 25-1-97-1; Abel 10-2-42-0; Pretty 4-1-15-0; Hayes 4-0-17-0.

Surrey	first innings	
Pretty	ht wkt b Smith	15
Brockwell	c Mitchell b Smith	29
Hayes	c Mitchell b Smith	6
Abel	c Smith b Jackson	193
Hayward	c Hunter b Jackson	273
Jephson	c Tunnicliffe b Jackson	23
Lockwood	c sub b Jackson	4
Key	not out	4
extras		4
	(7 wkts)	551

Fall of wickets: 1-23, 2-29, 3-59, 4-506, 5-529, 6-541, 7-551.
Bowling: Rhodes 28-11-58-0; Smith 55-16-141-3; Jackson 47.2-15-101-4; Hirst 22-5-63-0; Wainwright 31-7-100-0; Haigh 31-8-61-0; Denton 6-0-25-0; Tunnicliffe 2-0-5-0.

Sixth wicket – 276 by Morris Leyland and Emmott Robinson *v* Glamorgan at Swansea, 28 and 30 August 1926

Yorkshire's first visit to Swansea attracted a crowd of more than 10,000, despite the start of the Football League programme, and the spectators had plenty to celebrate throughout the first morning as four wickets fell for the addition of 14 runs. The pitch, which had been watered too much, was bare of grass and gave assistance to all the bowlers. In the conditions left-arm spinner Frank Ryan caused the ball to turn sharply from leg under the hot sun. Leyland and Robinson began their partnership at twenty past two, adding 173 runs in the two hours and five minutes to tea.

Leyland took time to assess the difficulties before raising the tempo smoothly to reach 50 out of 78 in seventy minutes. He gave one very sharp chance at 81 when mis-hitting a pull which sent the ball high on the leg side but just out of reach of the Glamorgan fielders who rapidly assembled in the vicinity of its return to earth. His fifth century of the season occupied only two and a quarter hours and Robinson appeared quite laboured by comparison. His innings, though less stylish and lacking the rich variety of stroke, contained some powerful blows, struck mainly through the offside. Even so, his half-century came in two hours, while he batted for four hours in making 124.

The superb Leyland hammered one six and nineteen fours in his 191 in more or less the same time against bowling and fielding which stood up bravely to the pounding. Glamorgan were thoroughly outplayed and finally destroyed by the skills of George Macaulay, who raced through their second innings on a drying pitch to earn a victory brought about by that superb stand and two well-timed declarations.

YORKSHIRE v GLAMORGAN
at Swansea
28, 30 and 31 August 1926

Yorkshire	*first innings*		*second innings*	
Holmes	b Ryan	27	c Bates b Mercer	3
Sutcliffe	lbw b Ryan	20	b Mercer	7
Leyland	lbw b Mercer	191	b Ryan	27
Mitchell	b Mercer	1	c Arnott b Ryan	25
Kilner	b Mercer	4	c Riches b Ryan	52
Stephenson	c Walters b Ryan	18	b Mercer	5
Robinson	not out	124	run out	9
Macaulay	not out	23	not out	13
Waddington	did not bat		not out	2
extras		12	extras	11
	(6 wkts dec.)	420	(7 wkts dec.)	154

Fall of wickets: 1-48, 2-51, 3-52, 4-62, 5-103, 6-379.

Bowling: Mercer 39-9-100-3; Arnott 16-2-55-0; Ryan 33-1-115-3; Bates 9-1-50-0; E. Davies 19-2-49-0; Clay 13-3-39-0.

Fall of wickets: 1-8, 2-17, 3-56, 4-91, 5-96, 6-134, 7-143.

Bowling: Mercer 22-8-34-3; Arnott 6-0-24-0; Ryan 20-2-77-3; Davies 4-1-8-0.

Glamorgan	*first innings*		*second innings*	
Riches	b Robinson	1	b Macaulay	1
Bell	b Robinson	59	c Lupton b Macaulay	5
Bates	c Stephenson b Robinson	66	lbw b Robinson	6
Turnbull	b Kilner	3	run out	7
Walters	b Macaulay	69	b Macaulay	2
Arnott	c Sutcliffe b Robinson	11	b Macaulay	25
E. Davies	b Waddington	25	not out	11
Clay	lbw b Waddington	1	c Sutcliffe b Macaulay	4
Mercer	c Waddington b Kilner	32	c Waddington b Robinson	8
Ryan	b Robinson	14	b Macaulay	0
Sullivan	not out	7	b Macaulay	4
extras		20	extras	3
		308		76

Fall of wickets: 1-18, 2-127, 3-136, 4-136, 5-150, 6-211, 7-215, 8-266, 9-304.

Bowling: Robinson 27.2-11-56-5; Macaulay 24-1-68-1; Waddington 19-1-54-2; Kilner 41-11-110-2.

Fall of wickets: 1-5, 2-14, 3-16, 4-22, 5-30, 6-36, 7-66, 8-72, 9-72.

Bowling: Robinson 19-5-41-2; Macaulay 18.1-4-32-7.

OPPOSITE Morris Leyland gives some advice to Doug Padgett at the Headingley nets. Padgett proved an apt pupil, becoming the youngest player to represent the county and eventually taking over himself as Yorkshire coach. (*Yorkshire Post*)

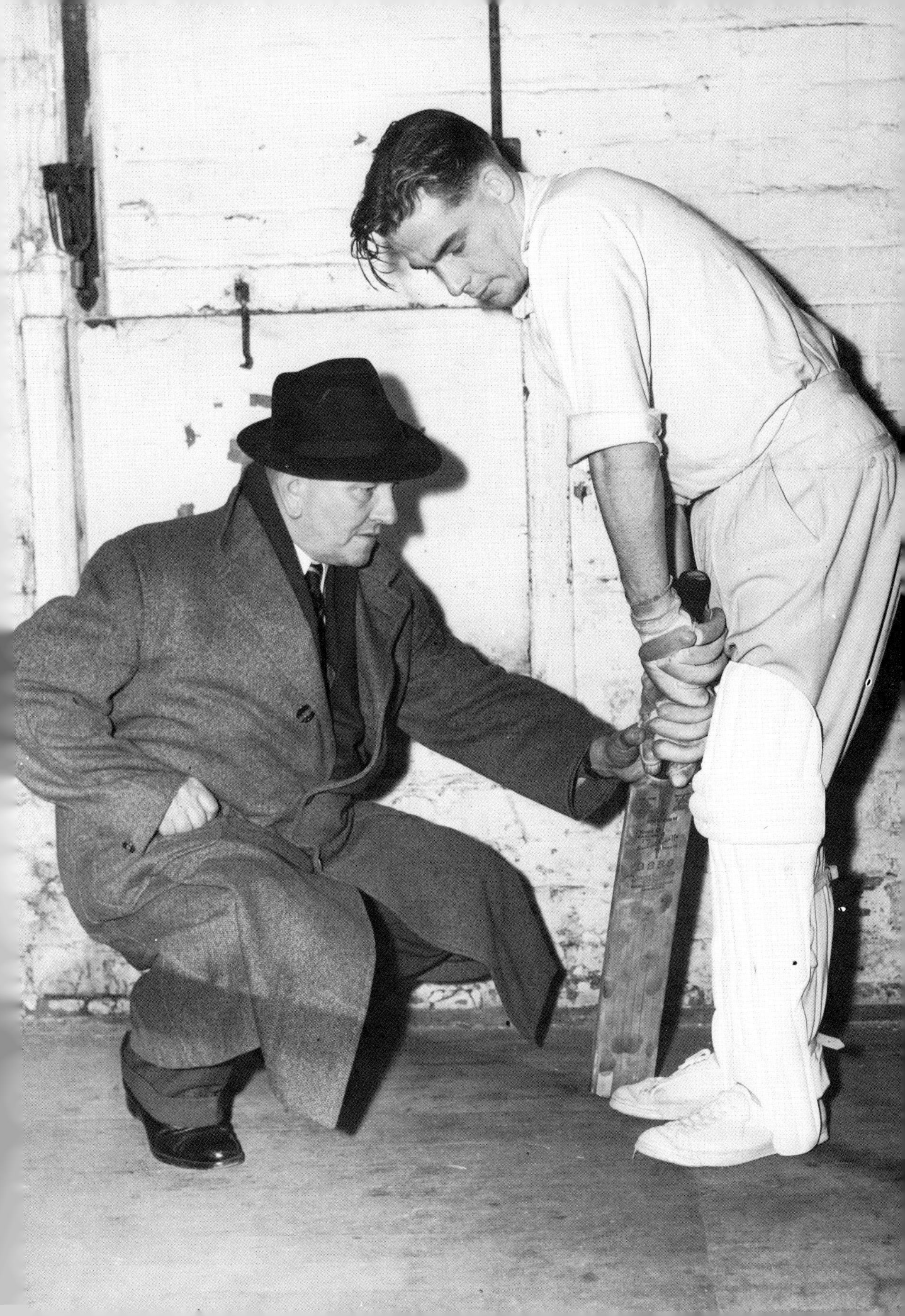

Seventh wicket – 254 by Derek Burton and Wilfred Rhodes *v* Hampshire at Dewsbury on 11 July 1919

Hampshire offered so little resistance in this match that they were defeated by an innings and 143 runs at ten minutes to two on the second day, yet they began positively and captured six wickets for

YORKSHIRE v HAMPSHIRE
at Dewsbury
11–12 July 1919

Yorkshire	*first innings*	
Holmes	b Kennedy	9
Sutcliffe	lbw b Jameson	46
Denton	c and b Melle	36
R. Kilner	b Jameson	0
Rhodes	c Kennedy b Newcombe	135
Hirst	c Kennedy b Melle	0
Robinson	lbw b Kennedy	12
Burton	not out	142
Waddington	b Jameson	1
extras		20
	(8 wkts dec.)	401

Fall of wickets: 1–14, 2–91, 3–91, 4–91, 5–91, 6–123, 7–377, 8–401.

Bowling: Brown 11–2–32–0; Kennedy 26–3–109–2; Tennyson 2–0–17–0; Ryan 11–1–44–0; Melle 20–6–42–2; Jameson 21.4–4–82–3; McGibbon 1–0–10–0; Black 5–0–26–0; Mead 2–0–9–0; Newcombe 2–0–10–1.

Hampshire	*first innings*		*second innings*	
Melle	b Williams	24	c Waddington b Rhodes	34
Brown	b Williams	1	b Rhodes	16
Newcombe	b Williams	1	c Robinson b Waddington	50
Mead	b Williams	23	c and b Waddington	1
Tennyson	c Kilner b Williams	5	st Dolphin b Rhodes	41
McGibbon	b Williams	0	not out	1
Kennedy	b Williams	5	st Dolphin b Rhodes	0
Jameson	b Williams	6	c Robinson b Rhodes	6
Black	b Williams	0	c Denton b Rhodes	0
Maartensz	c Holmes b Kilner	4	b Williams	21
Ryan	not out	5	b Waddington	0
extras		8	extras	6
		82		176

Fall of wickets: 1–8, 2–14, 3–45, 4–56, 5–56, 6–61, 7–65, 8–65, 9–76.

Bowling: Waddington 8–1–25–0; Williams 12.5–4–29–9; Kilner 5–1–20–1.

Fall of wickets: 1–37, 2–78, 3–89, 4–118, 5–124, 6–130, 7–131, 8–163, 9–167.

Bowling: Waddington 21–4–50–3; Williams 14.3–4–37–1; Rhodes 24–4–66–6; Robinson 5–0–17–0

123 before lunch on a mild pitch. In one two-over spell they dismissed Sutcliffe, Denton, Roy Kilner and Hirst, while the scoreboard remained stuck on 91, but Burton and Rhodes showed little concern for the situation.

They had to contend with a leg theory attack and were crowded by fielders, but they soon took full advantage of the wide open spaces in the outfield to change the complexion of things. They were in part aided by a strange captaincy of Lionel Tennyson, who switched his bowlers too often giving no one the chance to settle into length and line, and 216 runs flowed in two hours and twenty minutes, with Rhodes completing his only century of the summer in two and half hours.

Burton's hundred was his first for the county, but he came to it in a very quick time – two and a quarter hours. Neither batsman gave a chance until Rhodes, on 107, edged to third slip and escaped. Altogether the pair added their runs in 165 minutes. A feature of the game was the bowling of Ambrose Williams, who burst onto the scene with an incredible spell of nine for 28, with eight of his victims being bowled.

Eighth wicket – 292 by Lord Hawke and Robert Peel *v* Warwickshire at Birmingham on 8 May 1896

This was the match in which Yorkshire broke so many records, the principal one being for the biggest score in an English county championship match. They also became the first county to include four separate centuries in one innings, which lasted for all the first two days. By the time Lord Hawke and Peel came together, therefore, the Warwickshire bowling had rather lost interest and enthusiasm.

The score then stood at 448 for seven and they carried it to 740. Warwickshire called upon ten bowlers, who went through their paces with varying degrees of application. Peel remained circumspect throughout the slaughter, hitting only sixteen boundaries in his 210, but Lord Hawke managed twenty-one in his 166. Peel had fifty-nine singles to his credit and struck only two boundaries in more than an hour towards the end of his marathon – presumably surrendering to the air of lethargic inevitability which hung over the proceedings. Overall, Yorkshire batted for ten hours and fifty minutes – a long time by any standards – and they might well have won had they set their minds firmly on the main objective.

YORKSHIRE v WARWICKSHIRE
at Birmingham
7-9 May 1896

Yorkshire *first innings*
Jackson	c Law b Ward	117
Tunnicliffe	c Pallett b Glover	28
Brown	c Hill b Pallett	23
Denton	c W. G. Quaife b Santall	6
Moorhouse	b Ward	72
Wainwright	run out	126
Peel	not out	210
Milligan	b Pallett	34
Lord Hawke	b Pallett	166
Hirst	c Glover b Santall	85
Hunter	b Pallett	5
extras		15
		887

Fall of wickets: 1-63, 2-124, 3-141, 4-211, 5-339, 6-406, 7-448, 8-740, 9-876.
Bowling: Santall 65-9-223-2; Ward 62-11-175-2; Glover 30-1-154-1; Pallett 75.3-14-184-4; W. G. Quaife 8-1-33-0; Bainbridge 6-1-17-0; Hill 3-0-14-0; Lilley 6-1-13-0; W. Quaife 9-1-18-0; Driver 10-1-41-0.

Warwickshire *first innings* / *second innings*
Bainbridge	c Hunter b Hirst	5	b Wainwright	29
W. Quaife	b Hirst	0	not out	18
W. G. Quaife	not out	92		
Law	c Jackson b Hirst	7		
Lilley	b Hirst	0		
Hill	b Hirst	4		
Driver	b Peel	27		
Pallett	c Wainwright b Jackson	25		
Santall	b Hirst	29		
Glover	b Hirst	1		
Ward	b Hirst	3		
extras		10	extras	1
		203		(1 wkt) 48

Fall of wickets: 1-0, 2-7, 3-25, 4-25, 5-31, 6-78, 7-117, 8-170, 9-176.
Bowling: Hirst 40.1-16-59-8; Peel 31-21-27-1; Jackson 18-9-23-1; Wainwright 16-7-35-0; Milligan 13-5-14-0; Brown 4-0-24-0; Moorhouse 4-1-11-0.

Fall of wickets: 1-48.
Bowling: Milligan 5-1-15-0; Moorhouse 4-0-24-0; Peel 3-2-4-0; Wainwright 2.1-1-4-1.

Ninth wicket - 192 by George Hirst and Schofield Haigh v Surrey at Bradford on 7-8 June 1898

If any partnership completely turned the course of a game it must have been this one between two of the most reliable professionals. They came together in the gloom of the second evening - rain

Record Stands

YORKSHIRE v SURREY
at Bradford
6-8 June 1898

Surrey *first innings*

Abel	st Hunter b Wainwright	51
Brockwell	b Wainwright	19
Hayward	st Hunter b Rhodes	1
Baldwin	c and b Wainwright	3
Jephson	c and b Wainwright	4
Key	c Jackson b Rhodes	32
Street	c Tunnicliffe b Rhodes	0
Lockwood	st Hunter b Rhodes	2
Lees	b Wainwright	18
Wood	not out	8
Richardson	c Denton b Rhodes	0
extras		1
		139

second innings

	c Jackson b Rhodes	6
	lbw b Wainwright	5
	b Wainwright	2
	b Wainwright	0
	c Brown b Rhodes	0
	not out	8
	st Hunter b Rhodes	4
	c Hunter b Rhodes	0
	st Hunter b Rhodes	0
	st Hunter b Rhodes	0
	c Hunter b Rhodes	9
extras		3
		37

Fall of wickets: 1-42, 2-43, 3-52, 4-56, 5-111, 6-111, 7-111, 8-131, 9-137.

Bowling: Haigh 13-3-28-0; Jackson 16-6-21-0; Rhodes 30.3-12-46-5; Wainwright 27-11-43-5.

Fall of wickets: 1-8, 2-10, 3-10, 4-11, 5-13, 6-17, 7-17, 8-17, 9-23.

Bowling: Wainwright 20-14-10-3; Rhodes 19.1-9-24-7.

Yorkshire *first innings*

Brown	b Lockwood	0
Tunnicliffe	run out	21
Jackson	c and b Lockwood	3
Denton	b Lockwood	11
Wainwright	lbw b Richardson	5
Hirst	not out	130
Moorhouse	c Hayward b Lockwood	12
Lord Hawke	b Lees	5
Rhodes	c Jephson b Richardson	13
Haigh	c Abel b Brockwell	85
extras		12
	(9 wkts dec.)	297

Fall of wickets: 1-0, 2-6, 3-34, 4-44, 5-44, 6-70, 7-78, 8-105, 9-297.

Bowling: Lockwood 41-18-74-4; Hayward 13-3-36-0; Richardson 29-7-64-2; Lees 18-8-41-1; Jephson 8-0-30-0; Brockwell 6.2-1-18-1; Abel 4-1-8-0; Street 5-0-14-0.

washed out the first day – with Yorkshire in desperate trouble. Their score stood at 105 for eight in reply to 139 and Surrey were confidently expecting an important lead on a pitch that gave the bowlers a lot of hope.

Hirst and Haigh set themselves to see out the session, but despite strictly limiting their ambitions, managed to collect 37 in the last half hour – clear indication that they missed few chances to hit the indifferent delivery. On the resumption, Hirst signalled a continuation of Yorkshire's defiance by striking the underarm lobs of Mr Jephson, the amateur, to the boundary with widely appreciated vigour and the run-rate rose appreciably. Much of the Surrey bowling lacked accuracy in the face of this brutal challenge and they made a fatal error when Hirst was 83, a straightforward chance to square leg off Mr Jephson being put down.

Hirst reached his only county century of the season and by that stage Surrey were thoroughly upset about an umpire's decision which had gone in his favour when he might just have been run out at the start of the innings. The partnership realised 192 in 170 minutes as Surrey went through all manner of bowling permutations which involved sixteen changes. Haigh did not give a chance and thoroughly compensated for disappointing work in the Surrey innings.

The pitch played much easier while Hirst and Haigh were together, but Surrey, utterly dispirited, collapsed in total misery in their second innings, being bundled out for 37 in only eighty-five minutes, Yorkshire having plenty of runs and time to spare.

Tenth wicket – 149 by Geoff Boycott and Graham Stevenson *v* Warwickshire at Edgbaston on 20 May 1982

The one area in which Yorkshire managed a degree of improvement in comparatively modern times was in the depth of their batting, for during the 1980s they managed on occasions to put into the field eleven players each with a first-class century to his credit. Reasonably accomplished run-makers such as Arnie Sidebottom and Phil Carrick regularly found themselves denied much room for manœuvre except in the desperate circumstances of an early-order collapse and often what would normally be described as 'the tail' responded effectively to the demands of a tricky situation on a difficult pitch. Graham Stevenson, in fact, has supportable claims to being the best batsman to have appeared on the card at number eleven as a matter of policy, for there are few harder strikers of the ball.

Yorkshire's last-wicket record of 148, held by Lord Hawke and the faithful David Hunter from 1898, had been in danger in 1977, when Sidebottom and the determined Arthur Robinson squeezed 144 runs from the Glamorgan attack at Cardiff before the former celebrated his maiden first-class century by running himself out with suicidal deliberation. The drama of Edgbaston, therefore, did not quite assail the senses as it might have done, although the prospects were not encouraging on a pitch of uneven bounce.

Warwickshire, clinically destroyed after being put in to bat, fought back with commendable spirit as Gladstone Small achieved his best bowling figures, aided by poor light on the first evening. Yorkshire's troubles followed them into the second day as they wrestled to narrow the gap on the first innings. Sidebottom and Chris Old helped Boycott, who had given one chance when 14 to the slips, to hold things together. From 91 for seven, Yorkshire clawed their way to 143 before Stevenson marched into the arena.

He took deliberate aim and pulled Willie Hogg firmly for six, but under the influence of his senior colleague, resisted all temptation against the leg spin of Asif Din, who made it clear he was prepared to buy the wicket. The higher Asif Din flighted the ball the more exaggerated became Stevenson's defensive push, but he still managed to reach 50 in twenty overs, mostly at the expense of the seamers, who were much more to his liking.

Gradually gaining in confidence he reached his century out of 131 in 42 overs in 130 minutes with fourteen fours and two sixes. As 100 runs came from thirty-six overs, Boycott contented himself with pushes and nudges, picking up ones and twos without serious risk, and Warwickshire were waiting on events when they got the last wicket. It fell in amazing fashion as Boycott aimed an extravagant sweep to be bowled by Asif Din.

Stevenson's 115, the highest unbeaten innings by the last man in the first-class fixture, destroyed Warwickshire, who collapsed for a second time, leaving Yorkshire with the simple task of winning the match before lunch on the last day. 'It was my brains and experience and Graham's skill that saw us through,' said Boycott, and, while some thought he had taken too much of the credit, there was a lot in what he said. Without Boycott's calm authority Stevenson may well have been persuaded to chance everything in a do-or-die assault on Asif Din or to lash out indiscriminately. As it was, in much of their association the pair observed the standards of an earlier age.

YORKSHIRE v WARWICKSHIRE
at Edgbaston
19–21 May 1982

Warwickshire *first innings*

Amiss	c Bairstow b Stevenson	39
Lloyd	b Stevenson	12
Kallicharran	b Sidebottom	11
Humpage	b Boycott	4
Oliver	c Hartley b Boycott	16
Asif Din	c Athey b Old	13
Smith	c Bairstow b Old	15
Small	b Old	22
Willis	b Stevenson	12
Cumbes	c Lumb b Sidebottom	4
Hogg	not out	0
extras		10
		158

Fall of wickets: 1–21, 2–43, 3–58, 4–87, 5–92, 6–114, 7–121, 8–148, 9–158.

Bowling: Old 20-7-52-3; Stevenson 18-5-41-3; Sidebottom 15.1-4-30-2; Carrick 5-1-10-0; Boycott 6-1-15-2.

second innings

	c Boycott b Old	75
	b Old	5
	c Bairstow b Sidebottom	8
	c Sidebottom b Old	18
	b Stevenson	9
	c Boycott b Old	5
	c Boycott b Sidebottom	16
	c Bairstow b Old	5
	not out	2
	c Sharp b Old	0
	c Bairstow b Sidebottom	8
extras		15
		166

Fall of wickets: 1–7, 2–21, 3–50, 4–77, 5–94, 6–148, 7–148, 8–152, 9–156.

Bowling: Old 27-8-76-6; Stevenson 9-2-30-1; Sidebottom 21.3-7-34-3; Carrick 2-1-1-0; Boycott 4-0-10-0.

Yorkshire *first innings*

Boycott	b Asif Din	79
Lumb	lbw b Small	1
Athey	lbw b Small	0
Sharp	c Smith b Willis	0
Hartley	c Amiss b Willis	7
Bairstow	c Humpage b Small	30
Carrick	lbw b Small	0
Whiteley	c Humpage b Small	1
Sidebottom	c Humpage b Small	13
Old	b Small	27
Stevenson	not out	115
extras		19
		292

Fall of wickets: 1–2, 2–2, 3–9, 4–35, 5–89, 6–89, 7–91, 8–108, 9–143.

Bowling: Willis 23-4-71-2; Small 29-7-68-7; Hogg 7-0-41-0; Cumbes 20-8-34-0; Asif Din 12-4-27-1; Smith 5-0-32-0.

second innings

not out		21
lbw b Small		4
not out		5
extras		3
(1 wkt)		33

Fall of wickets: 1–26.

Bowling: Willis 2-0-3-0; Small 7-0-13-1; Hogg 6.3-2-14-0.

Chapter 18

ALL IN A DAY'S WORK

Matches completed in one day without the aid of declarations are a freak of first-class cricket. They rely on an error or bad luck in the preparation of the wicket or on some interference by the weather which cuts across all the groundsman's plans immediately before the game. There has to be a marked advantage for the bowlers if at least thirty wickets are to fall in around six hours and such circumstances, rare as they are, inevitably create argument.

There have been five instances since the Second World War, the most recent being in 1960, when Kent beat Worcestershire, and overall Yorkshire have taken part in three such matches, winning them all, although it has to be noted that in each case the opposition was mediocre.

Poor Somerset completed the most embarrassing of doubles at Huddersfield on July 19, 1894, for they had suffered a similar indignity in their previous fixture with Lancashire at Old Trafford. Without being really adequate, the conditions did not explain entirely Somerset's inability to make a worthwhile impression. Yorkshire's fielding reached impressive heights, with some brilliant catches being held, and they won by an innings and 5 runs with five minutes of normal playing time remaining.

They hurried things to an even speedier conclusion in accounting for Hampshire at Southampton on May 27, 1898, and, together with the weather, they made something of a mess of Harry Baldwin's benefit. Heavy rain prevented play on the scheduled first day, but the downpour ensured a treacherous pitch on which the ball reared and moved unpredictably.

Hampshire lacked the services of their Army officers, who made up the backbone of their batting, four leading scorers being absent on military duties, and they could make nothing of Schofield Haigh on a soft strip that had 'caked' sufficiently on top to make batting a lottery. Haigh, in gathering a rich harvest of fourteen wickets for 43 runs, hit the stumps ten times.

John Tunnicliffe took the remaining honours with a disciplined half-century. First in and last out for Yorkshire, he waited patiently

YORKSHIRE v SOMERSET
at Huddersfield
19 July 1894

Somerset *first innings*
Hill	c Hunter b Hirst	25
L. Palairet	c Hunter b Wainwright	1
Hedley	c Moorhouse b Wainwright	0
R. Palairet	c Hunter b Wainwright	1
Fowler	c Hunter b Hirst	14
Nichols	c Sellers b Wainwright	0
Woods	c Mounsey b Jackson	19
Evans	c Wainwright b Hirst	10
Ebdon	c Tunnicliffe b Hirst	1
Tyler	b Hirst	0
Wickham	not out	2
extras		1
		74

second innings
	b Hirst	9
	c Jackson b Wainwright	7
	c Jackson b Wainwright	18
	b Hirst	0
	b Wainwright	14
	c Peel b Wainwright	5
	c Wainwright b Hirst	9
	c Jackson b Hirst	2
	b Jackson	5
	c Moorhouse b Hirst	21
	not out	0
extras		4
		94

Fall of wickets: 1-1, 2-1, 3-9, 4-40, 5-41, 6-41, 7-71, 8-71, 9-71.

Bowling: Peel 9-2-18-0; Wainwright 13-3-42-4; Hirst 6.1-4-9-5; Jackson 2-0-4-1.

Fall of wickets: 1-16, 2-22, 3-31, 4-45, 5-52, 6-68, 7-68, 8-92, 9-92.

Bowling: Hirst 17-4-44-5; Wainwright 14-4-43-4; Jackson 2-0-3-1.

Yorkshire *first innings*
Hawke	b Woods	56
Jackson	c and b Tyler	9
Tunnicliffe	c R. Palairet b Tyler	0
Sellers	b Tyler	1
Brown	c R. Palairet b Tyler	9
Peel	c Hill b Hedley	44
Wainwright	c Hill b Hedley	4
Moorhouse	c Tyler b Woods	2
Mounsey	b Woods	6
Hirst	not out	31
Hunter	c Ebdon b Hedley	4
extras		7
		173

Fall of wickets: 1-12, 2-12, 3-26, 4-46, 5-101, 6-106, 7-111, 8-123, 9-161.
Bowling: Tyler 21-4-68-4; Hedley 15.2-5-37-3; Woods 13-2-43-3; Nichols 8-2-18-0.

All in a Day's Work 215

YORKSHIRE v HAMPSHIRE
at Southampton
27 May 1898

Hampshire	*first innings*		*second innings*	
Ward	c Denton b Haigh	6	b Haigh	5
Barton	b Haigh	7	c Brown b Rhodes	3
Hill	c Jackson b Rhodes	0	b Haigh	7
Andrew	b Haigh	0	b Haigh	0
Webb	c Jackson b Rhodes	0	b Jackson	7
Lamb	b Haigh	0	b Jackson	3
Heseltine	b Haigh	6	not out	5
Steele	c Jackson b Haigh	10	run out	0
Robson	not out	6	b Haigh	0
Baldwin	b Haigh	6	b Haigh	0
Light	b Haigh	0	st Hunter b Haigh	4
extras		1	extras	2
		42		36

Fall of wickets: 1-10, 2-13, 3-13, 4-14, 5-14, 6-18, 7-23, 8-30, 9-36.

Bowling: Haigh 15.4-10-21-8; Rhodes 15-8-20-2.

Fall of wickets: 1-8, 2-13, 3-15, 4-24, 5-27, 6-28, 7-28, 8-28, 9-28.

Bowling: Haigh 13.2-7-22-6; Rhodes 7-3-10-1; Jackson 6-4-2-2.

Yorkshire	*first innings*	
Brown	b Baldwin	4
Tunnicliffe	b Baldwin	58
Jackson	b Andrew	9
Denton	c Barton b Baldwin	3
Wainwright	st Robson b Light	8
Hirst	st Robson b Light	18
Milligan	c Barton b Hill	2
Rhodes	c Andrew b Hill	28
Hawke	c Ward b Hill	0
Haigh	c Lamb b Baldwin	17
Hunter	not out	4
extras		6
		157

Fall of wickets: 1-5, 2-18, 3-21, 4-41, 5-72, 6-79, 7-121, 8-123, 9-152.
Bowling: Andrew 15-4-30-1; Baldwin 12.1-1-37-4; Light 11-0-44-2; Hill 18-6-34-3; Heseltine 2-0-6-0.

YORKSHIRE v WORCESTERSHIRE
at Bradford
7 May 1900

Worcestershire *first innings*

H. Foster	b Rhodes	6
Howard	b Haigh	0
Arnold	c Hunter b Rhodes	20
Bowley	b Haigh	5
Fereday	run out	0
Isaac	st Hunter b Rhodes	2
Bird	b Haigh	2
Bannister	b Rhodes	0
Wilson	c Washington b Haigh	1
Straw	not out	0
Gethin	absent	0
extras		7
		43

second innings

b Haigh		6
c Tunnicliffe b Rhodes		1
b Rhodes		13
st Hunter b Rhodes		12
c Hawke b Haigh		0
c Haigh b Rhodes		12
st Hunter b Rhodes		0
not out		4
c Denton b Rhodes		0
lbw b Rhodes		0
b Haigh		1
extras		2
		51

Fall of wickets: 1-0, 2-18, 3-29, 4-32, 5-35, 6-40, 7-40, 8-43, 9-43.

Bowling: Rhodes 13-6-16-4; Haigh 12.3-5-20-4.

Fall of wickets: 1-4, 2-10, 3-27, 4-34, 5-34, 6-34, 7-47, 8-47, 9-47.

Bowling: Rhodes 11.1-4-20-7; Haigh 11-0-29-3.

Yorkshire *first innings*

Tunnicliffe	b Wilson	5
Brown	c Bowley b Wilson	2
Denton	b Wilson	0
Washington	c Sub b Wilson	0
Wainwright	c Straw b Bannister	34
Hirst	c Bird b Bannister	24
Haigh	b Bird	15
Rhodes	c and b Bannister	0
Hawke	c Foster b Bannister	0
Brown (jun.)	c Bird b Bannister	9
Hunter	not out	6
extras		4
		99

Fall of wickets: 1-2, 2-3, 3-8, 4-9, 5-56, 6-75, 7-79, 8-79, 9-85.

Bowling: Arnold 10-4-21-0; Wilson 15-7-25-4; Bannister 13.5-5-30-5; Bird 8-2-19-1.

for the bowling mistakes and punished them efficiently.

Worcestershire arrived at Bradford in 1900 in a very confused state, savagely weakened in terms of both quality and quantity, for they had only ten men at the start, a situation brought about by late changes and travel difficulties which delayed one member of their party. This may have persuaded them to bat first on winning the toss, for they were well aware they faced a mountainous task against Yorkshire's strong and experienced attack.

The match did not start until twenty past twelve because of rain, but it was all over by six o'clock, the two Worcestershire innings lasting seventy minutes and an hour respectively as Wilfred Rhodes and Haigh mowed them down. Yorkshire had their own anxieties with four wickets falling for nine runs and they were indebted to a solid stand between Ted Wainwright and George Hirst for a modest total of 99, which allowed them to win by an innings and 5 runs.

Chapter 19

THE ONE-DAY GAME

The lifeblood of Yorkshire cricket flowed from a league system that has from its formative days created circumstances in which the potential county players have been tested to the full and prepared for the most exacting examinations at the highest level. These leagues, in turn, fed on the schools, where keen competition has flourished and winning mattered. Teachers tended to ignore the old Corinthian maxim that playing the game according to the spirit of a well-defined tradition was an end in itself. Pride has been a driving spur in the side of progress.

Behind the major organisations such as the Bradford League, the Yorkshire League, the Central Yorkshire League and the Huddersfield League, the smaller bodies, often operating under artificial restrictions in the evenings, have been pushing forward, raising the standards because no one wanted to fall behind. Nowhere in the world has there been quite the same passionate involvement in cricket.

In the circumstances, tactics have been studied closely with captaincy involving more than just tossing up and making routine bowling changes to suit the members of the team and keep everybody happy. Field placing developed as an art in Yorkshire over a century ago and defensive bowling is nothing new to the area, where, not so long ago, even the smaller clubs would expect to have a full ground of committed spectators for virtually every match.

The introduction of limited-overs cricket should, therefore, have enabled Yorkshire to add easily to their long list of honours. The Sunday League and the two cup competitions are, after all, no more than the league game dusted and lifted to first-class surroundings. The trophies were, most people thought, likely to come the county's way on a reasonably regular basis, for their players had cut their teeth on the sharp edge of Saturday afternoon rivalry.

The opposite, however, has been the case, for, with three notable exceptions, Yorkshire have stumbled along in a daze, persistently finding it impossible to live up to optimistic pre-season predictions that they could compensate for shortcomings in the championship

The One-Day Game

with success in this direction. The team have failed to come to terms with one-day requirements and have competed without real enthusiasm.

Brian Close, as captain, summed up the general opinion when, before the Sunday League had begun, he said: 'Frankly I would not go very far to watch the form of cricket that will be served up on Sundays. It holds very little interest for me.' Although he received an immediate blast from Lord's, who were anxious to legitimise their brainchild, he echoed the thoughts of the majority of senior cricketers.

Undeterred, Close hammered at the theme. 'Limited-overs cricket is workshop cricket,' he claimed. 'It is the same as saying to golfers like Jack Nicklaus, Gary Player and Tony Jacklin, here is a wonderful and challenging course – you have to be back in an hour and ten minutes. They would play no better than greenhorns. In real cricket, the player who has developed imagination and skill makes the game, but in the one-day match it is the other way round. The match dictates to the player, telling him what he has to do.'

In the end, when Yorkshire sacked Close in 1970, they said: 'His resignation has been requested in view of his often stated dislike of one-day cricket – a form of the game which becomes increasingly important as the years go by.' They had, of course, a point, but the county have continued to rub shoulders with disappointment.

Their three great moments brought victories in the 1965 and 1969 Gillette Cup Finals, and the Sunday League in 1983. The oldest of the limited-overs events, the Gillette Cup, also caused them considerable grief when they lost to Durham, who became the first representatives from the Minor Counties to topple first-class opposition when they triumphed by five wickets at Harrogate in 1973.

Yorkshire's first Gillette victory path was smooth and untroubled. Leicestershire were beaten by six wickets at Grace Road, while Fred Trueman's six for 15 spell earned a seven-wicket margin at Taunton over Somerset. Warwickshire, made of much sterner stuff, might well have won at Edgbaston, where Yorkshire were dismissed for 177, but Ray Illingworth and Don Wilson bluffed their way through twenty-six overs for 44 runs in the middle of the home team's reply, and there were 20 runs to spare in the end.

No game in the merry-go-round of one-day competition has captured the imagination or caused so much debate as the final between Yorkshire and Surrey, for the tie was dominated entirely by one man – Geoff Boycott, who struck three sixes and fifteen fours

A powerful stroke from John Hampshire, who scored heavily in one-day competitions and, along with Geoff Boycott, dominated Sunday League batting. (*Yorkshire Post*)

in his 146, an innings that destroyed the opposition.

There is a good deal of sneering among the purists about the quaint improvisations that have been welded on to the average batsman's technique at this admittedly lower technical level, and many refuse to accept that a limited-overs game allows for true greatness, but on this occasion Boycott raced along without recourse to the ugly or the wildly speculative. He made no concessions to the unorthodox, although he may have hit 'on the up' a shade more readily than he would with more time at his disposal.

Heavy rain and the inevitably saturated ground delayed the start and Yorkshire laboured under a serious handicap in having to bat first. 'We would have settled for around 170 without batting,' said Boycott, who kept his self-control when a subdued beginning to the

YORKSHIRE v SURREY
at Lord's
4 September 1965

Yorkshire

Boycott	c Storey b Barrington	146
Taylor	c Barrington b Sydenham	9
Close	c Edrich b Gibson	79
Trueman	b Arnold	24
Hampshire	not out	38
Wilson	not out	11
extras		10
	(4 wkts)	317

Fall of wickets: 1–22, 2–214, 3–248, 4–292.
Bowling: Arnold 13-3-51-1; Sydenham 13-1-67-1; Gibson 13-1-66-1; Storey 13-2-33-0; Tindall 3-0-36-0; Barrington 5-0-54-1.

Surrey

Stewart	st Binks b Wilson	33
Edrich	c Illingworth b Trueman	15
Smith	lbw b Trueman	0
Barrington	c Binks b Trueman	0
Tindall	c Wilson b Close	57
Storey	lbw b Illingworth	1
Edwards	b Illingworth	0
Gibson	lbw b Illingworth	0
Long	b Illingworth	17
Arnold	not out	3
Sydenham	b Illingworth	8
extras		8
		142

Fall of wickets: 1–27, 2–27, 3–27, 4–75, 5–76, 6–76, 7–76, 8–130, 9–132.
Bowling: Trueman 9-0-31-3; Hutton 8-3-17-0; Wilson 9-0-45-1; Illingworth 11.4-1-29-5; Close 3-0-12-1.

innings exposed the nerve ends of others. He had one brush of good fortune when a slight mis-hit lofted the ball dangerously close to square leg, but otherwise he marched forward with a lofty disdain for all poor Surrey could offer.

Brian Close promoted himself for tactical reasons and Fred Trueman and John Hampshire enjoyed the pleasure of a late thrash against dispirited men reduced to the roles of mere labourers. The bowling presented itself for the benefit of the master craftsman and his supporting cast and Yorkshire reached an unbelievable 317 for four wickets. They stood on the heights and took in the view as Ray Illingworth quietly dismantled the Surrey batting after Trueman had undermined the foundations.

Forgetting momentarily his heartfelt convictions, Close admitted: 'This is a proud moment for a fine team,' and so it was.

Yorkshire had done things the hard way by being drawn away in all the rounds and they almost repeated the feat in 1969, for they were given a solitary home tie – the semi-final at Scarborough with Nottinghamshire as their opponents. They had a trouble-free run, too, only once having to worry about the danger of defeat.

Norfolk, as expected, were thoroughly outplayed at Lakenham, where the margin amounted to something more than the 89 runs in the scorebook, while Lancashire collapsed at Old Trafford and went down by seven wickets. Don Wilson led the bowlers with three for 32 and he also wore down Surrey at the Oval, taking four for 31 in a total of 134 which was 138 too few.

That brief flicker of alarm came at the seaside, where the ball swung about enough in the early morning sea fret for Gary Sobers and Barry Stead to beat the bat. Boycott and Barrie Leadbeater were caught at the wicket off Leeds-born Stead with only three on the board, but Deryck Murray, the West Indian Test wicket-keeper, then missed the easiest of chances from Doug Padgett first ball. Thus reprieved, Padgett helped Phil Sharpe to add 101 for the third wicket and Yorkshire breathed again.

In the blazing heat of a brilliant afternoon, with 15,242 spectators crammed into every nook and cranny of North Marine Road behind firmly locked gates, and with anxious spectators peering out of boarding-house windows around the ground, they squeezed the life out of Nottinghamshire with accurate bowling that made their total of 191 perfectly adequate, success coming by 68 runs.

The final never got off the ground. Derbyshire won the toss and put in Yorkshire, pursuing their normal policy by embarking on a purely defensive operation, although their thinking may have been slightly influenced by the knowledge that Boycott was missing with a damaged hand and that Leadbeater was playing with a broken finger. This injury occurred at Hove on the previous day and Leadbeater had to fight his way through the proverbial pain barrier in inching his way to 76.

At that time uncapped, Leadbeater presented himself as an obvious candidate for the Man of the Match award, but Close again forgot about his likes and dislikes to orchestrate the whole affair superbly.

He hammered the bowling in blistering fashion to make up for lost momentum during the opening partnership and then handled

The One-Day Game

his attack shrewdly to keep Derbyshire on a tight rein. Tony Nicholson went straight through his allocation of twelve overs for just 14 runs, while Close himself conceded the same number from ten as Derbyshire fell irretrievably behind the clock.

YORKSHIRE v DERBYSHIRE
at Lord's
6 September 1969

Yorkshire			**Derbyshire**		
Leadbeater	c Taylor b Ward	76	Gibbs	b Nicholson	19
Woodford	c Taylor b Eyre	15	Smith	b Close	26
Close	c Page b Ward	37	Morgan	run out	5
Sharpe	b Ward	3	Ward	c Close b Hutton	17
Padgett	c Buxton b Rumsey	30	Burton	c Close b Wilson	34
Hampshire	c Morgan b Rhodes	2	Harvey	b Wilson	3
Hutton	not out	29	Page	c Wilson b Close	16
Binks	b Rhodes	4	Taylor	c Leadbeater b Close	2
Wilson	c Ward b Rumsey	2	Eyre	not out	14
Old	not out	3	Rumsey	b Wilson	1
extras		18	Rhodes	c Hampshire b Old	6
			extras		18
	(8 wkts)	219			150

Fall of wickets: 1-39, 2-103, 3-107, 4-154, 5-154, 6-177, 7-192, 8-195.
Bowling: Ward 12-1-31-3; Rhodes 12-2-47-2; Buxton 12-6-24-0; Eyre 12-0-53-1; Rumsey 11-0-33-2; Morgan 1-0-13-0.

Fall of wickets: 1-37, 2-49, 3-54, 4-77, 5-83, 6-112, 7-128, 8-129, 9-136.
Bowling: Old 9.4-1-25-1; Nicholson 12-5-14-1; Close 11-2-36-3; Wilson 12-0-38-3; Hutton 10-1-30-1.

From that point, Yorkshire went into rapid decline. They tripped red faced over the first hurdle in 1970, 1971, 1972 and 1973, when Durham's incredible victory by five wickets followed the cheap dismissal of Boycott, who was bowled for 12, by Stuart Wilkinson, an unassuming young man who found himself immortalised in a rash of newspaper headlines for one delivery - 'I wish,' he said, 'I could watch it again and again for ever.'

Between 1970 and 1978, in fact, the only success against first-class opposition came at the expense of Hampshire at Bradford in 1974.

In step with this depressing catalogue, the Sunday League results were poor, with second place in that ill-fated year of 1973 raising a modest flicker of hope among the faithful followers. Throughout the 1970s, Yorkshire failed to link bowling tactics to the field placing

Paul Jarvis became the youngest player to appear for Yorkshire in first-class cricket. He was 16 years and 75 days when he made his debut against Sussex at Hove on September 12, 1981. He also claimed the county's first Sunday League hat-trick against Derbyshire at Derby in June 1982. (*Yorkshire Post*)

patterns, so that in 1976 they lost six games in which they topped 200 runs.

At the heart of their concern was the destructive influence on young bowlers who were expected to attack and take wickets in the championship and then adjust to become entirely defensive on a Sunday. The bewilderment was very evident.

Chris Old crystallised the difficulties. 'The trouble is that the wicket-taking ball is the one which moves away late and forces the batsman to play. Often he will be driving and might well get an edge to slip. This ball which we try to produce, however, is entirely wrong for Sunday when it gets hammered for four or edged through what should be the slips but is usually open space. You have to bowl a different line and length and if I find it hard with a lot of experience and confidence after playing for England, it has got to be next to impossible for youngsters.'

Yorkshire did reach the final of the Benson and Hedges Cup in its first year – 1972 – but injury to Boycott, who carried the whole weight of the batting, as well as tactical responsibility, on his shoulders, ruined their chances against Leicestershire. The Midlands county, aided substantially by Chris Balderstone and guided by Illingworth, two Yorkshire rejects 'getting their own back in the best possible way', won by five wickets. Thereafter Yorkshire struggled to get beyond the qualifying stages.

They failed most noticeably in 1976, when the unconsidered students from Oxford and Cambridge Universities thrashed them at Barnsley to heap ignominy on bowed heads. In more than ten years Yorkshire only had to rely on semi-final appearances in the two knockout cups to sustain them through some dark hours before finally raising their game to capture the Sunday League title in 1983. Predictably, Boycott and Illingworth were the leading figures

The end of fourteen years in the wilderness as Yorkshire celebrate their Sunday League championship at Chelmsford. Enjoying their moment of success Ray Illingworth hoists the John Player trophy aloft. (*Press Association*)

although Bill Athey contributed important runs. Illingworth took twenty wickets for 259 runs and was the most successful bowler in the competition, while Boycott, in addition to scoring steadily, got through some important overs at critical times. Yorkshire, too, were fortunate in that Illingworth won the toss eleven times out of fourteen – two fixtures were abandoned – and was able to field first. Thus the vulnerable bowlers were protected from the greatest pressure.

This proved important since the only logical explanation for a shocking record generally is that the pressures have been too great. It is something which is often overlooked when people talk glibly about the skills required for the three-day game. The 'sudden-death' atmosphere created by the limitation on overs and the knowledge that there is no possibility of a draw has unnerved many a young cricketer. Yorkshire have simply not been able to cope with the special demands, and the theory is supported by their performances in semi-finals in more recent years when they have played a long way below their known form and by moments of ragged uncertainty once they found themselves at the top of the Sunday League. If the one-day competitions have proved anything, it is that there is more to sport than the ability to look good going through the motions with little or nothing at stake.

Chapter 20

THE OUTSIDERS

The claim Yorkshire's fortunes are directly linked to England's prospects, supported, as we have seen, by prominent figures from other counties, does no more than scratch the surface of a first-class theory. The truth goes much deeper, for the Broad Acres have always produced a surplus of talent which has gone forward to improve the quality of other counties less well endowed with natural resources, thus raising overall standards. It would, for example, be easy to select a useful eleven from the men who have represented their country after being released by Yorkshire and in the last seventy or so years over a hundred players have earned their living by moving to other areas.

No attempt has been made to adjust the balance, for Yorkshire stubbornly maintain a policy of relying on only those born within the county, resisting the easy options of importing overseas Test stars to the point at which many of their followers believe that Lord Hawke is the one man to break through this particular qualification barrier. Indeed, the birthright restriction was defended fiercely by members, who backed it almost nine to one in a poll taken in 1982, but it has been ignored or overlooked by accident in at least twenty-four instances and a number of other cases have been the subject of protracted enquiry. The players who played for Yorkshire despite being born in another county are:

Player	*Birthplace*	*Matches*	*Batting*	*Bowling*
W.E. Blackburn	Clitheroe	10 (1919–20)	3.71	24.73
M. Burrows	Chesterfield	6 (1880)	8.20	
T. Darnton	Stockton-on-Tees	13 (1864–68)	14.95	29.16
T. Foster	Birkdale	14 (1894–95)	9.20	16.41
G. Gifkins	Thames Ditton	2 (1880)	10.00	
J. Hall	Nottingham	1 (1863)	2.00	
Lord Hawke	Willingham, Lincs	510 (1881–1911)	20.25	0–16
W.G. Keighley	Nice, France	35 (1947–51)	26.67	0–18
C.W. Landon	Bromley	9 (1878–82)	3.92	0–74
W. Law	Rochdale	4 (1871–73)	7.28	
E. Loxley-Firth	Hope, Derbys	2 (1912)	10.75	
F.W. Milligan	Aldershot	81 (1894–98)	18.24	24.42
C. Parkin	Eaglescliffe	1 (1906)	0.00	12.50
E.J. Radcliffe	Tiverton	64 (1909–11)	10.86	62.50

Player	Birthplace	Matches	Batting	Bowling
H. Rhodes	Hennerton, Berks	10 (1878–83)	17.93	
C.M. Sharpe	Codicote, Herts	1 (1875)	15.00	0–17
H.M. Sims	Tavistock	5 (1875–77)	12.11	
W. Smith	Darlington	11 (1865–74)	16.25	
R.T. Stanyforth	Chelsea	3 (1928)	8.66	
F.H. Sugg	Ilkeston	8 (1883)	10.00	
W. Sugg	Ilkeston	1 (1881)	9.00	
H.W. Verelst	Claughton, Cheshire	3 (1868–69)	22.00	
W.F. Whitwell	Stockton-on-Tees	10 (1890)	5.58	20.72
A.J. Wilkinson	Mount Oswald, Co. Durham	5 (1865–68)	21.50	0–57

It can be seen that few of them made much difference to the club's fortunes, for they were mostly amateurs of no great standing who appeared once or twice, did little or nothing, and then disappeared. Their claim to fame is simply that they beat the system and it is sufficient to mark their existence and observe that the majority lived in the distant past when the chance of exposure was slim. Blackburn, though, did threaten one curious journalist with legal action if anything appeared in the press about his background, which indicates how keen the officials were to cover their tracks.

Five men, however, merit consideration, with, of course, Lord Hawke leading the list. He was born in Lincolnshire at Willingham-by-Stow, near Gainsborough, where his father was rector, but he always said: 'Wherever I go, whatever I do, I am a Yorkshireman.' His famous ancestor, Admiral Hawke, about whom Sir Henry Newbolt penned his stirring line 'When Hawke came sweeping out of the West,' settled in Yorkshire when he married the heiress to Burton Hall, Catherine Brook, in 1737. From that point, the family had their roots buried deep in the county's soil and it was Lord Hawke who introduced the white rose emblem to the Yorkshire cap.

His casual introduction to the side through the influence of the Reverend Edmund Carter, though, goes some way to explaining why so many others slipped through the net.

It is also worth noting that he played only infrequently in his early years with Yorkshire. During his first season as captain he took time off to figure in such fixtures as Cambridge University *v* MCC, North *v* South, and Cambridge University *v* Orleans Club and did not feature in the Yorkshire ranks until July 2, when Nottinghamshire provided the opposition. He appeared only six times in 1884 for the county, while his solitary game in 1885 came

The Outsiders

against MCC at Scarborough in September. Apparently the demands of militia service may have had something to do with this unsettled state of affairs, but the fact that it aroused little comment gives another insight into the way Yorkshire conducted their affairs.

Frank Milligan took part in eighty-one matches, although no secret seems to have been made of his birthplace, possibly because he also represented the Gentlemen against the Players. He earned a reputation as a dashing late-order batsman and bowled at a lively medium pace. He was also an exceptional fielder and captained the team on some of those occasions on which Lord Hawke had other engagements.

Everard Radcliffe also led the side, owing his place purely to the amateur captain convention, for he made no progress as a player. As Lord Hawke admitted: 'His position is not an easy one, but I am sure we all admire the pluck with which he has stuck to his post.'

Captain R.T. Stanyforth enjoyed the distinction of leading England before earning selection for the county. Born at Chelsea, he played most of his cricket for the Army, taking over the leadership of the MCC team to South Africa in the winter of 1927–28 at the last minute. As a wicket-keeper his value to Yorkshire was strictly limited in the shadow of Arthur Wood, so he made only three appearances in 1928.

Potentially the best player in this group, Geoffrey Keighley gained acceptance despite being born in France because his family, like Lord Hawke's, had very strong Yorkshire connections. He could have become a long-standing captain, for he led the Colts in 1949 and 1950, impressed the right people and possessed the necessary credentials, having been educated at Eton and Oxford.

His qualities as a batsman were evident when he made a century for the university as a freshman against the 1947 South Africans, but business interests captured his attention and in 1952 he emigrated to Australia, where he took up sheep farming at Springdale, an outpost some three hundred miles from Sydney.

We should not close this chapter without reference to A.J.A. Wilkinson, who cheerfully played for both Yorkshire and Middlesex without official complaint.

Even in the most casual of times, however, it is difficult to accept that Wilkinson managed to play for Yorkshire against Nottinghamshire at Bradford and then travel down to Trent Bridge, where he turned out against Nottinghamshire again – but this time for

Geoffrey Keighley, one of the best known of the Yorkshire players born outside the county. (*Yorkshire Post*)

Middlesex! The records for 1866 indicate that this, in fact, is what he did.

Whether the demands of an ever-changing world will create circumstances in which Yorkshire find themselves forced to open wide the door to outsiders is a question that will be debated for a long time. The precedents are clearly established, but it is unlikely that the county will take the controversial step in the foreseeable future.

Their self-reliance is compensation for the success enjoyed by the other first-class counties and there is a lot of truth in the argument that they would again be dominant if the championship were to be restricted to Englishmen. That, at least, is a strongly held contention in the dressing-room and, for all their widely publicised squabbles, Yorkshiremen still band together when threatened by a third party.

APPENDIX
COUNTY RECORDS

Highest scores by Yorkshire
v Derbyshire 662 at Chesterfield in 1898
v Essex 555 for one declared at Leyton in 1932
v Glamorgan 579 for six declared at Huddersfield in 1925
v Gloucestershire 504 for seven declared at Bradford in 1905
v Hampshire 585 for three declared at Portsmouth in 1920
v Kent 559 at Canterbury in 1887
v Lancashire 590 at Bradford in 1887
v Leicestershire 660 at Leicester in 1896
v Middlesex 575 for seven declared at Bradford in 1899
v Northants 548 for four declared at Harrogate in 1921
v Nottinghamshire 562 at Bradford in 1899
v Somerset 549 for nine declared at Taunton in 1905
v Surrey 704 at the Oval in 1899
v Sussex 681 for five declared at Sheffield in 1897
v Warwickshire 887 at Birmingham in 1896
v Worcestershire 560 for six declared at Worcester in 1928
v Australians 377 at Sheffield in 1953
v Indians 385 at Hull in 1911
v New Zealanders 393 for four declared at Bradford in 1969
v Pakistanis 433 for nine declared at Sheffield in 1954
v West Indians 312 for five declared at Scarborough in 1973
v Cambridge University 540 at Cambridge in 1938
v Oxford University 453 at Oxford in 1935

Highest scores against Yorkshire
Derbyshire 491 at Bradford in 1949
Essex 521 at Leyton in 1905
Glamorgan 349 for seven declared at Middlesbrough in 1976
Gloucestershire 528 at Cheltenham in 1876
Hampshire 521 for eight declared at Portsmouth in 1927
Kent 493 at Tonbridge in 1914
Lancashire 509 for nine declared at Manchester in 1926
Leicestershire 458 at Hull in 1937
Middlesex 527 at Huddersfield in 1887
Northants 405 for six declared at Northampton in 1952
Nottinghamshire 492 for five declared at Sheffield in 1949
Somerset 630 at Leeds in 1901
Surrey 560 for six declared at the Oval in 1933
Sussex 566 at Sheffield in 1937
Warwickshire 536 for seven declared at Birmingham in 1929
Worcestershire 456 for eight at Worcester in 1904
Australians 470 at Bradford in 1893
Indians 490 for five declared at Sheffield in 1946

New Zealanders 370 for seven declared at Bradford in 1949
Pakistanis 356 at Sheffield in 1954
West Indians 358 for nine declared at Sheffield in 1963
Cambridge University 425 for seven at Cambridge in 1929
Oxford University 422 for nine declared at Oxford in 1953

Lowest scores by Yorkshire
v Derbyshire 44 at Chesterfield in 1948
v Essex 31 at Huddersfield in 1935
v Glamorgan 83 at Sheffield in 1946
v Gloucestershire 35 at Bristol in 1959
v Hampshire 23 at Middlesbrough in 1965
v Kent 30 at Sheffield in 1865
v Lancashire 33 at Leeds in 1924
v Leicestershire 47 at Leicester in 1911
v Middlesex 43 at Lord's in 1888
v Northants 64 at Northampton in 1959
v Nottinghamshire 32 at Sheffield in 1876
v Somerset 73 at Leeds in 1895
v Surrey 26 at the Oval in 1909
v Sussex 42 at Hove in 1922
v Warwickshire 49 at Huddersfield in 1951
v Worcestershire 62 at Bradford in 1907
v Australians 48 at Leeds in 1893
v Indians 146 at Bradford in 1959
v New Zealanders 189 at Harrogate in 1931
v Pakistanis 137 at Bradford in 1962
v West Indians 50 at Harrogate in 1906
v Cambridge University 51 at Cambridge in 1906
v Oxford University 141 at Oxford in 1949

Lowest scores against Yorkshire
Derbyshire 20 at Sheffield in 1939
Essex 30 at Leyton in 1901
Glamorgan 48 at Cardiff in 1924
Gloucestershire 36 at Sheffield in 1903
Hampshire 36 at Leeds in 1904 and Southampton in 1898
Kent 39 at Sheffield in 1882
Lancashire 30 at Holbeck in 1868
Leicestershire 34 at Leeds in 1906
Middlesex 45 at Huddersfield in 1879
Northants 15 at Northampton in 1908
Nottinghamshire 13 at Nottingham in 1901
Somerset 35 at Bath in 1898
Surrey 31 at Holbeck in 1883
Sussex 20 at Hull in 1922
Warwickshire 35 at Sheffield in 1979 and at Birmingham in 1963
Worcestershire 24 at Huddersfield in 1903
Australians 23 at Leeds in 1902
Indians 66 at Harrogate in 1932
New Zealanders 134 at Bradford in 1965
Pakistanis 150 at Leeds in 1967
West Indians 50 at Leeds in 1928

Cambridge University 30 at Cambridge in 1928
Oxford University 46 at Oxford in 1956

Highest individual scores for Yorkshire
v Derbyshire 300 by J.T. Brown at Chesterfield in 1898. Most centuries G. Boycott (eight).
v Essex 313 by H. Sutcliffe at Leyton in 1932. Most centuries H. Sutcliffe (nine).
v Glamorgan 197 by L. Hutton at Swansea in 1947. Most centuries P. Holmes and H. Sutcliffe (five).
v Gloucestershire 182 by D. Denton at Bristol in 1912. Most centuries G. Boycott (five).
v Hampshire 302 not out by P. Holmes at Portsmouth in 1920. Most centuries H. Sutcliffe (six).
v Kent 248 by W. Barber at Leeds in 1934. Most centuries L. Hutton (five).
v Lancashire 211 not out by M. Leyland at Leeds in 1930. Most centuries G. Boycott and H. Sutcliffe (nine).
v Leicestershire 341 by G. Hirst at Leicester in 1905. Most centuries H. Sutcliffe (ten).
v Middlesex 315 not out by P. Holmes at Lord's 1925. Most centuries P. Holmes and H. Sutcliffe (seven).
v Northants 277 not out by P. Holmes at Harrogate in 1921. Most centuries H. Sutcliffe (five).
v Nottinghamshire 285 by P. Holmes at Nottingham in 1929. Most centuries G. Boycott (fourteen).
v Somerset 213 by H. Sutcliffe at Dewsbury in 1924. Most centuries G. Hirst and W. Rhodes (five).
v Surrey 255 by W. Barber at Sheffield in 1935. Most centuries H. Sutcliffe (nine).
v Sussex 311 by J.T. Brown at Sheffield in 1897. Most centuries L. Hutton (eight).
v Warwickshire 275 by P. Holmes at Bradford in 1928. Most centuries H. Sutcliffe (eight).
v Worcestershire 259 not out by F. Lowson at Worcester in 1953. Most centuries M. Leyland (six).
v Australians 167 by J.T. Brown at Bradford in 1899. Most centuries G. Boycott and D. Denton (two).
v Indians 183 not out by L. Hutton at Bradford in 1946. Most centuries D. Denton, S. Haigh, L. Hutton, E. Lester, R. Illingworth and C. Old (one).
v New Zealanders 175 by P. Holmes at Bradford in 1927. Most centuries L. Hutton and B. Close (two).
v Pakistanis 197 by P. Sharpe at Leeds in 1967. Most centuries P. Sharpe (two).
v West Indians 112 not out by D. Denton at Harrogate in 1906. Most centuries D. Denton, L. Hutton and R. Lumb (one).
v Cambridge University 207 not out by G. Boycott at Cambridge in 1976. Most centuries H. Sutcliffe (four).
v Oxford University 183 not out by F. Lowson at Oxford in 1956. Most centuries M. Leyland (four).

Highest individual scores against Yorkshire
Derbyshire 219 by J.D. Eggar at Bradford in 1949. Most centuries W. Storer (four).
Essex 219 not out by D.J. Insole at Colchester in 1949. Most centuries F.L. Fane and D.J. Insole (three).
Glamorgan 156 not out by A. Jones at Middlesbrough in 1976. Most centuries A. Jones and P. Walker (two).

Gloucestershire 318 not out by W.G. Grace at Cheltenham in 1876. Most centuries W.G. Grace (nine).
Hampshire 268 by E.G. Wynyard at Southampton in 1896. Most centuries P. Mead (ten).
Kent 188 by F. Woolley at Bradford in 1931. Most centuries F. Woolley (five).
Lancashire 200 not out by R. Spooner at Manchester in 1910. Most centuries C. Lloyd (six).
Leicestershire 186 by N.F. Armstrong at Leicester in 1928. Most centuries C.J.B. Wood (five).
Middlesex 243 not out by A.J. Webbe at Huddersfield in 1887. Most centuries E. Hendren (six).
Northants 186 by W. Larkins at Middlesbrough 1982. Most centuries W. Larkins (four).
Nottinghamshire 210 by W.W. Keeton at Sheffield in 1949. Most centuries C.B. Harris, A Shrewsbury and W. Whysall (four).
Somerset 217 not out by I.V. Richards at Harrogate in 1975. Most centuries L.C.H. Palairet (five).
Surrey 273 by T. Hayward at the Oval in 1899. Most centuries J.B. Hobbs (eight).
Sussex 234 by C.B. Fry at Bradford in 1903. Most centuries C.B. Fry (seven).
Warwickshire 206 by C. Charlesworth at Dewsbury in 1914. Most centuries H.E. Dollery, R.B. Kanhai and W.G. Quaife (four).
Worcestershire 259 by D. Kenyon at Kidderminster in 1956. Most centuries D. Kenyon and G. Turner (five).
Australians 193 not out by B.C. Booth at Bradford in 1964. Most centuries N. O'Neil (two).
Indians 244 not out by V.S. Hazare at Sheffield in 1946. Most centuries V.S. Hazare, V. Mankad, P. Umrigar and D. Gaekwad (one).
New Zealanders 126 by W.M. Wallace at Bradford in 1949. Most centuries H.G. Vivian, W.M. Wallace and J.G. Wright (one).
Pakistanis 139 by A.H. Kardar at Sheffield in 1954. Most centuries A.H. Kardar (one).
West Indians 164 by S. Bacchus at Leeds in 1980. Most centuries S. Bacchus, P. Goodman and G. Sobers (one).
Cambridge University 171 not out by G.L. Jessop at Cambridge in 1899 and 171 by P. May at Cambridge in 1952. Most centuries G.M. Kemp (two).
Oxford University 201 by J. Raphael at Oxford in 1904. Most centuries A.A. Baig and Nawab of Pataudi (two).

County Records

Championship record

Yorkshire's proudest record, which is likely to stand for a long time yet, is that they have overall a marked advantage in terms of results over all their Championship rivals. Their full record between 1863 and 1983 is:

	P	W	L	D	Abd
Derbyshire	171	92	13	66	3
Essex	136	74	17	45	
Glamorgan	85	45	10	30	
Gloucestershire	178	96	36	46	1
Hampshire	125	61	14	50	1
Kent	167	77	31	59	4
Lancashire	215	68	45	102	
Leicestershire	136	75	10	50*	2
Middlesex	203	76	44	82*	
Northamptonshire	110	59	17	34	1
Nottinghamshire	212	80	38	94	5
Somerset	127	77	12	38	
Surrey	211	81	58	72	2
Sussex	166	76	24	66	1
Warwickshire	151	71	16	64	
Worcestershire	111	58	16	37	1

*Yorkshire also tied with Leicestershire and Middlesex.

Yorkshire also met Cambridgeshire in eight first-class fixtures over this period, winning three games, losing four and drawing one. In addition, they figured in twenty matches between 1833 and 1862 which were accorded full status. These were:

6 *v* Surrey (won 2, lost 4)
5 *v* Norfolk (won 3, lost 2)
4 *v* Lancashire (all won)
3 *v* Kent (won 1, lost 2)
2 *v* Sussex (won 1, lost 1)

With regard to their other major opponents, Yorkshire's record is:

	P	W	L	D	Abd
Australians	54	6	19	29	1
Indians	12	5	0	7	
New Zealanders	9	1	0	8	
Pakistanis	4	1	0	3	1
South Africans	17	1	3	13	
West Indians	15	3	6	6	1
Cambridge Univ.	83	41	17	25	2
Oxford Univ.	39	20	3	16	1
MCC	152	54	38	60	4

INDEX

Abbeydale Park, 27
Abel, Bobby, 201
Ackworth, 115
Action Group, 111
Allen, David, (West Indies), 140
All England, 21, 25, 28
All India, 133
Amiss, Dennis, 106
Anderson, George, 28, 31, 32
Appleyard, Bob, 89, 90, 92, 95, 96, 170, 180, 189
Arsenal, 103
Aspinall, Ron, 85
Athey, Bill, 156, 225
Atkinson, George, 28
Australia, 48, 58, 92, 118, 129–136, 148, 164, 167, 168, 174, 175

Badcock, Charlie, 134
Bailey, Trevor, 153
Bairstow, David, 110, 121, 190
Balderstone, Chris, 225
Barber, Alan, 68, 69, 71
Barber, Wilf, 79, 83, 84, 155, 197, 198
Barker, T. R., 26
Barnsley, 21, 37, 225
Bath, 48
Batley, 35, 36
Berry, John, 28
Binks, Jimmy, 95, 106–109, 140, 189
Birmingham, 42, 207
Blackburn, W.E., 227
Booth, Arthur, 82, 85, 174
Booth, Major, 51–55, 167, 168
Bowes, Bill, 68, 73, 77–85, 134, 143, 164–69, 174, 197
Boycott, Geoff, 15, 35, 103, 105, 109–128, 135, 142, 143, 146–150, 156, 187, 210, 219, 225
Bradford, 15, 21, 26, 28, 36, 37, 46, 56, 71, 72, 75, 99, 110, 112, 125, 126, 129–131, 145, 167, 169, 189, 208, 217, 223

Bradford League, 58, 76, 113, 143, 168, 180, 218
Bradford P.A. F.C., 189
Bradman, Don, 133, 134, 148, 165, 175
Bramall Lane, 11, 25, 26, 61, 90, 133, 175, 197
Bray, Charles, 194
Brennan, Don, 90, 118
Brighton, 36, 55, 82
Bristol, 49, 69, 101
Brown, J.T., 41, 42, 44, 47, 130, 150, 151, 193, 196
Brown, J.T., junior, 47
Burnet, Ronnie, 96–101, 124
Burrows, M., 227
Burton, Derek, 55, 56, 154, 206

Cambridge University, 35, 41, 55, 59, 85, 156, 225, 228
Canterbury, 36
Cardiff, 210
Cardus, Neville, 9
Carew, Joe, 140
Carlisle, 36
Carrick, Phil, 116, 120, 210
Carter, Rev. Edmund, 35, 228
Cayley, George, 29
Central Yorkshire League, 218
Cheltenham, 126
Chesterfield, 44, 121, 150
Close, Brian, 11, 87–89, 92, 100–111, 116, 135, 140, 170, 178, 180, 219, 221, 222
Colchester, 99, 116
Connell, Arthur, 118, 120
Cooper, Howard, 112, 113, 116
Cope, Geoff, 108, 109, 113–119
Cordingley, Albert, 163, 164
Cowan, Mike, 95, 174
Cox, George, 87
Coxon, Alec, 85, 86, 89, 180
Crawford, Michael, 120

Dalton, 25, 28
Darfield, 47
Darnall, 21, 22, 25
Darnton, T., 227
Dawson, Edwin, 28

Denton, David, 41, 48, 50, 152, 153, 199, 201, 207
Derbyshire, 54–56, 71, 80, 81, 121–124, 161, 190, 222
Dewsbury, 37, 42, 46, 102, 129, 174, 206
Dolphin, Arthur, 51, 57, 63, 65, 187, 188
Doncaster, 20
Drake, Alonzo, 51, 53, 54, 167, 173
Durham, 112, 219, 223

Eastman, Lawrence, 193
Edgbaston, 59, 106, 117, 145, 187, 210, 219
Ellison, M.J., 26
Emmett, Tom, 12–16, 28–31, 35, 173
Essex, 52, 74, 75, 79, 99, 108, 116, 145, 176, 193

Farnes, Ken, 75
Fender, Percy, 117
Fisher, Horace, 75
Foster, T., 227
Freeman, George, 28–30, 173, 177
Fry, C. B., 87, 186

Gibb, Paul, 189
Giffen, George, 129
Gifkin, G., 227
Gilligan, Arthur, 66
Glamorgan, 103, 198, 203, 210
Gleeson, John, 136
Gloucestershire, 31, 36, 40, 49, 69, 72, 79, 101, 110, 125, 126, 145, 156, 172
Gower, David, 118
Grace, W.G., 13, 16, 17, 29, 40, 152, 153, 165, 168, 173
Greenhough, Tommy, 105
Greenwood, Frank, 71, 72, 76, 77
Greenwood, Luke, 16, 29, 32
Gregory, Jack, 56
Griffith, Charlie, 140
Grimmett, Clarrie, 132

Groves, Charles, 117

Haigh, Schofield, 42, 45–52, 130, 166, 187, 202, 208, 213, 217
Halifax, 21, 28, 37
Halifax Courier, 12
Hall, J., 227
Hall, Louis, 35, 36, 152
Hammond, Walter, 72, 143,151
Hampshire, 50, 52, 58, 74, 80, 102, 104, 105, 125, 152, 187, 199, 206, 213, 223
Hampshire, John, 103, 112, 118–124, 140, 156, 221
Harrogate, 21, 46, 47, 103, 112, 120, 127, 131, 172, 219
Hartley, Neil, 121, 124
Harris, Lord, 152
Harvey, Neil, 135
Hassett, Lindsay, 133
Hawke, Lord, 32–36, 40–43, 50–52, 56, 61, 65, 72, 76, 80, 120, 130, 151, 163, 187, 207, 210, 227
Hayward, Tom, 166, 201
Headingley, 14, 26, 50, 51, 57, 61, 72, 74, 87, 96, 141, 169
Hendren, Patsy, 197
Hickleton Main, 179
Hill, Alan, 30, 173, 177
Hirst, George Herbert, 40–58, 120, 130, 131, 160–169, 176, 187, 199, 201, 207, 208, 217
Hobbs, Jack, 65, 142, 143, 146
Hodgson, Ikey, 28, 29
Hogg, Willie, 211
Holmes, Percy, 56, 59–63, 68, 74–79, 84, 116, 127, 133, 142–146, 150, 156, 169, 193–198
Hornby, A.N., 30
Hove, 99, 122, 232
Howell, Harry, 59, 60
Huddersfield, 15, 21, 37, 42, 46, 79, 88, 93, 98, 129, 198, 213
Huddersfield League, 71, 156, 218
Hull, 37, 46, 59, 64, 69, 131–33, 154, 189
Hunt, Tom, 22
Hunter, David, 41, 42, 47–52, 130
Hunter, Joe, 186
Hunter, William, 186
Hutton, Len, 15, 18, 79–92, 95, 134, 135, 142–150, 175
Hutton, Richard, 11, 106, 109, 136

Hyde Park, Sheffield, 7, 24, 25

Iddison, Roger, 28, 31
Illingworth, Ray, 11, 16, 92, 100–108, 115, 118–125, 136, 147, 170, 219, 221, 225
India, 95
Ingham, Alderman R., 66
I. Zingari, 35

Jackson, Hon. F.S., 37, 41, 45–48, 85, 130, 131, 163, 168, 174
Jarvis, Paul, 122
Jephson (Surrey), 210
Johnson, Colin, 113
Johnson, Ian, 134
Johnson, Mark, 191
Johnston, Bill, 135
Jones, Jeff, 103

Kanhai, Rohan, 117
Keighley, 16, 21, 40
Keighley, Geoffrey, 88, 227, 229
Kent, 14, 25, 47, 49, 52, 55, 106, 108, 118, 142, 187, 213
Kettering, 145
Kilner, Roy, 47, 51, 55, 59–63, 68, 155, 165, 170, 207
King, Lance, 140
Kingston, W.H., 49
Kirkheaton, 7, 44, 160
Knaresborough, 22, 25, 173

Lancashire, 25, 26, 30, 41, 45, 47, 52, 56, 58, 64, 71, 74, 87, 101, 105, 117, 132, 169, 213
Landon, C.W., 227
Langridge, James, 87
Lascelles Hall, 7, 13, 16, 28–30, 165
Law, W., 227
Lawry, W., 136
Leadbeater, Barrie, 222
Leadbeater, Eddie, 88
Leeds, 20, 27, 28, 37, 46, 47, 59, 130, 131
Leeds United, 103
Leicester, 48, 57, 160
Leicestershire, 42, 57, 75, 93, 96, 108, 112, 160, 219, 225
Lester, Ted, 77, 85, 87, 117, 162, 170
Leyland, Morris, 14, 63, 64, 68, 75–84, 145, 153, 197–203
Leyton, 74, 169, 176, 193
Lindwall, Ray, 17, 147, 148
Lloyd, D., 11

Lockwood, Ephraim, 13, 29, 31, 152
Lord's, 15, 17, 30, 51, 62, 80, 112, 156, 174
Love, Jim, 117
Lowson, Frank, 87–90, 96, 156
Loxley-Firth, E., 227
Loxton, Sam, 135
Lumb, Richard, 116, 120, 121
Lupton, Major Arthur, 61, 63–65
Lyon, Beverley, 71, 72

Macaulay, 58–63, 73, 77, 79, 84, 169, 176, 177, 187, 203
Malton, 67
Manchester, 21, 25
Manchester United, 120
Marlar, Robin, 100
Marsden, Tom, 22
Marylebone C.C., 21, 30, 46, 47, 58, 61, 65, 101, 146, 168, 174, 228
May, Peter, 8
McGahey, Charles, 193, 194
Mead, Phil, 199
Melbourne, 188
Mercer, Jack, 199
Metcalfe, Ashley, 128, 156
Middlesbrough, 50, 101, 104, 124, 129, 140, 156
Middlesex, 43, 45, 51, 55–57, 61, 62, 80, 81, 85, 86, 112, 173, 190, 197
Miller, Keith, 17, 134, 148, 160
Milligan, Frank, 227, 229
Mitchell, Arthur, 13–15, 73, 77, 81–84, 155, 175, 198
Mitchell, Frank, 41, 156
Moxon, Martyn, 121, 128, 156
Murray, Deryck, 222

Nash, John, 96
Newstead, J.T., 50
Nicholls, Maurice, 79
Nicholson, Tony, 11, 12, 102–105, 109, 113, 116, 135, 189, 223
Norfolk, 23–25, 222
Northampton, 49, 56, 77, 117, 120
Northamptonshire, 49, 77, 117, 123, 124, 127, 145, 150, 199
Nottingham, 16, 17, 21, 22
Nottinghamshire, 28, 36, 38, 41, 45, 47, 49, 50, 59, 68, 72, 74, 89, 101, 116, 126, 222, 228
Nurse, Seymour, 140

Index

Old, Chris, 108, 109, 112–125, 181, 211, 224
Oldroyd, Edgar, 17, 52, 60, 63, 153, 169, 198
Old Trafford, 41, 61, 101, 105, 116, 132, 213
O'Reilly, Bill, 155
O'Shaughnessy, Steve, 117
Otley, 21
Oval, 28, 50, 57, 63, 64, 81, 101, 148, 164, 166, 201, 222
Oxford University, 87, 156, 225

Paddock, 15, 156
Padgett, Doug, 90, 100, 101, 104, 140, 222
Parkin, C., 227
Peate, Edmund, 18, 36, 173, 187
Peel, Robert, 36, 41–43, 129, 187, 207
Pilch, Fuller, 22, 24
Pinder, George, 13, 30, 32, 186, 190
Pudsey, 7, 79, 146, 150, 170
Pudsey Britannia, 143, 150
Pullar, Geoff, 11

Radcliffe, Everard, 51, 227
Ranjitsinhji, 87
Redcar, 21
Reform Group, 118, 120
Rest of England, 48, 62, 79, 101
Rhodes, H., 228
Rhodes, Wilfred, 36, 44, 45, 48, 50, 55, 56, 59–68, 130, 160–169, 176, 180, 187, 206, 217
Richardson, Tom, 25
Ringrose, Billy, 193, 194
Ripon, 21, 28
Robins, Walter, 80
Robinson, Arthur, 112, 113, 116, 210
Robinson, Ellis, 83, 85
Robinson, Emmott, 9, 55–58, 63, 64, 68, 72, 74, 134, 168–170, 203
Rotherham, 21
Rowbotham, Joe, 17, 28, 31, 32
Ryan, Mel, 203

Sainsbury, Peter, 147
Sandham, Andy, 146
Scarborough, 21, 26, 35, 37, 58, 75, 79, 101, 108, 121, 123, 131, 145, 147, 167, 190, 222, 229
Sellers, Arthur, 40, 41, 76, 77

Sellers, Brian, 14, 18, 71, 75, 79–86, 96, 99, 111, 120, 133–135, 165, 189, 193
Selvey, Mike, 113
Sharpe, C.M., 228
Sharpe, Phil, 11, 98, 104, 111–116, 222
Sheffield, 7, 8, 22, 25, 26, 28, 30, 36, 37, 41, 43, 46, 57, 71, 75, 80, 81, 89, 99, 122, 124, 129, 132, 135, 141, 152, 173, 187, 197
Sheffield Amateur Sports Club, 27
Sheffield Wednesday, 24, 26
Sidebottom, Arnie, 120, 210
Simms, H.M., 228
Slinn, William, 28, 29
Smailes, Frank, 79–86, 134, 135, 173
Small, Gladstone, 211
Smith, Ernest, 37, 41, 49
Smith, Neil, 190
Smith, Tiger, 193
Smith, W., 228
Smithson, Gerry, 85
Sobers, Gary, 140, 160, 222
Somerset, 47–49, 54, 75, 90, 101, 109, 213, 219
South Africa, 88, 131, 156, 176
Southampton, 58, 125, 199, 213
Spencer, Terry, 93
Spen Valley League, 153
Spofforth, Frank, 129, 152
Staffordshire, 173
Staincliffe, 153
Stanyforth, R.T., 228, 229
Stead, Barry, 222
Steele, David, 191
Stephenson, Edwin, 28, 30
Stevens, Greville, 198
Stevenson, Graham, 112, 119, 187, 210
Stott, Bryan, 98, 100, 104, 140
Stringer, Peter, 11
Strudwick, Herbert, 188
Studd, Charlie, 18
Sugg, F.H., 228
Sugg, W., 228
Surrey, 8, 25–30, 38, 41, 44, 50, 52, 57, 64, 85, 87, 92, 95, 117, 196, 201, 208, 219, 222
Surridge, 85
Sussex, 21, 24, 25, 36, 42, 59, 62, 79, 80, 82, 87, 99, 122, 140, 150, 154, 174
Sutcliffe, Billy, 95, 96
Sutcliffe, Herbert, 35, 55, 56, 59–67, 74–79, 82, 84, 87, 133, 134, 142–146, 150, 193, 194–199, 207
Swansea, 203

Taunton, 90, 219
Taylor, Ken, 12, 98, 104, 108
Taylor, T.L., 96
Tennyson, Lionel, 154, 207
Thewliss, John, 28, 29, 32, 152
Thirsk, 21
Thomson, Ian, 100
Todmorden, 16
Tong Park, 58
Trent Bridge, 68, 190
Trueman, Fred, 87–89, 92–98, 101–108, 135, 136, 140, 177–181, 189, 219, 221
Trumper, Victor, 130
Tunnicliffe, John, 41, 44, 150, 151, 167, 193, 194, 196, 213
Turner, Cyril, 83
Tyldesley, Richard, 61
Tyson, Cecil, 58, 122

Ulyett, 'Happy Jack', 36, 40, 41, 129, 152

Verelst, H.W., 228
Verity, Hedley, 36, 68, 72–84, 169, 173, 175, 181, 189

Waddington, Abe, 55, 56, 59, 61, 63, 64, 68, 169
Wainwright, Ted, 41, 42, 129, 173, 201, 217
Waite, Mervyn, 134
Wakefield, 37, 41
Ward, William, 22, 62
Wardall, Thomas, 40
Wardle, Johnny, 36, 85, 86, 88, 90, 92–98, 113, 135, 179, 181
Warwickshire, 42, 59, 64, 72, 79, 88, 99, 106, 112, 117, 121, 145, 152, 207, 210, 219
Watson, Willie, 15, 17, 85–88, 92, 95, 96, 156
Ward, Brian, 28
West Indies, 132, 137, 140, 141
Weston-super-Mare, 54
Whitaker, James, 118
White, Sir Archibald, 51
Whitehouse, John, 117
Whiteley, Peter, 115
Whitwell, W.F., 228
Whitwood, 58
Wilkinson, A.J., 228
Wilkinson, Stuart, 223
Williams, Ambrose, 207

Willis, Bob, 112, 117
Wilson, Benny, 52
Wilson, Don, 98, 100–105, 109–116, 136, 219, 222
Wilson, Geoffrey, 59, 61, 64, 65
Wilson, Rockley, 52, 57, 59
Wilson, Vic, 85, 87, 89, 98, 101–103
Wisden, 8, 30, 50, 61, 117, 163, 193
Wolves, 179

Wood, Arthur, 65, 77, 81, 82, 84, 90, 134, 188, 189
Woodhouse, 21
Woolley, Frank, 189
Wootton, G., 28
Worcestershire, 49, 79, 104, 169, 213, 217
Worksop, 116, 126
Worsley, William, 67, 68, 71, 103
Wyatt, Bob, 73

Yardley, Norman, 82, 84, 85, 88, 90, 92, 95, 134
Yeadon, 29, 98
York, 20, 25, 26
Yorkshire Council, 58
Yorkshire Evening News, 175
Yorkshire Evening Post, 175
Yorkshire Gentlemen, 35, 64
Yorkshire League, 218

Zimbabwe, 124